THE REDEMPTION OF THE ANIMALS

the Redemption of the Animals

of the Animals

their evolution, their inner life,
and our future together

AN ANTHROPOSOPHIC PERSPECTIVE

Douglas Sloan

Lindisfarne Books | 2015

2015 | Lindisfarne Books
An imprint of SteinerBooks/Anthroposophic Press, Inc.
610 Main Street, Great Barrington, MA 01230
www.steinerbooks.org

Cover image © by Audran Gosling (www.500px.com/ajgosling)
Book and cover design: William Jens Jensen

LIBRARY OF CONGRESS CONTROL NUMBER: 2015947686

ISBN: 978-1-58420-194-6 (paperback)
ISBN: 978-1-58420-195-3 (eBook)

CONTENTS

Dedicated to

Frosty
Heba
Susie
Lassie
Sandy
Peter
Zephyr
Koshka
Rachel
Sammy
Gunner
Maggie

ACKNOWLEDGMENTS

I want to express my special gratitude to the following persons: Professor George Russell of Adelphi University regularly alerted me over recent years to important aspects of Rudolf Steiner's insights into our kinship with the animals. Dr. Stephen Sagarin of the Great Barrington, Massachusetts, Rudolf Steiner School, let me bend his ear many times over lunch and coffee to try out some of my thoughts as the book proceeded. And Professor Robert McDermott of the California Institute of Integral Studies, who first urged that I take on the task of exploring our responsibilities for the redemption of the animals in the light of Anthroposophy, and, at some critical moments, insisted that I not flag in the effort. Finally, I also want to express my gratitude to Gene Gollogly and Christopher Bamford of SteinerBooks for their encouragement, and to William Jensen of SteinerBooks for his thoughtful editorial guidance. Obviously none of these persons is responsible for the positions I have taken or for any mistakes I have made.

Introduction

Rudolf Steiner and
the Human–Animal Connection:
Animal Evolution, Rights, and Redemption

Many persons, if not most, who write on behalf of animal welfare, begin their accounts by relating how from early childhood they loved animals, were deeply moved by the suffering of animals, and were intent from the very beginning to look after and protect animals. I cannot make that claim. Perhaps in the eyes of many this in itself disqualifies me from saying anything persuasive on behalf of animals. Of course, as a boy I loved my pets dearly and was heartbroken when they died or were killed. My great old Springer Spaniel Frosty and my one-eyed, blue Maltese tomcat Heba still have a fond and unassailable hold on my memory. With them is the little, pale yellow kitten Susie, who would play "stalking and chasing" with me for as long as I could keep it up, only to die one weekend from distemper, the scourge in those days of nearly all barnyard cats. My mother and I both cried as we tried vainly to pull Susie back from her seizures and gasping for breath. So, yes, my pets were the few animals in my early life with whom I had a deep and feeling connection.

During my years of grade school I grew up on an agricultural experiment station in western Kansas. The experiment station, common in agricultural states, was an extension project in western Kansas of Kansas State College for the purpose of conducting agricultural research, and to help the local farmers learn to respect that research as the latest in "scientific agriculture." My father was the superintendent of the experiment station. These were the days within only a year or two after western Kansas had been ravaged by the dust storms of the 1930s. The specific purposes of the experiment station were to conduct research in soil conservation, develop new varieties of crops most suitable at the time for dry-land farming—mainly wheat—and to pioneer new approaches in animal husbandry.

For a young boy, the experiment station was an idyllic place to grow up. In the midst of the dry, hot, windswept Kansas summers and freezing winter blizzards, it was like a little Garden of Eden for a boy. There was a pond, surrounded by trees, to swim in during the summer and to play ice hockey on with friends from town during the winter. There were trees, a rarity in that part of the state, to climb and swing from and that provided shade from the searing Kansas sun, as well as nesting for all kinds of birds. And there were animals as part of the experiment station research projects: cattle, pigs, horses, mules, sheep, and poultry. So in my grade school years I was not unacquainted with animals. On the contrary, I was surrounded by animals, was curious about them and even, when it was possible, played with them. But I did not develop the close feeling for the animals of the kind many animal advocates point to in their own early years.

This does not mean that I was unmoved, and often even deeply disturbed by the suffering of animals that is a part of any farming experience—most of it not deliberately inflicted but simply an unavoidable fact of farm life. I witnessed the veterinarian having to reach up to his shoulder into the birth canal of a ewe to reach its incorrectly positioned fetus; I saw my father having to plunge a butcher knife into the stomach of a bloated cow to save its life by releasing trapped gas from the foundering animal; and I saw animals having to be killed because they had become too sick or too injured to recover. I have a vivid memory of stepping off the school bus one evening near the barn to witness the heifers of the future dairy herd milling about in panic in the barnyard pen, bellowing in confusion and fear, with ten-foot spurts of arterial blood shooting from their heads—it was an experiment in scientific dehorning that had not gone quite as planned (dehorning of cattle I learned years later is neither necessary nor desirable, but at the time, and still is for most dairy herds, *de rigeur*). There were also the days of slaughter and butchering. These and many other incidents constituted a kind of ever-present, dark background of my otherwise light-filled Garden of Eden.

In whatever moments one may have been touched in pity by these and other incidents of animal suffering, one learned quickly not to be sentimental and to accept the suffering as something to be faced up to. This is an attitude essential for the successful medical treatment of animals, just as for human beings. But the avoidance of sentimentality can be difficult to distinguish from an ever deepening and pervasive indifference, or suppression of feeling. On all farms a procedural indifference is reinforced by usage and tends to become an accepted—even encouraged—attitude. This may have been still more the case for the agricultural experiment station because it was committed, at all costs, to be unmovedly scientific.

Indifference to animal suffering also flows easily from the main purpose of animals in agriculture. They exist to serve the needs of humans—for food, for clothing, for work. Anything that stands in the way of using animals for human desires and purposes smacks of sentimentality and is, in most cases, suppressed as a matter of course. Natural feelings of love and pity for the farm animals—apart from our pets—make their appearance from time to time, but soon evaporate in the all-pervasive assumption that the animals exist for our use and that this is beyond question.

Making it even more difficult for me during these early years to develop a feeling connection to animals in general was the ever-present hunting culture. Every boy had a BB gun to shoot sparrows with, and by my teenage years owned a .22 rifle and usually a 12- or 16-gauge shotgun. We hunted rabbits, quail, ducks, and pheasants. By the time I left high school, jack rabbits, once ubiquitous in western Kansas, had been all but exterminated, as had pheasants except in some of the most remote areas. Although I never questioned that all boys and men hunted, and found delight in the kill, some experiences did cause me a temporary pang of regret. One winter, for example, I shot a small cottontail rabbit. The .22 caliber bullet pierced its stomach but failed to kill it, and as I approached to view my kill, the silent rabbit looked up at me with wide eyes that seemed to me, then and still now, to ask, "Why?" Perhaps that was an early glimmer of hope, but it soon passed, and the importance of hunting reasserted itself. It never occurred to me to face one of the obvious questions about the hunting culture, promoted as sport by all involved: What is, at bottom, sporting about it? Equipped with high-powered, precision-tooled guns, and telescopic sights, rising from hidden blinds from which to suddenly ambush unsuspecting deer or ducks, shooting sleeping crows nestled down in trees for the night simply for the sake of the kill—this, and one could multiply the examples, is not sporting in any sense of the word. Now, as I look back, I am appalled at these, and other instances, of my lack of consciousness and feelings for the creatures at my mercy.

When I began high school we moved from the experiment station to a small wheat farm, also in western Kansas. Since by that time a "small wheat farm" in western Kansas was already an oxymoron, it was also necessary for my father, who had a wife and four children to feed, to teach in the local high school and to raise a small number of animals to supplement his income. We had a couple of cows for milking and a steer for meat, some pigs, many chickens, and occasionally a sheep for mutton. My gentle father loved animals—that had always been apparent to me, and perhaps the later recall of that was a main influence in awakening me from the slumber of my unconsciousness. Nevertheless, he wanted to be a no-nonsense farmer and to do the things required of farmers. Accordingly, we did our own butchering and engaged in the other things attendant to feeding meat to one's family. It was my job, therefore, to help my father castrate the pigs that would have become young boars. My assignment was to hold them down as they squealed and screamed, with my knee on their neck and my free hand trying to control their kicking, while my father performed the quick surgery with a scalpel-honed pocket knife, and with a can of pine tar as a primitive disinfectant and covering against maggot infestation. Castration was thought to be necessary to prevent the young male pigs from fighting and also to ensure that their buttocks, deprived of the requisite male hormones, grew fat and tender, rather than lean and tough. So there were cruelties, but we tried to avoid as many as possible, and butchering day was somber and a little sad. The cruelties were limited, however intense for the moment, and of course apart from their doomed end, our animals were treated well and with respect—my father saw to that. And they lived well and enjoyed their limited time.

Occasionally an unexpected light-ray of feeling would break through, throwing everything out of kilter and threatening to reveal the presence of a whole other reality. One such instance remains especially vivid. My father had bought a young sow with the intention of fattening her for butchering. He, unfortunately however, became quite attached to her, and she to him. He even made the mistake of naming her—"Margery, " as I recall. Every time he would approach her barnyard area, Marge would come grunting and running to him, not to be fed as that had already been taken care of, but to be scratched by him behind her ears and patted, rather robustly, on her flanks. This became almost a ritual, acted out on more than one occasion during the day. But, as he was a no-nonsense farmer, the time came for him to see to it that Marge met her destined end. A few days later at supper, as my mother put some of Marge on my father's plate, he looked at it for a moment in silence, then placed his hands on the table and pushed his chair back mumbling, "I can't eat this." That, however, was only a momentary crack in the usual, and life and farming soon returned to normal.

College did little to awaken me to our relationships with the animals. They were never mentioned in class, not even in classes in philosophy, which was my major. The only exception was comparative anatomy, premed being my other major, in which we were required to dissect dogfish sharks and cats. Sometimes I did wonder if this cat I was cutting open might once have been someone's pet, but I would quickly put that thought aside. Fortunately, we did not have to kill our dissection specimens ourselves. If we'd had to, as some such classes must, I don't know if that would have jolted me into a new sensitivity to the being before me, or simply would have driven me deeper into my hardened feelings—difficult to say which.

With respect to animals, little changed after college. I had received a scholarship to attend Yale University Divinity School, and there, for three years, heard nothing whatever about animals—much less about the divine-human–animal relationship. My professors were highly intelligent and theologically and socially liberal, but the animals were not of their concern. It was as though the animals had been created by God for the use of humankind, and there would have been no point in enquiring further. It seems to me in retrospect, that the dominant conventional view of the larger culture was simply accepted and shared as a given by these intelligent, erudite, and liberal professors. The situation seems to have changed somewhat since then, however, with the rise in some theological seminaries of courses in what has been called "creaturely theology" or "animal theology."

I have spent this much initial space on my own story—perhaps inordinately so—with two hopes in mind. In the first place, one hope is that it can indicate that even when the odds are stacked pretty high against it, a fundamental change in basic attitude and orientation is possible. In addition, I hope it will be evident to others, as it is to me, that my early experience of the human–animal relationship is not entirely out of the ordinary in our culture. Perhaps through the personal narrative the deep-rooted attitudes and assumptions of our dominant culture and the challenges they pose for meaningful change can be clearly illuminated.

A number of influences helped me leave behind more and more of my conventionally assumed attitudes and behavior. My change in consciousness was slow in coming, but, nevertheless, a basic turnaround has gradually resulted. Of great importance has been the presence of long-forgotten memories, some of which I have touched upon. My childhood love of my pets—my desolation at their deaths, my joy in playing with them, and, above all, our mutual affection for one another—all this was always in me, but seldom recognized and engaged. With the memories of my pets were also memories of standing in the barn in the company of the cows and pigs, sensing their own conscious presence and their joy in being alive.

These memories were rekindled in me by several new events and experiences. Of crucial importance was when my wife and I adopted three new kittens, whose intelligence, playfulness, and affection placed whole new demands on us and conferred rewards of the kind we had forgotten. Especially powerful was the kittens' response to our emotional states, especially when these took an unsuspected turn—whether we were angry, owing perhaps to a little spat, or sorrowful at the loss of a friend or family member, the kittens would be present to us immediately, clearly and deeply affected by our emotional squalls.

Such memories and feelings as these began to surface in force as I became aware and affected by two developments in the larger world of human–animal relationship. One of great importance for me was the revealing of the horrors visited relentlessly on millions of animals—pigs, cows, poultry, all the gentlest of our animal companions—in factory farming (the very kind of "scientific agriculture," I realized many years later, that was, and is, being promoted by the college-sponsored, experiment station). Fond memories of our own farm animals arose afresh, along with a beginning sense of what they would have undergone and suffered in modern agriculture.

This also made me aware as never before of the burgeoning field of ethology—the scientific study of animal behavior. Studies in this field had begun to appear in ever-increasing numbers during the past half-century. Their discoveries and detailed descriptions of animal behavior, consciousness, cognition, emotions, and social life made unavoidable, for anyone with the slightest interest, a confrontation with the rich, inner life of animals.

And, finally, a third influence for me was the discovery of the work of the Austrian philosopher and spiritual scientist, Rudolf Steiner and the movement he founded, which he called Anthroposophy. As part of his investigations into the nature of reality and the possibilities of human knowing, Steiner presents, among many other things, a picture of the fundamental kinship of humans and animals from the very origins of earth evolution. In his account of this relationship, Steiner describes the rich spiritual and emotional lives of animals and our human responsibility for them, now and into the far future.

All of these influences served to awaken me ever more to the increasingly desperate plight of the animals in our time, and to our inseparable kinship with them. What follows is my beginning attempt to explore Rudolf Steiner's help in understanding and meeting our responsibility to the animals. I am painfully aware of the beginning nature of this exploration, and of its deficiencies. It is offered as an invitation for others to enter into the dialogue— and, of course, to correct and to extend this beginning.

PART I

TWO PERSPECTIVES ON EVOLUTION

DARWINIAN PERSPECTIVE

The concept of evolution was not new with Charles Darwin. The general idea was already in the air when he wrote and had long been entertained by a variety of thinkers. Nevertheless, the still dominant, anti-evolutionary view of the different animal forms was strong and held not only in traditional religious circles, but also by many prominent philosophers and scientific thinkers. The anti-evolutionists maintained that the multitudinous life forms that we find in the world around us have not changed and evolved over time, but were created—by God or nature itself—once and for all in fixed, unchanging forms. Darwin's importance was not so much that he advanced the general concept of evolution, but that he provided a theory to explain how it took place. In his major work, *The Origin of Species,* published in 1859, Darwin set forth his theory, buttressing it with copious, painstaking observations and his own careful weighing of evidence and arguments for and against. The richness and honesty of Darwin's presentation in *Origin of Species* continue to win great admiration even from among many of his critics.

The center of Darwin's theory is what he called "natural selection." From time to time, he argued, small changes will occur randomly in a plant or animal. Most such random changes will be deleterious to the animal, that is, they will not be to the organism's advantage in making the most of the resources necessary for life offered by the environment. Occasionally, however, a change will take place that works to the advantage of the organism in "the struggle for existence." In other words, those organisms with the small advantageous change will adapt to the given environmental conditions more successfully than those lacking the change. These changes will then tend to be subsequently reinforced by the environment and persist from one generation to another. In this sense, such advantageous, random changes in the organism will be "selected"—favored and reinforced—by the given environmental circumstances, and will be passed on, by virtue of their superiority in fostering survival, to the organism's offspring. Most important, the gradual accumulation of such small, random, but "selected" changes would lead over long stretches of time to the emergence of fundamentally new, life forms. The origin of species as Darwin presented it was not the result of supernatural creation, but the result of a fully natural process of, as he put it in one of his favorite expressions, "descent with modification," and, as he also held, of descent from a common ancestor.

As biologist Michael Denton has put it, this was Darwin's *special* theory of evolution, "the origin of new species from preexisting species," made possible by natural selection. This was a theory of "microevolution," the development of many species from and among earlier species. Microevolution in this sense has become largely non-controversial as the evidence for it is abundant and strong, and for nearly all biologists indisputable. But what about what can be called macroevolution, the development not only of new species from preexisting species, but the appearance of the entirety of all the great diversity and complexity of the myriad life forms on earth? As Denton points out, Darwin extended his special theory to a general theory of all evolution: changes at the level of microevolution also lead by the same process—small adaptive changes favored by natural selection—to the major and very different life forms at the level of macroevolution. All present living things, as far distantly related, for instance, as worms and primates, mollusks and mammals, amoebas and elephants, have descended through small, gradual changes occurring over long periods of time and have originated from a simple, common ancestor (Denton, 46ff.).

Darwin's main emphasis was on "descent with modification" through natural selection working on small, random changes in the organism. But how the changes and subsequent modifications complexity, and remarkable functionality of the organic world. It should be noted that from the perspective of neo-Darwinism the randomness of mutation means that it is not guided or aimed in any way to favor the organism, or to further its better adaptation to the environment. Random means that, as one evolutionary biologist has put it, "mutations are random with respect to the organism (Eldridge, 252). That is to say, they are not intended (intentions having no place in this view) to help organisms adapt better; it is just that by chance and natural selection some do. The fact that most random mutations are deleterious, or ineffectual, further strengthens the assumption that they are not designed in any way to express, on the one hand, any purposeful activity or aim inherent in nature, or, on the other hand, any subjectivity or conscious purpose on the part of the organism.

Evolutionary change as described by orthodox neo-Darwinism is, therefore, without purpose in any sense. The organism is conceived essentially as matter in motion, with the various material elements related mechanistically as the parts of a machine. The dominant framework and vocabulary of neo-Darwinism is materialistic and mechanistic. Purpose, subjectivity, and intention have no place in this view. When these do make an appearance in evolutionary understanding, they signal departure—sometimes radical, sometimes less so—from strict neo-Darwinism.

In a relatively short time after the pronouncement of "the central dogma," strains, even cracks, began to appear in the neo-Darwinian edifice. Here we can examine only a few examples of these problems.

In the first place, the question, "What is a gene?" has acquired a new urgency (Pearson; Commoner; Holdrege 1996). In popular portrayals of neo-Darwinism—written often by scientists who ought to know better—genes are presented as little, self-contained bits of matter, self-enclosed and unaffected by the environment. In actuality, genes are not isolated, self-contained entities, but segments of DNA consisting of combinations of certain chemicals. As the biologist Francisco J. Ayala has written, "The process of mutation that provides the raw materials for natural selection is now known to be much more complex than it was thought a few decades ago" (Ayala, 73).

This complexity involves a number of discoveries that provide no support for the "central dogma." One such complexity is the discovery, as Craig Holdrege has pointed out, that mutations exist that involve many genes, and others that involve only DNA segments within what was once considered a single, separate gene. Genes have been known to move from chromosome to chromosome, and in the new position to function differently than before. Scientists are unsure as to which position on a chromosome the beginning and end of hereditary factors are found. Holdrege has described this as "the position effect" in which genes function differently according to their location in the DNA segment and in their relation to other genes. "Evidently," writes Holdrege, "Genes are not as immune to their context as had been thought" (Holdrege, 77).

The notion that there is a one-to-one correspondence between a particular gene and specific characteristics, or traits (such as, for examples, in humans: eye color, intelligence, sexual orientation, or bodily defects and diseases, etc.), is no longer seen to hold, except in a few particular instances, as in sickle cell anemia. The popular hope, hyped in the original promotion of the "human genome project," that everything about a person would be understood by a detailed knowledge of their genetic makeup has been abandoned by most scientists—except, perhaps, those scientists and institutions with financial interests in promoting the idea. The idea that "a person's character is written in the genes" has been dubbed by leading biologists as "genetic astrology" (Jablonka and Lamb, 58–59, 67).

Far from being isolated, self-contained units, the genes stand in a multifaceted relationship with the totality of the organism, including with its proteins, its fats, and other organic connections. It is now clear that no one gene governs processes that give rise to a particular protein, but that one gene may be involved in the production of hundreds, even thousands of different types of proteins. As Commoner writes, "The DNA gene clearly exerts an important influence on inheritance but it is not unique in that respect and acts only in collaboration with a multitude of protein-based processes." It has been shown also that very different kinds of cells develop from the same DNA depending on their location in different parts of the body (Commoner).

Discussing the increasingly new ferment in genetic research and conceptualization is a recent book by two microbiologists, Eva Jablonka and Marion Lamb entitled *Evolution in Four Dimensions*. One dimension involves genetic changes that seem to be not so much random as targeted, that is, as being related and limited to particular characteristics of the organism. A second dimension of inheritance Jablonka and Lamb point to is the influence of *epigenetics*, that is, the hereditary influences that stem not primarily from the genes at all, but from factors external to the genes and that can be affected by non-DNA elements. The remaining two dimensions of evolution they describe as behavioral and symbolic inheritance systems, both of which they argue play crucial roles beyond DNA in inheritance. Throughout their book, the authors point to the renewal of a kind of—albeit, reconstructed—Lamarckism, involving the inheritance of "acquired characteristics." They do not see this reintroduction of a revised Lamarckism as a repudiation of Darwin or even all neo-Darwinism, but certainly as demanding a revision of the "ultra neo-Darwinism" guided exclusively by the "central dogma." In their view "natural selection" is to be placed in a wider context than usual, but still remains in the end for them the decisive, guiding factor at the microbiological level.

Other discoveries also have pointed to the need for the rethinking of orthodox neo-Darwinism. An important discovery has to do with the emphasis placed by neo-Darwinians on the one-sided influence of the environment on the organism. This emphasis has viewed the organism as being one-sidedly and passively influenced through natural selection by a largely separate and independent environment. Richard Lewontin has argued that this view ignores the large body of evidence about "the actual complexity of the relationship between organisms and their [environmental] resources."

Instead of seeing the organism as being passively worked upon by an independent, outside environment, biologists, Lewontin says, should recognize that organisms also help *construct* their environment, one more suitable to the organism's survival requirements. In this the sharp separation between the animal and its environment begins to fade. As Lewontin writes, "Organisms help create effective environments through their own life activities." Although there is ample evidence for it, Lewontin writes, the idea of the organism shaping its environment has not had much influence on most evolutionists. The reason for this neglect, he says, is because it does not fit well with the mechanistic assumptions that dominate neo-Darwinian theory (Lewontin 2000, 2011; Cobb 2008).

The realization of the full range and complexity of the relationships between and among genes, the cells, the organs, the whole body, and the environment is beginning to emerge, and to make its way fitfully into aspects of orthodox neo-Darwinian theory. Most biologists, it seems however, have been able—or at least have attempted—to accommodate new discoveries without making fundamental changes in the theory itself. Signs do exist, nevertheless, that new-Darwinism may be on the verge of—or approaching—a new evolutionary phase of its own. The new discoveries and reconceptualizations together suggest that inheritance is built out of a number of interacting components, and that these are combined and recombined among themselves, even "interpreted," transformed, and guided by the organism itself (Talbot). It may be that the *whole* organism can be brought more and more into the center of research and that the extreme reductionism of neo-Darwinnism can be transcended. Meanwhile, however, other weighty issues and problems remain and need to be addressed.

Some Persistent Problems

About fifteen years ago, the renowned Cambridge paleontologist, Simon Conway Morris commented, "When discussing evolution, the only point of agreement seems to be: 'It happened,' and thereafter there is little consensus" (Morris 2000).

Beyond the currently emerging, new views in genetics, examples of which we have touched upon, there remain persistent and perplexing questions for the large Darwinian perspective as such. As we have seen, Darwin insisted that evolution has taken place through a gradual process of small, biological changes guided in adapting to the environment—or not—by natural selection. He was insistent on the gradual, step-by-step and continuous nature of evolutionary change. This however, posed a problem for Darwin himself because it required the existence of innumerable, transitional organic forms leading gradually from the simplest of one-celled organisms to the immense complexity and diversity of our present-day animal kingdom. As Darwin himself put it, "the number of intermediate and transitional links, between all living and extinct species [going back, as Darwin maintained, to a common ancestor] must have been inconceivably great" (Denton).

Unfortunately for Darwin at the time, the fossil record did not provide the evidence he needed. It revealed only highly differentiated and well-defined types appearing all at once with no linking, transitional forms. Darwin himself recognized the problem and its serious challenge to his theory. In the *Origins* he wrote, "the case at present must remain inexplicable and may be truly argued as a valid argument against the views here entertained" (Denton, 188). As we noted, he rejected any suggestion, however, that evolution proceeded by sudden jumps (saltations) because he thought that would represent a miraculous intrusion into the process and would vitiate his whole naturalistic theory of evolution based entirely on chance and natural selection. He had to explain the lack of the "inconceivable numbers' of transitional forms required by his theory of gradualism. The gaps in the fossil record, he maintained, could be explained—and this seemed reasonable at the time—because the record was still incomplete or imperfect, and the postulated innumerable transitional forms would eventually be discovered.

This has not happened. The fossil record has been expanded enormously, and as Denton points out, one of its most striking features is that "most new kinds of organisms appear abruptly as distinct types" (Denton, 165, 157–198). Darwin was supported in his theory by the fact that natural selection working on random genetic variations does figure prominently in evolutionary development at the level of micro-evolution—the emergence of new species from preexisting species. Thus he was encouraged to extend his theory to the whole of evolution—macroevolution—explaining the gradual development of all the diversity of life forms on earth from a simple, common ancestor. This picture of gradual development disappears, however, once we move from the level of species to that of the appearance of a new genus, and still more so as one moves up the classification ladder from species to genus to family, and so forth. There the gaps between the types of organisms become ever wider and sharper (ibid.; Griffin 2000, 277–279).

At the level of interspecies evolution there are transitional forms, but as Denton comments, "there are fewer transitional species between the major divisions than between the minor." And he goes on to say, "The gaps that separate species: dog/fox/rat/mouse/etc., are utterly trivial compared with, say, that between a terrestrial reptile and an Ichthyosaur; and even these relatively major discontinuities are trivial alongside those that divide major phyla such as mollusks and arthropods (Denton, 193). Denton writes, "the first representations of each major group appears in the fossil record already highly specialized and highly characteristic of the group to which they belong" (Denton 163). As even Niles Eldridge, himself a leading paleontologist of neo-Darwinian persuasion comments, newness in evolution "usually shows up with a bang" (Eldridge, 95).

Darwin's insistence on evolution by means of innumerable, small, step-by-step changes has always been haunted by the views of the nineteenth-century biologist, Georges Cuvier. In his pioneering work in comparative anatomy, Cuvier very early laid the foundations for modern vertebrate paleontology (Bowler, 106). Cuvier rejected Darwin's notion of small, continuous inherited changes resulting in innumerable transitional forms for two reasons, empirical and conceptual. Empirically, the fossil record revealed overwhelmingly, not transitional forms but, as Darwin also realized, abrupt changes from one well-defined type of organism to another. Conceptually, this was explained, Cuvier thought, by his view of what he called "the correlation of parts." Cuvier insisted that all parts of the organism are interdependent, that they are all interrelated and must change together. Small, independent changes would either have no survival value and be eliminated by natural selection, or, not being integrally related to the rest of the organism, would prove lethal to its survival. As Bowler summarizes Cuvier's theory, "Bodily interactions were balanced so delicately that any significant change would upset the system and render the animal inviable" (Bowler, 107). Though Cuvier was very much a nineteenth-century biologist and man of his time, his emphasis on the "correlation of parts" continues to raise a difficult problem for the Darwinian emphasis on small, independent, incremental, and gradual changes.

The problem is further exacerbated conceptually by what has been called "the functional problem." This is the necessity that every change in the animal has to be functional—has to work—in concert with the rest of the animal's body. In the words of one biologist, "certain modifications cannot greatly precede or lag behind others but must keep pace if the performance of the machine is not to become sloppy...the task is to improve a machine while it keeps running" (Taylor, 113). As David Ray Griffin has summarized the problem, "several changes would have to occur at once if the new organism is to be viable, and the possibility that these coordinated changes could occur by chance is remote" (Griffin 2000, 284). Darwin himself said, "If it could be demonstrated that any complex organ exists that could not possibly have been formed by numerous, successive, slight modifications, my theory would absolutely break down" (quoted from *Origin*, Denton, 213). Denton, Wesson, and others give numerous examples, such as the avian lung and feather, that in Denton's words, "bring us very close to answering Darwin's challenge" (ibid.).

Here arises an even more serious difficulty. According to the theory, the adaptation of animals to their environment through natural selection means that the animal becomes increasingly specialized in relation to that environment in order "to fit" better into the environment's particular conditions and demands, and to make the most effective use of what it has to offer. The more well adapted, the more specialized. Some of these specialized animals may begin to split up into other specialized varieties more adapted to other, particular aspects of a changing environment. This process has been called "adaptive radiation" in that there is a kind of radiating out from the original of newly specializing varieties adapted to different aspects of the surrounding environment. Thus a great variety of organisms can begin to appear, related to the original but variously adapted to a variety of environmental conditions. In each case, those that are successful and dominate particular environmental conditions are those that are most specialized in that environment—those most highly adapted to it. At the level of microevolution this process seems to hold: selection→ specialization→ adaptation→ species variations.

This process, however, raises a fundamental question: How does a highly specialized, and now fixed and securely adapted organism give rise to a decidedly new organism that is highly divergent with respect to the original? And this raises a still further question about the adequacy of natural selection as the determining factor in the evolutionary process leading to new animal forms. Of course, natural selection is important in successful adaptation, but its reach and role are not really clear. Does natural selection, as the German biologist Bernd Rosslenbroich has asked, have as its main role merely that of keeping animal populations healthy, by eliminating the weaker members and retaining the stronger (and more specialized)? Or, is natural selection, as Darwinists hold, what gives rise not only to new species in microevolution but also to new organisms in macroevolution (again, not just new species, but new genera, families, orders, and so forth)? Rosslenbroich comments: "To see evolution as a whole solved by the selection process remains a hypothesis." Rosslenbroich adds that the concept of "adaptation" is itself unclear. Obviously organisms adapt successfully on many different levels of the environment, else they could not live and survive (Rosslenbroich 2006). However, as we have noted, the paleontologist Lewontin has shown that adaptation is only one aspect of the many interactions between organisms and the environment. Besides adapting, organisms also choose their environment, transform it, and balance out its fluctuating changes (Lewontin 2000, 2011).

Moreover, if evolution were primarily about the survival of the fittest through natural selection, change would be rare. As Niles Eldridge, himself a Darwinist, observes, "once they appear, species tend not to accumulate much anatomical change through the remainder of their existence" (Eldridge, 75). This is sometimes referred to as "species stasis," the fact that, once they appear, new organic forms tend to remain static. So again we come back to this question: How do new major changes in animal forms originate?

Obviously, change does occur, bountifully and often relatively rapidly. Here we have, then, two problems with the concept of natural selection, related but in tension with one another. One has to do with what it is that holds the forms of many groups of animals constant over millions of years. The other is equally difficult: How do new forms arise in the first place? To put it more sharply: How do new forms arise from already highly specialized, well adapted, and fixed animal forms? It is in light of this question that biologist Wesson observes, "Innovation is the central problem that has troubled evolutionists ever since Darwin" (Wesson, 53).

The Mechanical Worldview

It is crucial to recognize that neo-Darwinism is committed with most of modern science, to a certain worldview that determines the way nature and the empirical data of evolution, and of all nature, are to be interpreted and understood. This view emerged in force in the seventeenth century and was articulated especially by leaders of the scientific revolution, such as Galileo, Descartes, Boyle, and others, including most notably the English philosopher John Locke. This view held that nature is "a law-bound system of matter in motion" governed and functioning according to the laws of mechanics. This idea Darwin inherited, so to speak, in that by his time it was increasingly being taken for granted as the only basis for the truly scientific understanding of nature. Although this worldview has undergone some changes—some might say, refinements—since that time, in its essence it still provides the dominant, conceptual framework, employed by most scientists, in many cases perhaps unconsciously, for understanding nature.

Central to this materialistic mechanistic worldview is the philosophic assumption that we can only know what is given in sense experience or abstractions from sense experience. In other words, it is the claim, as Owen Barfield has described it, that "nothing really exists except what is actually or notionally perceptible by the senses." Barfields adds, "This is not very often explicitly affirmed nowadays, but it is almost everywhere implicitly assumed" (Barfield 1982). This sense-bound view of what and how we can know means that non-sensory realities, such as immaterial forms and formative laws, archetypes and typological ideas in general, as well as all the things we have to assume in practice, even if we deny them in theory, including meaning, purpose, beauty, consciousness and subjectivity, and so forth, have no place in scientific theory in general, and in evolutionary theory in particular. This is the persistence of seventeenth-century materialism with a vengeance, and was taken for granted by Darwin in his evolutionary thinking (he seems personally to have been of a broader persuasion).

The mechanistic assumptions endemic to Darwinism, especially to neo-Darwinism, actually make the whole idea of evolution itself problematic. In the mechanistic view nature has no inner reality, only the outer mechanical combination of material parts. Decades ago the noted twentieth-century biologist, Adolf Portmann, urged that we begin seriously to recognize and take into account that nature has not only a material outside, but also an inside of meaning, which finds expression in the outer. "By an extraordinary reversal of attitudes," he urged, "we should turn our minds inward so that we may have a chance of recognizing a far more comprehensive reality behind our experience" (Portmann, 218). Without a recognition of the inner reality—the qualitative reality within the quantitative, material outside—evolution loses its meaning. In the mechanical view change can take place but it merely refers to the replacement of material parts for other material parts, or their rearrangement—as in, for example, the replacement in a machine of one cogwheel for another. Evolution, however, refers not merely to change in the outer but, rather, the persistence of an inner reality that lends meaning, purpose, and coherence from one changing "outer form to another.

Owen Barfield has pointed out that evolution involves change, but a particular kind of change, change that is meaningful and is more than just a change or rearrangement of parts. Barfield writes:

> It [evolution] is a particular kind of change.... There are other kinds of change—one-damn-thing-after-another, for instance. I would call that kind mere substitution, whereas evolution implies a process of *transformation*. The difference between transformation and substitution is that transformation involves the persistent presence of something common to both the old form and the new. But where there is a total transformation of the material form, the something that persists must itself be immaterial. (Barfield 1965, 96)

That which persists belongs to the qualitative, inner side of nature.

Alfred North Whitehead, the twentieth-century mathematician and philosopher has written similarly:

> The aboriginal stuff, or material, from which a materialistic philosophy starts is incapable of evolution.... Evolution, on the materialistic theory, is reduced to the role of being another word for the description of the changes of the external relations between portions of matter [as in one cogwheel—or DNA unit—impinging on another]. There is nothing to evolve, because one set of external relations is as good as any other set of external relations. There can be merely change, purposeless and unprogressive. (Whitehead, 157)

In exposing the lack of purpose and progress in Darwinian evolutionary theory, Barfield and Whitehead have also identified a major point of contention among present-day evolutionary theorists themselves, who differ on the question: "Is there such a thing as progress in evolution?" Some answer in the negative, others tend, perhaps more tentatively, toward the positive.

Those who reject the idea of evolutionary progress do so for both social and scientific reasons. The social reason for the rejection has been in many respects healthy. For one thing, an optimistic interpretation of Darwinian evolution had by the end of the nineteenth century encouraged an uncritical faith in the inevitable progress and steady advancement of modern society. This "Victorian faith in progress" was suddenly shattered by the outbreak and brutalities of World War I. More lasting, however, was the fact that Darwinian theories of "the struggle for existence" and "the survival of the fittest" carried strong overtones of nineteenth-century (and twentieth-century) colonialism, which posited the existence of higher, superior, more advanced races and nations (essentially white and Western) over and against lower, inferior, and retrograde peoples (mainly the colonized of Africa and Asia). As historian of science, John C. Greene, has pointed out, Darwin, as a man of his time, shared with most of his contemporaries this view of racial and national differences in intellectual and moral capacities. Greene cites a letter written by Darwin a year before his death to his friend William Graham saying, "The more civilized so-called Caucasian races have beaten the Turkish all hollow in the struggle for existence," and he predicted that, as Greene quotes him, "the lower races will soon be eliminated by the higher races throughout the world" (Greene 1981, 122, 150). Greene adds, however that Darwin was careful, to recognize "the obligations of enlightened humanity" and the promptings of "sympathetic impulses toward all people" (Greene, 263).

The evolutionary idea of superior peoples led certain persons, including a number of leading scientists, to attempt to ensure the improvement of the hereditary line of human beings through eugenics—the adoption of a program of coercive social control to eliminate the weak, the socially unfit, and the imbecile through birth control and sterilization. The nightmare extension of eugenics in the Nazi attempt to create its own version of the superior race seems to have played an influential role among some biologists to simply deny the idea of "progress" in evolution, lest it be misused.

In a comprehensive look at the history of the idea of progress in evolutionary theory, Bernd Rosslenbroich has pointed out Darwin's actual ambivalence toward the idea of progress in evolution (Rosslenbroich 2006). Because natural selection was for Darwin not guided, it would produce change and variety of organic forms without any particular direction or purpose. At the same time, Darwin couldn't escape the feeling, as Bowler has written, "that modern forms of life are more advanced than their earliest ancestors" (Bowler, 18). And John Greene notes that while Darwin's *Origin* makes little mention of "progress," it abounds with words like "improvement," "improving," "improved" (Greene 1991). Rosslenbroich also writes that, while Darwin repeatedly "warned himself never to speak of 'higher' or 'lower', it was a warning that even he repeatedly disregarded" (Rosslenbroich 2006). And though for Darwin natural selection is undirected, he wrote in the final paragraph of *The Origin*, "Thus, from the war of nature...the most exalted object we are capable of conceiving, namely, the production of the higher animals directly follows" (Darwin).

The tension and ambivalence Darwin felt remains unresolved among present-day biologists. Two main contrasting emphases play in the modern debate among biologists: "trends" and variations." Some see "trends" appearing within the manifold of variations in nature that suggest directional transformation that can be characterized as "progress." Against them, other biologists, especially radical neo-Darwinians, will stress only the appearance of chance variations with no discernible trends within them because in the materialistic view there can be no "higher" or "lower." From their perspective there can be only the reorganization of parts governed by chance—random modifications. Hence the majority view among most contemporary neo-Darwinists is that there are no trends, that is, no directionality, no progress—and no purpose or meaning.

The biologist most famous for arguing against the notion of progress in evolution is the late, Yale paleontologist, Stephen J.

Gould. For Gould, radical contingency, chance, is the essence of evolutionary change. If there had been, Gould maintains, tiny, indiscernible alterations, "little quirks," at the beginning of life, then the subsequent development of life forms would be entirely different from what we have now. One of Gould's favorite metaphors is the image of "the tape of life" (Gould 1989, 320-1, 233-4). If we could rewind the tape and play it again from the beginning—a million times over even—the ensuing results would always be entirely different each time. And the appearance of the human being itself "is the product of massive historical contingency, and we would probably never arise again even if life's tape could be replayed a thousand times" (ibid.). As for the human being, he pushes even harder. Changing his metaphor he writes, "we are, whatever our glories and accomplishments, a momentary cosmic accident that would never arise again if the tree of life could be replanted from seed and regrown under similar circumstances" (Gould 1996, 18). For Gould, talk about purpose (as in trends) merely distracts us from recognizing the real importance of radical contingency (random variations). "Progress," wrote Gould, "is a noxious, culturally embedded, untestable, non-operational, intractable idea that must be replaced if we wish to understand the patterns of history" (Nitecki, 319). The whole of nature is what it is by chance; it could just as well have been something else.*

Perhaps even more extreme than Gould in stressing the meaninglessness and nihilism of neo-Darwinism have been a number of philosophically inclined proponents of neo-Darwinism. William Provine, neo-Darwinist and historian of science has, for example, written: "Science reveals to us only chance and necessity.... There are no purposive principles whatsoever

---

* During the past few decades neo-Darwinism with its assumption that all life forms are the result of chance has provided the ideological rationale for unrestrained genetic engineering. If all of nature is the product of chance, then existing life forms have no intrinsic value and there is, therefore, little reason not to alter them at will by transferring genetic material from species to species—or even from kingdom to kingdom—with patents taken out on the results and profits payable to the research universities and their associated biotech and agribusiness industries.

in nature" (ibid., 58, 71). This metaphysical meaninglessness extends also to ethical and moral nihilism. Two neo-Darwinian philosophers, themselves of the neo-Darwinian persuasion, have made this clear:

> Darwinism thus puts the capstone on a process that since Newton's time has driven teleology to the explanatory sidelines. In short it has made Darwinians into metaphysical Nihilists denying that there is any meaning or purpose to the universe, its contents and its cosmic history. But in making Darwinians into metaphysical nihilists, the solvent algorithm should have made them into ethical nihilists, too. For intrinsic values and obligations make sense only against the background of purposes, goals, and ends that are not merely instrumental. (Summers and Rosenberg, 653)

Representing the other side in the debate, and a major critic of Gould and the radical contingency and meaninglessness that Gould espouses, is the Cambridge paleontologist Simon Conway Morris (Morris 1988, 2003). Conway Morris argues that rather than rampant divergence, the history of life reveals strong evidence of repeated patterns of convergence. He gives many examples of how otherwise very different animals show similarities in structure and function and in other biological properties. "Convergence," he writes, "demonstrates that the possible types of organism are not unlimited but may in fact be severely constrained.... Put simply, convergence shows that in a real world not all things are possible" (ibid., 139, 202). In other words, replaying Gould's tape of life would produce not a widely different world each time, but one, not exactly like but very similar to the one we in fact have. Constraints of the physical and chemical world and the limited possibilities "under the scrutiny of natural selection result in repeated patterns of evolutionary convergence" (ibid.).

Elsewhere he writes, "remarkably similar end points can be arrived at from quite different starting points.... Despite different starting points, different lineages converge on particular destinations" (ibid., 9).

As for progress, Conway Morris has recently written: "Life has trajectories (trends if you prefer), and progress is not some noxious by-product of the terminally optimistic, but simply part of our reality" (ibid., xiii). And he goes further:

> Simply because evolution has delivered us to a point where only now can the word *progress* make any sense, need not mean that it either has no relevance to the human condition or that it lacks an evolutionary reality.... Neither is progress a question of the sheer number of species, nor the supposed number of body plans. What we do see through geological time is the emergence of more complex worlds.... Nor is this a limiting view.... Nor need we imagine that the appearance of humans is the culmination of all evolutionary history. Yet, when within the animals we see the emergence of larger and more complex brains, sophisticated vocalizations, echolocation, electrical perception, advanced social systems including eusociality, viviparity, warm-bloodedness, and agriculture—all of which are convergent—then to me that sounds like progress. (ibid., 307)

Toward the end of his book, Morris says, "The principle aim of this book has been to show that the constraints of evolution and the ubiquity of convergence make the emergence of something like ourselves a near-inevitability (ibid., 328). We will return later to this question of the place and role of the human being in evolution.

In a comprehensive overview of more than 125 leading biologists since 1900, Bernd Rosslenbroich has identified many patterns proposed by the various authors as measures of development, sometimes viewed as measures of progress—patterns such as increasing morphological complexity, increasing differentiation, improvement in adaptation, increasing centralization and differentiation of the nervous system, increasing capacity for homeostasis, enhancement of ecological possibilities, increasing autonomy and emancipation from the environment, and many other patterns (Rosslenbroich 2006). He notes that, while such large-scale patterns are rarely addressed explicitly, "they are often embedded in general discussions and textbooks." As a general way of describing such large-scale evolutionary patterns,

Rosslenbroich concludes that it will not be possible to eliminate the term *progress* in the future, "just as it has not been possible to eliminate it in the past." "Eliminating it from the vocabulary of evolutionary biology" he writes, "is not the solution but rather a moratorium" (ibid., 54, 58).

The debates and discussions surrounding the notion of progress point to perhaps the most significant and fruitful insight of Darwin; namely, his vision of the essential unity of all nature—plants, animals, and human beings. Darwin's theory, however, has sought to understand this unity solely in terms of the relations between and among the external, material, and mechanistic elements of nature. It has accordingly striven to reduce the unity of nature to the materialistic and mechanistic. But biological research over the past two centuries, often brilliant and dogged, has continued to discover—turn up—aspects of nature that do not fit easily into the orthodox theory. We have seen in the discussion of "progress," for example, patterns and relationships of nature that seem to involve not only external, mechanical relationships but also internal, participatory relationships, both among organisms and between organisms and their environment. Such participatory, internal relationships, in which each participant is transformed in a mutual interaction with the others, point strongly to the presence in nature of an inside of meaning, purpose, value, formative principles and forces, and subjectivity—consciousness—of varying degrees and levels.

As Barfield and Whitehead point out, without the inner reality of nature, together with the outer, there can really be no evolution as transformation—change with inner connection and continuing identity, only substitution and rearrangement of material parts. Thoroughgoing neo-Darwinians deny this inwardness and hold fast to the meaninglessness and ethical nihilism that is thus entailed. Other biologists, perhaps the majority, continue to wrestle, often brilliantly, to understand the unity of nature and to live in tension with discoveries and puzzles that do not rest comfortably with the materialistic metaphysics that have accompanied the theory. In the long term, perhaps the great gift of Darwinism will not be the set of metaphysical assumptions with which it has been unnecessarily invested, but the vision of the unity of nature that continues to inspire.

One striking example of the influence of the Darwinian vision of the interrelationships of all life has been the emergence and growth of the relatively new field of ethology—the study of animal behavior and emotions. The Austrian scientist, Konrad Lorenz, is often seen as having given the field its modern form with the publication of his book, *King Solomon's Ring* in 1949. The field, however, actually owes its modern origins to Darwin himself who brought his own deep interest in animal intelligence and emotions to bear in his book, *The Emotional Lives of Animals,* a work still studied and referred to appreciatively today (Darwin 1949). During the past half century the field of ethology has grown enormously, with countless studies being made of animal behavior, emotions, and intelligence, both in the laboratory and in the wild. Besides the interest of Darwin and the growing numbers of ethologists like Lorenz, advances in modern genetics have probably also given the field an important impulse. The discovery of the existence of the genome in nearly all organisms has heightened the sense that the kinship of all animals, including the human being, runs very deep indeed.

Animal researchers have made important, and frequently striking, discoveries in the realm of animal consciousness, including intelligence, tool use, symbolic communication and language capacities, problem solving abilities, and play—all involving a wide range of emotions: fear, pain, curiosity, joy, depression, sorrow, and many others. Besides revealing the richness and significance of animals' inner experience, these studies also strongly reinforce the idea that, along with natural selection and contingency, animals themselves play an active part in the evolutionary process.

Most ethologists count themselves staunch Darwinists. The irony in this, which is becoming increasingly evident, is that the metaphysical strictures of Darwinism do not allow for consciousness or subjectivity of any kind. An exclusive emphasis on the material and mechanistic cannot recognize these inner experiences, and certainly can accord them no role in the evolutionary process. To be sure, scientists of animal consciousness and emotions continue to make many new and important discoveries that enrich our knowledge of the animals, but it is in spite of, not because of, the received Darwinism to which they appeal as a matter of course (filial devotion?). Outwardly and publicly, they affirm their support for a Darwinian theory of the animal as a mechanistic product of chance; in actuality, they have moved ever closer to an understanding of the animal as a living organism with its own inner experience of intrinsic worth expressed in the qualitative/quantitative wholeness of its being.

This irony is further compounded by the fact that many of these scientists of animal consciousness are serious and active advocates of animal rights and animal welfare. Again the dominant neo-Darwinian theory, apart from its central vision of the connections of all life, offers them no real support. A consistent materialistic and mechanistic Darwinism must by its nature be totally indifferent either to animal welfare or animal suffering. Moreover, if followed out to its actual consequences, Darwinian theory offers no resistance whatever to the worst kinds of cruelty to animals, whether in factory farming or in "scientific" animal experimentation and vivisection.

Recently the philosopher Thomas Nagel has argued that current Darwinian theory is fundamentally flawed and false. The title of his book is, *Mind and Cosmos: Why the Materialist Neo-Darwinian Conception of Nature is Almost Certainly False* (Nagel 2012). It is false he says because it totally ignores and cannot deal with three of the most important realms of experience—including we might add, the experiences of neo-Darwinian scientists themselves; namely, consciousness, cognition, and value.

None of what has been said should be taken to imply that the material and quantitative are unimportant or to be ignored. Indeed, no reason exists why biologists, including microbiologists, should not concern themselves chiefly with these if their primary interests so incline them. This would be their methodological preference, and we could expect it to continue to yield interesting and important results. What is essential, however, is that the material and mechanical not be inflated into all-inclusive explanations of everything. We could also hope that these biologists, even if methodologically they choose to limit their inquiries to the quantitative and material, would maintain a vital sense that they are working with the outer, material manifestations of the inner life and form of the whole organism.

To neglect or disparage the inner and qualitative out of a (perhaps most often unconscious) pre-commitment to materialistic metaphysical principles that originate from nonscientific sources is itself patently unscientific. It is in the end a barrier to knowledge. It restricts the possibility of knowledge exclusively to the sense-bound, material world. It is self-contradictory because it denies (though this is seldom recognized) the basic non-sensory, immaterial realities without which empirical science itself would be impossible—a sense for truth, the grasp of meaning, and such moral characteristics as respect for the evidence, honesty, freedom, and others.

The neo-Darwinian William Provine has provided a vivid example of what is at issue. "Science," Provine asserts, "reveals to us only chance and necessity.... We humans are just complex machines without free will that have been poorly programmed for moral behavior" (Nitecki, 71). Although Provine denies the possibility of freedom in theory, here he assumes it in practice simply by taking pen in hand and giving public expression to his ideas (another realm of the non-sensory and immaterial). Apart from the self-contradiction, Provine helps lay bare the fact that an exclusively materialistic/mechanistic science is not only metaphysically and ethically nihilistic, it is at bottom also *epistemologically nihilistic*. It stymies the pursuit of knowledge and denies inquiry into the inner life and meaning of nature. To free science of the hold of these hobbling metaphysical notions that are not actually inherent to it, would help restore science to its original ideal of the unfettered quest for truth and knowledge.

2.

EVOLUTION FROM THE PERSPECTIVE
OF RUDOLF STEINER

Throughout his life, Rudolf Steiner was both a champion and a critic of Charles Darwin, and also of Ernst Haeckel, Darwin's foremost German disciple. This was not inconsistent on Steiner's part because, while he was ready to affirm important aspects of the Darwinian theory, he also held that it is incomplete in itself and deals with only one side of the evolutionary process. What is required, Steiner maintained, in addition to the outer processes of natural selection, adaptation, and environmental specialization ("adaptive radiation"), is a concrete grasp of the inner life and reality of nature, the inner, non-sensory realities of being, life, and organic wholeness and development, which alone make true transformation and any coherent conception of evolution possible.

As Steiner wrote in his autobiography toward the end of his life, he had been convinced early on that, if taken seriously, Darwin's theory, along with Haeckel's appropriation of it, would in itself point to the need for its own inner deepening. "I saw," he wrote, "in the thinking of Lyell, Darwin, Haekel something that, although incomplete as it issued from them, is nevertheless capable of becoming sound in the course of *its* evolution." And he wrote further: "To seek for understanding of the physical structure of man by tracing his forms from the animal forms, as Haeckel does in comprehensive fashion in his *Anthropogenie* [*The Evolution of Man*], appeared to me a good foundation for the future development of knowledge" (Steiner 1951, 247–8).

Steiner regarded the outer picture of evolutionary change, built up by scientists during the nineteenth century through devoted and painstaking work with the fossil record and comparative anatomy, as a great and valuable achievement. Accordingly he emphasized the importance of seeing that plants and animals, including the human being, stand in a universal evolutionary process with genealogical connections between different organic forms. Commenting in his autobiography on a series of lectures he had given to workers at the Berlin Workers' School on understanding Haeckel's book, *Welträtsel (World Riddles)*, Steiner said, "In the positive biological third of this book, I saw a brief compendium of the kinship among living beings. My general conviction that mankind can be led from this direction to spirituality, I held to be true of the workers also" (ibid., 286). Steiner was to extend and deepen this vision of the kinship among living beings, and especially the kinship between animals and the human.

The inner aspect of evolution, which Steiner refers to here as the spiritual, he sees as demanded by the sense-bound, outer facts themselves, if they are ever to be adequately understood. Rudolf Steiner was concerned to show that the materialism of the scientific revolution, and of today, is not intrinsic to science as such, but, moreover, stands in the way of a genuine scientific understanding of the world. "Materialism," Steiner wrote, "was imported into natural science, and naturalists such as Ernst Haeckel accepted it unconsciously. Darwin's discovery *per se* need not have tended to materialism" (quoted, Davy, 119). Many philosophers have made a similar criticism of the purely quantitative, mechanical worldview, but Steiner also took a crucial further step. As insightful as their critiques of the material worldview may be, the critics have almost all failed to take the positive next step of indicating how to develop an actual, concrete science of qualities and of the non-sensory.

Steiner did take this next step. He not only criticized the adequacy of the materialistic world view, as have a number of others, but he showed that it is possible to develop actual ways of knowing the qualitative, inner, immaterial realities of the world. It is not only possible, it is essential if the qualitative beauty, meaning, and future of the earth are to be preserved. Central to Steiner's

Anthroposophy, therefore, is his providing a path of inner discipline necessary to develop the cognitive capacities for coming to know the qualitative realities of the world. (Steiner 1986, 1997, among others). Steiner was himself gifted from an early age with capacities for perceiving and understanding the non-sensory and qualitative, and he continued to deepen and strengthen these capacities throughout his life.

During his life Steiner reported extensively on his own investigations of the qualitative dimensions of the world, and of their potential for enriching our understanding of ourselves and of the world. He was thus able to provide fundamental new insights, and new directions for further research by others, in such fields as education, agriculture, medicine, the arts, and social life and organization, as well as in many fields of science, including the science of evolution. The method he developed for investigating the qualitative Steiner called "spiritual science"— in German *Geisteswissenschaft,* the same term still used today in German universities for what we call the "humanities," presumably even for us the subjects dealing mainly with the qualitative. These realms of the qualitative, Steiner was convinced, could be investigated with the same rigor that marks our present quantitative science. The philosopher of science, Nicholas Rischer, has written: "One can never be sure that the science of tomorrow will not endorse what the science of today rejects.... Even if X lies outside the range of science as we nowadays construct it, it by no means follows that X lies outside science" (Rischer). "Spiritual Science," as Steiner laid the basis for it, is his concrete effort to show that the science of today, predominantly sense-bound and quantitative, can be extended to include the non-sensory and the qualitative.

Of extraordinary importance for Steiner in his development was his discovery as a young man of the scientific method and work of Johann Wolfgang von Goethe. By the time of his death in 1832, Goethe was acclaimed as the greatest poet and writer in German literature. What was not so well known then, as well as now, is that Goethe also worked for some thirty years in the fields of science, and that he himself considered his scientific investigations just as important (or more so) as his literary accomplishments. The range of Goethe's scientific work was broad, extending to botany, biology, morphology, meteorology, and color theory. And in each of these fields, his approach was unique because Goethe was exploring and developing a qualitative method of scientific inquiry as distinct from the dominant quantitative science of his and our day.

As a young man Rudolf Steiner's own philosophic and scientific abilities had drawn the attention of some leading Goethean scholars and he was invited to edit and write commentaries for two major editions of Goethe's scientific writings. Beginning at the age of 21, Steiner edited Goethe's scientific work for the Kurshner series on German National Literature and then was called to the Goethe–Schiller archives in Weimar in 1890 where he spent many years editing the important Sophia edition of Goethe's scientific work (Steiner 1950, 1968).*

Goethe's scientific method was of great importance for Steiner. He saw in it a point of departure for conceptualizing and articulating the essence of a systematic science of qualities, which Steiner himself would develop and carry even further (Steiner 1986, 1968, 1997).

At the risk of considerable oversimplification, suffice it here to consider briefly some central features of Goethe's scientific method. Basic to Goethe is the importance of seeing the organism in its wholeness and inner coherence. This requires, first of all, that we observe the phenomena of nature with care, patience, and respect. It is essential that we allow the phenomena to present themselves in their own right; that we do not prematurely impose upon them our own preformed assumptions and theories. If we

---

* For decades Goethe's scientific investigations remained largely unknown, and, when they did come to the attention of orthodox scientists, were long dismissed as the work of an amateur or aesthete. Since World War II, however, a major reappraisal of Goethe's scientific work has been under way, perhaps triggered by Werner Heisenberg's challenge to the scientific community to reevaluate Goethe's scientific accomplishments and stop rejecting them out of hand because they did not fit the dominant Newtonian–Kantian worldview. (Heisenberg 1974, Amrine 1987, Bortoft 1986, Zajonc 1993, Seamon and Zajonc 1998, Holdrege 2013).

refrain from forcing the phenomena under our own already pre-conceived theories and thought models, we are then in position to begin to perceive and experience something new—to allow the plant or the animal to present itself to us in its own immediacy and wholeness. Holding fast in our careful observation to what the organism presents to us, we can then begin to bring an active, disciplined imagination of creative thinking and sensitized feelings to bear in our understanding of the plant or animal.

To the extent that we achieve this, it becomes a truly participatory way of knowing. It entails our entering into an active, interrelationship with the phenomena, bringing our own qualitative awareness and sensitivities into connection with the qualitative being of the plant or animal itself. Just as in knowledge of another person, if I want to come to know qualities in the other—say, of trustworthiness, generosity, and so on—I must also bring these qualities to birth within myself, else I would be unable to recognize or respond to their presence in the other. Similarly, I can begin to enter into and grasp the principles of life, form, and meaningful development of the organism only to the extent that I have been able to cultivate and bring to birth in my own thinking and cognitive–feeling capacities the requisite, qualitative sensitivity and awareness, By the same token, the plant or animal carefully observed and imaginatively contemplated will from its own side begin to call forth and strengthen my capacities for qualitative discernment and understanding. Goethe himself wrote, "Each new object, well contemplated, opens up a new organ within me." Thus through a concentrated and living, participatory, qualitative thinking and feeling, we can begin to enter into an awareness and understanding of the qualitative, inner life of the organism.

Steiner, in line with Goethe, did not regard the outer—the quantitative and the mechanical—as unimportant. On the contrary. He did insist, however, that these must be placed and understood within the context of organic, qualitative wholeness. Steiner wrote that "Darwin dealt only with the factors that cause the world of living things to develop in a certain way," that is, the various external forces that bind the organism to the earth and that help maintain a physical continuity from generation to generation. Among such factors are those described by Darwin as natural selection and specialized adaptation to the environment. Steiner went on to say, however, that Darwin did not deal with "the something upon which these factors take their determining action." Steiner insisted, "The investigation of the external factors alone cannot possibly lead to a complete theory of organism" (Kranich 1999). With the external must also be brought that essential, internal "something"—the inner, qualitative reality that gives to the organism its life, its coherence, its meaning, and its ultimate identity. In this regard, Goethe and Steiner, as does Whitehead as well, pointed to the "archetype"—the living, dynamic, but immaterial principle, which is the source of both diversity and identity in the ongoing process of the organism's evolution. It is this immaterial, formative reality, that we have earlier seen emphasized by Barfield and Whitehead that makes genuine evolutionary transformation—identity through change—possible, rather than a mere substitution and rearrangement of parts, which is no true evolution.

Rudolf Steiner was, indeed, an early supporter of Darwin's emphasis on the interrelated evolution of the living world of plants, animals, and humans. But he was a far more radical and thoroughgoing evolutionary thinker than Darwin or any of his scientific followers from Huxley to the present. For Steiner evolution is a cosmic process involving the whole of existence. The kingdoms of nature—plants, animals, and humans are all caught up in the evolutionary process, but so, too, is everything else. Substances themselves, along with the laws that govern them, are not fixed and forever unchanging, but are also evolving, and come to radically different manifestations at different stages of the cosmos and of the earth. Consciousness itself is also evolving, and the changing forms of consciousness find expression in the successive stages of the development of the earth and its kingdoms of nature. And the immaterial, spiritual world—with its many forms and levels of cosmic being (cosmic intelligences, consciousnesses) is also evolving. The entire cosmos—the physical and the spiritual—is in a constant state of evolutionary development.

From this encompassing view of cosmic evolution, four perspectives that Steiner brings will be of special importance in our explorations. First is Steiner's all-important view that the human being stands at the center of earth evolution. From this perspective the animals can in large part be seen, as Steiner presents them, as branches from the human in the course of general evolution. A second perspective, seemingly, perhaps, at odds with the first, comes in Steiner's many explicit descriptions of how the animals go through their own independent developments, and have their own inherent value and meaningful experience. A third perspective has to do with Steiner's many descriptions of how the human and the animal have been joined from the beginning in a deep and intimate relationship, a relationship that is destined to continue into the far future. A fourth perspective that Steiner brings, one that enters into all of the other perspectives, is contained in his many, detailed descriptions of the presence of high spiritual beings—again, agents and levels of cosmic intelligence—working with the human and the other creatures in the processes and events of evolution.

We shall return as we go along to aspects of each of these four perspectives. Let us begin with some preliminary considerations of Steiner's view of the centrality of the human being in earth evolution. The great spiritual traditions have almost all seen the human being as central among the other beings of the world. And precisely because of this, most of the great spiritual traditions have commanded the human to exercise a special responsibility for the wellbeing of the earth and its creatures. Steiner shares both these emphases with the traditions—the central importance of the human being and the special responsibility of the human for the other beings of the earth. The traditions, however, have almost all lacked an evolutionary perspective; in fact, many have been hostile to the idea of evolution. Steiner went far beyond the traditions by placing the earth and all its beings within an evolutionary context.

As central to earth evolution, the human being is also a primary source, the indispensable starting point, for our understanding of the earth, as well as of ourselves. To leave the human being out is to leave a yawning gap in the possibilities of our knowledge of our selves and of the world. Other modern thinkers, besides Steiner, have argued this. Goethe, for example, said that the human being is the most accurate instrument of our knowledge. The late-nineteenth- and early-twentieth-century American philosopher, William James, wrote: "If we survey the field of history and ask what feature all great periods of revival, of expansion of the human mind, display in common, we shall find, I think, simply this: that each and every one of them have said to the human being, 'The inmost nature of the reality is congenial to powers that you possess'" (James 1950). The modern biologist L. Charles Birch, has vividly depicted the central position of the human in our understanding of the world. Birch is deeply influenced by the philosopher Alfred North Whitehead in his insistence that an adequate understanding of the world must take into account the realms of life, feeling, qualities, and creative archetypes as realities. Birch, following Whitehead, maintains that the place to start in knowing is with the human being—with our selves. Birch stresses that if science is ever to know the inner qualities of nature and not only its quantitative outside, it must take seriously the human being as our primary clue to understanding the world. Birch has written:

> A universe that produces humans cannot be known apart from this fact. It is a *humiverse*. We only begin to know what it is by what it becomes. We do not start with electrons and atoms and build a universe. We start with humanity and interpret the rest in terms of that starting point. In the same way we know more about an oak tree by studying the tree and how it has become a tree from an acorn, than we can by confining our studies to the acorn.... Human experience is a high level exemplification of reality in general. There the subjective world of feeling is real for us. But that world extends beyond the human when we see everything through this window, be it cats or elephants or electrons.... To bring the human being into the picture is to bring in mind and consciousness and purposes, sensations of red and blue, bitter and sweet, suffering and joy, good and bad. Because exclusive mechanism cannot deal with these human qualities, its framework is incomplete. (Birch 1979)

The emphasis on the centrality of the human for an adequate understanding of the world in general contains the further implications that the human is also an essential clue to our understanding of evolution and to our relationship with the animals. Rudolf Steiner took this next step: in his perspective the human being is present at the beginning of Earth evolution and contains within its own being all the kingdoms of nature.

Put bluntly, without further explanation, such a statement cannot help but raise questions to the modern mind. One such question is: If the human being is present and active from the beginning of Earth evolution, why is it the last to make its appearance in the fossil record? And in what form or forms was the human present in the evolutionary process if it did not appear physically—that is, leave fossil traces—until very late in the course of evolution? A second related question is: Is there any empirical evidence in what we know of animal development from the fossil record that in any way suggests the presence and influence of the human being on this development? And, finally, not so much a scientific question as an ethical one: Is this view of the importance of the human being not just another version of the century-long, widespread assumption that the human being is superior to the animals, and can, therefore, exercise "dominion" over them in any way the human sees fit to satisfy human desires and purposes? We will return to these questions.

Let us, however, first turn to Rudolf Steiner's account of the human and animal emergence and of their interrelationships in in the course of Earth evolution. In Steiner's view all was contained together in the primordial foundations of the origins of the Earth. Separation then began to take place and the result, broadly viewed, was the gradual emergence of the Earth and the four kingdoms of nature—the mineral, the plant, the animal, and the human. What in Steiner's view distinguishes the human as a fourth kingdom beyond the others is the possession by the human of an individual, independent "I"-being, or Self. This "I" is a spiritual reality that lives in each human being and is reflected in the human "personality." Because of the presence of the "I"-being, each individual human being is unique and of intrinsic value along with every other individual human. It is the "I" that gives to each individual the potential for genuine freedom. This potential for freedom has many dimensions and possibilities, for examples: the freedom of creative thinking beyond the givens of sensory experience; the freedom for self-knowledge and self-transformation beyond the constraints of habit, instinct, the physical body, and the social and natural environment; and the freedom for care and responsibility for the other—for other people, for the Earth and its creatures, for the spiritual world and its ideal possibilities. Of course, this freedom is a potential—it must be won again and again and made a reality by the individual—by the "I"-being itself.

An independent, individual "I" required for its presence and expression on Earth the development of a physical body capable of serving as a suitable vehicle for it. This meant, among other things, a body capable of uprightness as its primary posture, a body thus raised above the horizontal and released thereby, to an important degree, from the constraining, downward pull of earth forces. It also meant a body generalized in its capacities and structures and not subject to dead-end specialization in any particular environmental conditions. And it required a body capable of serving as an instrument for language and meaningful communication. Only in such a body can an independent, individual self begin to realize its potential for freedom.

Steiner's account of Earth evolution is difficult for the modern mind on several counts, not least of which is his description of three major, cosmic stages preceding the appearance of our Earth, on which we now find ourselves (Steiner 1997, ch. 4). These earlier stages preceding and laying the foundation for our Earth he calls "planetary" stages. The first he called "Old Saturn," and following it two further stages named "Old Sun" and "Old Moon." These are not to be confused with the present planets of our solar system, though there is a relationship as the names suggest. Each of these planetary embodiments underwent smaller developmental stages of its own. When the development of each "Planet" was complete it receded into a purely spiritual existence and was followed by the next (Old Saturn, Old Sun, and Old Moon in that order). These three laid the foundations for our present Earth, which followed them.

The first planetary stage, Old Saturn, existed as a finely differentiated body of warmth only, enormous in size, extending roughly to the orbit of our present Saturn. It was on Old Saturn that the physical body began to be formed, existing at this point only as fine currents of heat, delicate "formations" of warmth. (Steiner 1997 and, for example, Steiner 1987b). Though it has since developed far beyond these earliest beginnings, the physical body is now the oldest and most developed of all the human members, and also of the animals.

Following Old Saturn was the second planetary embodiment called Old Sun, which existed as a kind of gaseous, light-filled radiant being. During all of these planetary incarnations, or stages, high spiritual beings were constantly at work bringing spiritual forces and patterns of form to bear on the shaping of the developing entity. On Old Sun there was added to the physical what Steiner has described as the etheric or life body. The etheric is what endows the physical with the capacities for life, growth, development, and reproduction, and for memory forces, such as those involved in physical inheritance. The planetary incarnation of Old Sun was followed by that of the third embodiment, Old Moon. Existing at first as an active being of great spiritual and physical energy, Old Moon began to take on a fluid element, and gradually over the course of its life to condense into a kind of colloidal or spongy consistency. On Old Moon a third component was added to the developing physical and life bodies. Steiner called this third component "the astral." The astral is the carrier of feelings and passions. It can be generally described as the feeling reality of the universe, the soul of the universe.

From this point on, humans and animals both came to possess in their developing archetypes not only the physical and etheric, but also the astral, the capacities for feeling and consciousness. Because the archetypes of the plants had begun to densify and separate out of the common development on Old Sun, though they were imbued with the etheric, they came to lack the astral.

The etheric consciousness of plants, therefore, would remain at the level of deep sleep. The animals and humans, however, possessing the astral, could come to experience subjective feelings and develop the potentials for a dreaming and even waking consciousness. In this regard, it should be noted, their possession of both the etheric and the astral means that the humans and the animals alike have, in a word, souls, that is, an inner life of feeling and consciousness.

By the middle of Old Moon the evolving bodily archetypes had reached a significant point of development and interrelationships. By then separation and distinction among them had brought about the emergence of three major kingdoms of nature. These were "mixed" forms: a "plant–mineral" kingdom; an "animal–plant" kingdom; and a "human–animal" kingdom. The lowest was the plant–mineral, which provided the basic physical surface of Old Moon. At this point there were no minerals such as we have today (no rocks), but some densification had taken place and the Old Moon's surface Steiner describes as "akin to a peat bog or boiled spinach" or as a "viscous sea," "living and bubbling" (Steiner 1997; 1987b). The animal–plants, the forerunners of our plants, subsisted on this plant–animal substance as their "ground."

Later on, with the appearance of our present Earth further densification of this plant–mineral realm would result eventually in the mineral kingdom as we now know it. The human–animal kingdom on Old Moon contained both the archetypes of our animals and of the human. These kingdoms were carried over into the earlier stages of Earth as it emerged after Old Moon. This suggests that as further separation and differentiation took place, as the human form and animal forms became more and more distinguished from one another, both human and animal can, nevertheless, be said to have descended from a common mixed form, though as we have seen the primordial human form on Old Saturn contained all. Even in the processes of separation and differentiation the kinship of all beings remains a common thread running through the whole of evolution, from its primordial Old Saturn beginnings to our present Earth existence.

Following Old Moon, the Earth—our present Earth—began to emerge. In its early stages it was necessary for the emerging Earth to recapitulate the conditions of the earlier old planetary incarnations, first something like the gaseous state of Old Sun, and, subsequently, the liquid state of Old Moon. As the science writer John Davy has remarked, gaseous and liquid here are only analogies for what were tremendous spiritual forces permeating the entire planet, which existed as a vast, living being in its own right (Davy 1985, 97). As the gaseous, fluid conditions of these early stages condensed further, the mineral began to precipitate out as the first kingdom to appear on Earth. Even then the minerals were far more plastic and malleable than they were to become, existing still in a kind of ductile, colloidal state. Gradually, however, increasing densification of the early mineral eventually formed our present "hard" matter of earth and rocks. Plants then also began to descend on Earth. The human and animal relationship, however, became ever-more complicated.

The human archetype remained for long ages in a spiritual state, not taking on a densified form on Earth until it could develop a body capable of receiving and carrying an independent "I," or self. This self, a gift from high spiritual beings, had to wait for the proper physical body. As early, embryonal forms of the human archetype began to densify and appear, they were discarded by the human archetype as too premature to serve as the vehicle for an individual, independent "I." Other beings sought to enter these embryonal forms as their "I"-beings, but could not do so precisely because these forms were too premature to support an "I"-being. These beings had to remain in the spiritual world to serve as group "I"-beings for groups of similar animal forms. Similar animals were guided by a group "I" and were united in a group soul, since their individual astral participated in the similar astral of the other animals in their group. The animals with their group "I"-beings and group souls represent premature human forms. We could put it figuratively: the animals wanted to be human with their own independent "I"-being, but acted too soon.

Eventually, more complex and more highly conscious animals began to appear. Finally, with the help of spiritual beings, a bodily form was attained by the complete human archetype that was suitable for an independent "I"-being, and human beings began to make their appearance on Earth—and, only then, of course, as the last to appear in the fossil record.

It would be misleading, however, to think of the human "I" holding back until just the right animal body had developed, and then slipping into it as a kind of readymade, completed garment. This view seems sometimes to be represented as Steiner's and the anthroposophic view, wrongly I think. For one thing, it involves a kind of spiritual–physical dualism in which the spiritual "I" suddenly enters into the physical without having had any real, previous relationship with it. This does not do justice to the difficulties and challenges—to the give and take—involved in any incarnation of the spirit into the material, whether it be the creation of a work of art or the realization of one's ideals into concrete, institutional forms. Nor does this readymade garment view take into account Steiner's own indications that the spiritual human being had to work over the ages directly with the emerging animal bodies in forming and fashioning its own proper "I"-bearing body. And, moreover, this view has a tendency to regard the animal forms as merely unimportant and discarded remnants of an otherwise completed process—much like the discarded shavings from a completed carving. This runs counter to healthy human sensitivities. And, it certainly conflicts with Steiner's own more comprehensive view that the animals have a value and integrity of their own; that we are, moreover, deeply indebted to the animals for our own development; and, finally, that we have an important, ongoing relationship with the animals, both physically and spiritually, for good and ill, and will continue to do so well into the far-distant future.

The biologist and anthroposophist, Stephen Stockmar, has stressed that Steiner's work has many pointers to the fact that the human being has won its present form through a step-wise, active transformation of an already existing, usually simpler, animal form (Stockmar 2009). Only through a direct engagement with preceding animal forms could the spiritual human "I" shape and unite with a physical body suitable for itself. As Stockmar puts it, the human being had to wrestle its humanness on the earthly-physical plane through experience, in an ongoing relationship with the animals in fashioning an adequate body for itself. Steiner himself gives a description of this "wrestling." In 1904, Steiner wrote:

> Simultaneously with its first incarnation in the Lemurian age,* the untarnished human spirit...sought its primal physical incarnation. The physical development of Earth with its animal-like creatures had not evolved so far at that time, the whole of this animal–human organism was not so far advanced then that it could have incorporated the human spirit. But a part of it, a certain group of animal-like beings had evolved so far that the seed of the human spirit could descend into it to give form to the human body. (Steiner 2000, 11–12)

All animal forms were first present in the original human archetype. We have seen that Steiner speaks of the early ancestors as human–animal and/or animal–human. In order to incarnate on Earth, the human had to take on and work its way through the animal nature. Stockmar writes, "The human is not spared the way through the animal world in order to appear on Earth" (17). As spiritual beings with the spiritual gift of the I, the human does not descend (or ascend) from the animals. But because we both separated from a common, mixed ancestral form, we are in body the closest of cousins with the animals, to whom we owe much.

Clopper Almon has succinctly summarized the emergence of the human being from the dynamic human and animal interaction described by Steiner:

> Thus, it appears, we have indeed cooperated with the animals in the development of both their bodies and ours. We gave them forms we could no longer use. Then, later perhaps, we worked with them to lift up their bodies. Then came a time when we entered some of those bodies more completely. Thereupon, we seem to have begun working the bodies into softer, more

---

* Steiner's terminology for a long period that covers roughly the Pre-Cambrian, Paleozoic, and Mesozoic periods of modern dating.

youthful forms, through the presence of the human etheric. This factor, not a struggle for existence, has led from animal-like ancestors to today's humanity. (Almon 1998, 95)

The transformation of the animal world, the biologist Bernd Rosslenbroich has observed, "must have played itself out, therefore, in a changing relationship between the evolution of the human, which at first took place in a 'finer material', and the already stronger formed animals" (Rosslenbroich 2006, 98).

This entire process of "wrestling the human form into existence," as Stockmar puts it, was not the seamless unrolling of a plan. Much less was it the application of the archetype as a fixed and rigid template, a kind of spiritual cookie-cutter, or die, stamping out the human form. It was much more a cosmic adventure, fraught with challenges and risks, and the possibility of failures and dead-ends. Our human origins were risky, our human presence is risky, and our human future will be risky. This risk is endemic to the essence of a free and independent spiritual "I"-being. And it is fitting that this "I"-being be able to fully embrace the risk in order to attain new levels of human and Earth existence.

In order to progress in evolution the human had to expel from its own being those bodily qualities and organizations that would hold the human back. Steiner, in many similar statements, expressed it this way:

> Imagine that all the qualities distributed throughout the animal kingdom were in man. He has purified himself from them. Through this he was able to develop further. If we take a muddy liquid and allow the gross matter in it to settle to the bottom, the finer part remains at the top. In the same way the grosser parts that man would have been unable to use for his present condition of development have been deposited like a sediment in the animal forms. Through man having cast out of his line of development these animal forms—his elder brothers, as it were—he has reached his present height. (Steiner 1977, 81–82)

Echoing Steiner, the anthroposophic physician, Werner Hartinger, has written: "Looking at the animal world today we therefore have to say: I once bore those creatures within me as a part of myself; for the sake of my higher development I expelled them from my being" (Hartinger 2005, 123). Another variation of this perspective views the animal forms as having lagged behind, densified earlier, and, therefore, remained at an earlier, premature human stage.

By taking on bodily forms that the human could not use, the animals also took on "astral forms"—passions and emotions—associated with those forms. In doing so, we can say, they removed from the developing human being excessive astrality, which would have proved more than the human I could handle or withstand. This astrality—this emotionality—became woven both into the animal's bodily form, its physiognomy, and into its group soul, the group's characteristic emotional life and expression, including its characteristic sounds and aspects of behavior. This was especially the case with the higher animals whose astrality was closest to that of the evolving human. Steiner writes:

> A large proportion of our present higher animals are nothing other than human beings who were so entangled in their passions that they became hardened and ceased to evolve further. The animals came into being as a consequence of the hardening of human passions. The feelings experienced by an individual who looks about him with real occult understanding are as follows: In the course of becoming a human being I have passed through what I encounter today in the form of lions and snakes. I have lived in all these forms because my own inner being has been involved with the traits that are expressed in these animal forms. (Steiner 1987, 94)

The animals do not take away emotions and passions entirely. Emotions and passions are necessary and are of the substance and nature of the soul, of the astral, which we have in common with the animals in many ways. By assuming excessive emotionality the animals gave to the human being the potential, not always realized, of maintaining a certain emotional balance and control (ibid., 95). But the human being can, as is substantiated by an abundance of empirical evidence, lose balance, fall back, and give in to extreme or uncontrollable passions. One interesting question here is whether the human being in giving into uncontrollable passions is sinking into a kind of "animality" or is actually diving into what is both subhuman and sub-animal: subhuman because the human "I" has been abdicated; sub-animal because the human lacks the animal's group "I" to guide its behavior. In either case, the "I" is missing. Further, Steiner cautions, "We should not, however, imagine that all the animal forms around us, which are representative of specific hardening processes, derived from wicked human passions" (ibid., 95). Some passions in the hands of human beings may be wicked, indeed, but in the animals they are not, simply because animals cannot be evil (see chapter 9). Moreover, and of great importance, the animals have much in common with healthy human emotions. In fact, some animals, especially the mammals and some birds, appear, taken all together, to share in various ways and degrees nearly the full range of emotions common to healthy humans. Steiner himself repeatedly gives instances of the rich soul life of animals: joy in living, contentment, affection, and, we should add, emotional intelligence, as well as fear, anger, depression jealousy, hurt, and so forth.

Ethologists, as we shall see in detail, have been documenting for some years the extensive soul life of animals. At the beginning, this posed for some of them a difficulty. According to the mechanical philosophy dominant in science, animals as machines were denied having souls. The mounting evidence of a rich emotional life on the part of the animals led many ethologists to begin to speak outright of the souls of animals, even though at first they seem to have been taken somewhat by surprise and some of their original reactions had a "golly, gee whiz, the animals have souls" quality to them. The surprise would be greatly lessened by the perspective explored here, which sees the humans and the animals both possessing an astral body, the essence of soul, as the source of all subjectivity, emotions, and passions.

It is of crucial importance to avoid the possible, and easy, misunderstanding that because the animals have made possible the human being they exist on the Earth simply for the sake of the human. The antidote to this misunderstanding has been set forth clearly by Dr. Karl König, founder of the anthroposophic Camp Hill movement for persons with special needs. König is also a remarkable student of animal life, and author of a number of excellent books on many different animals (König 2002; 2013). "Zoology," König has written, "cannot be made to suit one point of view alone, for example that man has separated the animals out of himself. This may be correct if seen from the human standpoint, but when looked at from the point of view of the Earth, I have to say that the Earth organism creates animals for itself as well" (König 2002, 91). Once having taken form and appearing in Earth existence, the animals have acquired their own value in themselves as beings of the Earth. Elsewhere König makes the point still more sharply:

> An object can be useful, but an animal is a being. Neither can human beings be judged as to whether they are useful or harmful; every human being is worthy to live on Earth, or he would not be born. In the same way, each animal group should be seen in the light of its own worth. Although animals always occur as members of their species, family, group and class, they have a task in the plan of creation that only they can carry out. To recognize and to describe this task would be the goal of a future zoology. Current behavioral research is just a door opening on this new vista. (König 2013, 99)

That is to say, animals have being and value in their own right. They do not exist simply for the sake of humans, for our use, our entertainment, our nourishment, our gastrocentric pleasures. That they have for millions of years served humans in these ways does not do justice to their place in the world. That the animals are actually the most vulnerable of creatures has often been seen as an open invitation to take advantage of their defenselessness, rather than as a call to our heightened responsibility for them.

The animals have their own intrinsic worth and value; they have their own spiritual reality and experience. As Steiner observes, this was once recognized by traditional peoples. They preserved a recognition that "spiritual activities and spiritual

laws are active in the life and development of the animal kingdom" (Steiner 1995, 29). This knowledge has largely been lost
in the modern world, which, since the scientific revolution, has
tended to treat the animals not as sacred and sentient beings, but
as unfeeling, soulless mechanisms. Affirming that animals have
their own intrinsic value and being, Steiner offers the possibility
of recovering the ancient respect and reverence toward them in a
way appropriate to modern consciousness,

In the general picture of evolution presented by Steiner, the
animals are seen as branches of the developing human being. But
he also describes explicitly how the animals go through their own
independent development. Once the animal forms began appearing on Earth in their own integral being, densified and physically formed, they immediately became subject to the influences
of the external, shaping environment. In other words, the external, shaping influences that Darwin identified and placed in the
forefront, such as natural selection and adaptive radiation, set in.
Worked upon by these forces and principles, the animal forms
diversified in many, different directions, and in great profusion.
It should probably be recalled in this connection that, contrary
to ultra-neo-Darwinism, not all animals were the entirely passive
recipients of outside environmental pressures, but frequently also
took (and still do) an active—albeit unconscious—part in fashioning the environment in ways more congenial to it (Lewontin
2000, 2011; Cobb 2008). In any case, nevertheless, the manifest
animal forms now faced the challenge of adapting and surviving.
Some survived, adapting and becoming specialized in relation to
the particular environment in which they found themselves. Others, not so successful in adapting, failed to survive and became
extinct. Steiner describes this process in broad brush strokes:

> At this time [during early ages of Earth] different forms of liv-
> ing beings must originate, living beings that were adapted to
> the old conditions, and that nowadays could no longer exist....
> We find (which is geologically demonstrable and shown by pale-
> ontology) that animals have lived that we have to imagine, were
> only adjusted to water, only coming into its present form....
> and animals that were adapted to the atmospheric conditions of

that time.... Aside from these, other forms originated that were adapted to the conditions, so to speak, in such a way that they really could no longer be shaped out of the unformed, moving matter by the original formative principle, but that were able to transform themselves through successive generations, and to improve themselves by means of heredity in such a way that they developed the later forms out of the older ones. The new ones were then adapted to the new Earth conditions. While those forms that in olden times were so strongly penetrated by the formative principle that they could not be reshaped had to die out, those organizations that had remained more movable in themselves, in which the living was not yet fashioned so strongly could remodel themselves and thus develop further on in successive generations. (Steiner 1912)

The transformation of the animal world occurred in a reciprocal relation between the evolution of the human being, which took place within a more delicate, not yet densified realm, and the more densely formed animals appearing on Earth. The appearance of the animals can be fairly accurately followed in the fossil record, with the human being appearing last.

This leads to a question raised earlier: Is there any outer evidence, in the evolutionary record of the appearance of the animals, of the presence and influence of the human being in the process from the beginning? One such sign, and it is a significant one, may be the step-wise formation, from the lowest to the "highest animals," of an ever-increasing release of successive animal forms from the constraints of the environment. Over the whole course of evolution, from the single-cell organism to the human being, the animals can be seen at major transition points to become progressively less limited by environmental constraints. This phenomenon has been described as "evolutionary emancipation," or "evolutionary autonomy" (Rosslenbroich 2009, 2012; Davy 1985; Schad 1977).

Although a few biologists have touched upon the phenomenon of emancipation, the topic has not played a major part in modern evolutionary theory. This neglect may be owing in part to there being no available concept in the dominant theory for explaining it, and, moreover, for neo-Darwinists it probably smacks too much of the controversial notion of progress and the rejected idea of purpose. Attention to the phenomenon of emancipation opens up in renewed form the whole question of the meaning of evolution.

The German biologist and anthroposophist, Bernd Rosslenbroich, has explored the phenomenon in illuminating detail. Rossenbroich gives a tightly formulated definition of emancipation as "an evolutionary shift in the system–environment relationship, so that the direct influences of the environment on the respective individual systems are gradually reduced and stability and flexibility of self-referential intrinsic functions within the system are generated and enhanced" (Rosslenbroich 2009b, 625). He and others give many examples that lend concrete life to this rather abstract definition.

The fish, for example, are almost totally dependent on water—for support, for food, for oxygen, for reproduction. The fish releases its eggs directly into the water leaving them there to develop on their own, vulnerable to whatever might befall them. With the development of limbs the amphibians have a certain independence from water, but are still dependent on moist surroundings, from the egg to the adult. The reptiles also have limbs to support them, but these are further developed to provide them with increased flexibility and mobility. The reptile's internal temperature, however, is still dependent on the environment since the reptiles depend directly on the sun and surroundings for bodily warmth. A major step in autonomy is the birds' and mammals' ability to maintain an even internal body temperature and the ability, thereby, to survive within limits in environments of various degrees of heat and cold. A major step in emancipation from the environment has been the development in the mammal of the amniotic egg, whereby the young are relatively protected inside the bodies of their mothers from conception to birth.

Davy and Rosslenbroich give many other concrete examples showing the increase in autonomy and independence from one major group to the next in a variety of different ways (Rosslenbroich; Davy; Schad). One major step in emancipation is the increase among mammals of flexible behavior. Most animals seem to have what is sometimes described as "fixed action patterns," but among many mammals, and birds also, there appear advanced patterns of flexible behavior that allow, as Rosslenbroich says, "for novel, individual, and non-determined solutions to problems and tasks" (Rosslenbroich 2009b, 637). Learning is perhaps the most widespread and significant example of flexible behavior, significant because learning enables the animal to change its otherwise restricted behavior patterns through experience. "Many mammals and birds," observes Rosslenbroich, "have broad learning dispositions. Well-known examples for animals with pronounced learning abilities are the octopus, dolphin, great apes, parrots and ravens."

Alongside learning, another behavior of high flexibility is play. Song birds and most mammals, especially the human being, engage in play at important stages of their lives, and humans throughout life. Play, Rossenbroich has noted, has been hard to understand from the perspective of Darwinian adaptation, but it is clearly an aspect of behavior leading to great self-control, learning and modification of behavior, and in itself expresses a certain degree of freedom. Imitation among some primates and birds is also an important example of flexible behavior lying outside the usual "fixed-action patterns."

Rosslenbroich also points to simple skills observed among primates and some ravens for planning and thinking ahead. Apes have been observed exhibiting insight into social relationships and, as we shall examine more closely later, even some forms of empathy. Dolphins, chimpanzees, and some ravens have also all shown high flexibility in experiments with signals as communicative tools. Many people are often surprised to learn of the high degree of flexibility in learning and play among some birds, especially song birds. "In song birds," writes Rosslenbroich, "different degrees of flexibility and degrees of freedom from innate song repertoires such as song learning, imitation, duet singing and counter singing can be described" (ibid., 637). We will explore animal learning, play, and communication further in part 2.

Emancipation, the increase in autonomy, should not be seen as a kind of linear sequence, one step leading directly to the next. There are too many complexities and differences in the manifestation of emancipation, including regressions and loss of autonomy at some points. For this reason the increase in emancipation from one level of organism to the next should not be seen as following a fixed linear sequence or the unrolling of a plan. As Rosslenbroich comments, it has been entirely all along a "drama of development" (Rosslenbroich 2012, 19). One is reminded of Steiner's stating that evolution cannot be entirely explained logically because it has not been strictly a logical creation but more an *artistic creation*. "I have often drawn attention," says Steiner, "to the fact that, if we are really to understand the world, we cannot remain at the stage of mere intellectual comprehension, but that what is intellectual must gradually change into an artistic conception of the world" (Steiner 1970, 17–8).

This drama of emancipation reached a decisive turning point with the human upright posture. The uprightness of the human freed the head, the arms, and the hands from the horizontal position of the animals and from the direct pull of the Earth. The arms are not needed for walking or running, unlike the forelegs of the animals. And the hands are freed for all kinds of activities: increasingly complicated use of tools, artistic activities, gesturing, and many others. The head, rather than being pulled down, as with many animals to form a snout, is freed to sit back, look upon the world, and to think. Scientists once held that the enlargement of the brain preceded the attainment of uprightness, which then made possible the freeing of the arms and hands. It is now well established that the erect posture came first, that the complete emancipation of the arms and hands had already taken place before the real enlargement of the brain had set in, only after the attainment of erect posture. The human brain is now the largest among the primates. Upright posture seems to be one of the clearest marks of the first appearance of human beings some 7 million years ago (Schad 2009; Rosslenbroich 2012).

Along with upright posture and a large brain, two other characteristics of human development are unique and particularly important. One is the presence in the human body from birth through adulthood of infantile- or embryonic-like features. These also appear in young anthropoid apes but disappear only after a year or so and are no longer present thereafter. The persistence in the human of infantile-like features is often known as paedomorphism, infantilism, and fetalization. The other unique and important human bodily feature is the opposite from the phenomenon of paedomorphism. Certain parts of the human body continue to grow well beyond what takes place in other mammals. This is called hypermorphosis, in contrast to paedomorphism. This hyper-growth includes among other things, the placement and length of the legs, which contributes to uprightness; the lowering of the larynx and arching of the hard palate, which makes speech possible; and the development of facial muscles, which enable the outer expression of inner feeling and thinking to a far greater extent than is possible for the higher animals. As Jos Verhulst has shown in great detail all these uniquely human developments interact with one another in many different ways. Together they help make possible the human capacities for upright posture and gait, for language, and ultimately for thinking and cognition (Verhulst 2003; Kipp 2005).

Emancipation reaches its crowning point in the human being who appears as the latest and least specialized of all creatures. Steiner wrote:

> For the human, development presented itself such that in olden times we could not perceive him with outer eyes, but we would find him in matter of such formless, mobile kind that in times when animals were already present, he could become everything. The human being was the very latest to descend out of the formless into formed form.... Because the human being was the latest to enter into the formed form, he therefore appeared in such a way that he is not adapted only to certain specific Earth conditions, but to the whole Earth. (Steiner 1912)

The human being is not adapted, bound narrowly, to one kind of environment, but today populates the Earth, from the most frigid to the most arid areas of the globe. Of course this autonomy is relative, in part because of the limitations of the human body, in part because there do exist extreme conditions in which few creatures at all could survive. But the human being can also create its own environments through human culture made possible by thinking and language. Thus in the human being the process of emancipation reaches its furthest point. This emancipation from the environment, of course, has its dark side, for it can lead to neglect of the care of the environment, to over-exploitation of the environment, and to ignorance of the demands of the environment.

The human being has evolved as the most generalized, least specialized of all the creatures. Wolfgang Schad discusses the human hand as a key element in the development of the generalized human being, a key element that can also be seen as emblematic of the whole, unspecialized human being. Schad writes of the hand:

> His hand, in its balanced five-fingered structure, is not limited to any one activity. In this sense, we could say that man's hand is perfected. Yet, biologically speaking, it must be called underdeveloped, for it needs tools in order to compete with abilities animals naturally possess. Man has no shovel-shaped limbs like those of the mole; he must use a spade. Neither are his hands shaped like paddles, as are those of the seal, but he requires oars. He has no hooves but needs shoes. It is nature that provides the tools necessary for an animal's existence. In this respect most mammals are morphologically superior to man. However, since the human hand has not adapted to any single element or purpose, it is also not limited to one capability: man can use one tool and put it down again so as to take up a second and a third. It is just the imperfection of man's hand that permits him a choice, a choice that no animal can make to the same extent. Man's perfection is his imperfection: he can learn to choose freely what nature has not decided for him. (Schad 1977, 259–260)

Of special importance is that the distinctive potentials of the human—standing, speaking, and thinking—can only be actualized in interrelationships with others—in human community.

Only through intensive imitation of other people can young children realize these potentials and make them their own. Here can be seen a particular characteristic of the human self, the "I." The human alone has a physical body that enables the presence and expression of an independent I in the physical world. And, yet, this independent "I"—because it is independent—can turn inward, can become "I"-centered and egoistic. The fact, however, that its most foundational potentials can only be realized in and through the imitation and company of others—other selves— reveals the central quality of true individuality, true humanity. The human only fulfills his or her true, full individuality in community, in relationship with others.

The community of which we are a part, however, reaches far beyond that of other human beings. All earthly creatures began as one, contained in the primal archetype of the cosmic human being. In order to begin our development as independent selves, we separated the animals from us, but by the same token we owe an enormous debt of gratitude for what the animals thereby made possible for us. And they remain our brothers and sisters, as part of our larger cosmic community, together with the spiritual beings who guide and sustain us all. This community, however, is violated and shattered when we forget or exploit our kinship with our companion creatures and with the Earth itself to which we all belong. How are we to understand and honor the kinship that binds us together? How are we to express our gratitude for all that we owe them?

PART II

THE INNER LIFE OF ANIMALS

I

INTRODUCTION

Both the human being and the animal in Steiner's view have a soul, an astral body of consciousness, and emotions. Steiner frequently pointed out that a wide range of emotions present in human beings also finds expression in animals. He spoke of the various animals expressing nervousness, courage, cowardice, rapaciousness, joy, fear, sorrow, and others.

Charles Darwin was another who early on was especially interested in the emotional lives of animals. In his book, *The Expression of Emotions in Man and Animals* (1872), he pointed to the similarities between human and animal emotions. Darwin described animals, especially monkeys, apes, cats, and dogs as experiencing pleasure, pain, terror, suspicion, fear, jealousy, self-complacency, pride, curiosity, anxiety, grief, dejection, despair, love, devotion, sulkiness, anger, disdain, disgust, patience, surprise, and astonishment (I take advantage here of Charles Birch's help in culling this list from Darwin's book; Birch 1995, 39–40). This is, indeed, a fairly comprehensive list of emotions, and Darwin may have been wrong on some of them, but, nevertheless, all are recognizable to us as humans.

Darwin's critics very quickly accused him of anthropomorphism—the unwarranted projection of solely human experiences and capacities onto the animals. The same charge is still leveled by critics at present-day ethologists who identify and study similarities in human and animal emotions. The response of most modern ethologists—and it is likely that both Darwin and Steiner would agree with them in this—is that identifying, that is, feeling, the commonality between human and animal emotions is unavoidable and necessary. It is not anthropomorphizing, if done carefully and self-critically. Our human feelings are indispensable, cognitive capacities for discerning feelings in others—human and animal (and the emphasis on care and self-critical awareness is essential in our relations with both). Konrad Lorenz, one of the pioneers of the study of animal behavior, said that nobody could understand a dog without having possessed the love of one. "What is truly anthropocentric," the moral philosopher Mary Midgely has commented, "is to assume that animals don't think and feel." "Anthropomorphism endures," writes leading ethologist, Marc Bekoff, "because it is a necessity, but it must also be done carefully, consciously, empathically, and biocentrically. We must make every attempt to maintain the animal's point of view" (Bekoff 2007, 125). In this spirit students of animal behavior in the lab and in the wild have produced an abundance of studies exploring and raising questions about the richness and complexity of animal feelings.

Darwin seems to have had three main reasons for holding that animals have feelings similar to ours. One reason was no doubt his own, natural sympathetic love of animals. A second reason was that humans and animals share similar aspects of the nervous and other bodily organ systems that are connected with feelings. A third reason why Darwin emphasized the similarity between human and animal emotions was that it seemed to him strong confirmation of his theory of the evolutionary kinship of human and animal. A critical difference between Darwin and Steiner on this score is that for Darwin the human–animal kinship comes about at the end-stage of a long evolutionary process, whereas for Steiner this kinship is, indeed, well established by the end-stage, but has also been present all along from the earliest beginnings of Earth evolution, when the human and animal were essentially one.

A clear split exists, however, between Darwin's interest in animal emotions and the materialistic–mechanistic principles at the heart of his evolutionary theory. These principles provide no support at all for affirming that animals have feelings, and afforded, therefore, no protection whatsoever against the treatment of animals as unfeeling automatons. By the time Darwin wrote *The*

Origins, the mechanical philosophy, which had emerged with the beginnings of the scientific revolution, was in full swing, and the vivisection of animals without anesthesia was being increasingly accepted as compatible with, if not demanded by, a proper scientific attitude.

Steiner provides a brief sketch of the emergence and consequences of the view of animals as unfeeling machines. He describes how well into the Middle Ages humans maintained vestiges of a sacred attitude toward animals and a sympathetic connection with them. With the triumph of the mechanical philosophy spurred and promoted by such leading scientists as Galileo, Boyle, and philosophers such as Descartes and John Locke, the world began to be seen as consisting of dead matter in motion, governed by the laws of mechanism. The French philosopher, Rene Descartes, was especially instrumental in depicting the animals as mere mechanistic automatons. Steiner and a few others have pointed out that, contrary to a common assumption, Descartes himself did not hold that animals are incapable of pain. Other scientists following him, however, soon drew the logical conclusion that, if the animals are machines and machines don't feel, neither, then, do animals. Very quickly, the practice of vivisection—the dissection of living animals, usually without anesthesia, burgeoned among the scientifically curious. Early on some objectors did come forth. The Enlightenment man of letters, Nicolas Fontaine, reported in 1798 on a physiology laboratory in France, which wholeheartedly took up the view that animals don't feel pain:

> They said that animals were clocks; that the cries they emitted when struck were only the noise of a little spring that had been touched, but that the whole body was without feeling.... They made fun of those who pitied the creatures as if they felt pain. (Birch 1995, 38–39)

The Enlightenment philosopher Voltaire saw the contradiction and lack of logic in the thinking of those scientists who denied that animals have feelings but, also wanted at the same time to open up the animals in order to show the similarity between certain animal organs and human organs responsible for pain:

There are barbarians who seize this dog, who so greatly sur-
passes man in fidelity and friendship, and nail him down to
a table and dissect him alive, to show you the mesaraic veins!
You discover in him all the same organs of feeling as in yourself.
Answer me, mechanist, has nature arranged all the springs of
feeling in this animal to the end that he might not feel? (Singer
2009, 202)

Reviewing the history of the consequences of the mechanical
philosophy for the treatment of animals, Steiner writes:

The idea advanced by a great body of Western philosophy, that
animals are automatons and possess no actual soul [in short,
no life of feeling] has trickled down onto those parts of the
population where there is no compassion for the animal and
where there is often no limit, either, to the cruelty meted out to
the animals. (Steiner 1995, 27)

The view that animals are unfeeling machines persists today
nearly unchanged in industrial agriculture—factory farming—
and in many a university and medical research laboratory.

Body, Soul, and Spirit: Human and Animal

1. Animal and Human

One way of speaking of spirit is to see it as the creative intelligence that is the source ultimately of all existence. Steiner often speaks also of this creative intelligence as the wisdom that shapes and permeates all of Earth existence. All the beings that come to life on Earth are permeated and shaped by the cosmic wisdom developed on previous stages of cosmic evolution. "That is why," Steiner writes, "we present-day earthly humans, if we observe closely, can discover wisdom in the nature of things around us. We can admire the wisdom in every leaf of every plant, in every human or animal bone and in the marvelous structure of the brain and heart" (Steiner 1997, 192). Throughout his life Steiner gave myriad examples of the working of this intelligence, the cosmic wisdom, in the beings of the world. This intelligence is the expression of the spirit in both humans and animals. Each, however, has access to the spirit—to this wisdom and intelligence—in different ways and degrees.

Both human and animal also possess an astral body. Steiner's use of *body* in this connection, may seem at first somewhat strange, but essentially it is simply a useful term for "whatever gives a being shape or form." The physical body is the only body perceptible by the senses; the etheric and astral bodies are particular, non-sensory, formative organizations of the cosmic etheric and astral. The astral is the "soul of the universe," the carrier of consciousness and feeling. An astral body as such is a particular form or formative organization or constellation of the universal astral. The plants have an etheric body, but, since they lack an astral body, they are only "conscious" of the spirit at a deep sleep level. Humans and animals, however, both have an astral body. "With respect to our astral body," writes Steiner, "we are of the same nature as animals" (Steiner 1997, 37). The astral body is of the essence or substance of soul. Whoever thoughtfully regards animal life, Steiner writes, "can hold that animals are soulless only with great difficulty. We need merely to point out that many animals in our environment perform actions, and enter into relationships even among themselves, which are difficult to imagine without a soul. One example is the faithfulness of the dog" (Steiner 1907).

The astral body is also the source of consciousness. "We can," Steiner says, "speak of consciousness even in connection with the lower soul stirrings. The most ordinary everyday sensation is a matter of consciousness. To this extent animals also have consciousness" (Steiner 1971, 24). (It is interesting that the mechanical philosophy has had such a strong hold on the scientific community that only two years ago—July 2012—a group of prominent scientists was able to bring itself to announce publicly that they had come to the conclusion that animals do actually have consciousness (Cambridge Declaration 2012; Bekoff 2012). What they will do with this, if anything, in relation to orthodox neo-Darwinism, which has no place for consciousness, and to their laboratory experiments, remains to be seen.

The individual "I" of the human and the group "I" of animals are both expressions of spirit, of the creative intelligence. The human soul and body have a different relationship to this intelligence, this wisdom, than do the animal soul and body. We can look more closely at each.

The group "I" of a particular species has formed the bodies of the animals belonging to that species. The closest of connections exists, therefore, between the group "I" and the physical bodies of that species. Because of this close connection, the intelligence of the "I" is built directly into the physical body of the animals. The animals live out this wisdom built into their bodies. It is their bodily wisdom that manifests the deep, pervasive spirituality of the animal. Steiner makes clear that it is a very high wisdom, indeed, initially far outstripping the given intelligence of the human being. Throughout his writings Steiner gives many examples of the wisdom incorporated in the soul and bodily existence of the various animal groups. Among the examples he gives are: the wasp's ability to make paper long before its discovery by humans; the beaver's highly complicated engineering feats in the construction of dams and the precision felling of trees, anticipating by millions of years similar engineering capabilities of humans; the knowledge of birds and animals in knowing when and where to migrate, finding the way over hundreds and thousands of miles by means of their own equivalents of radar, sonar, or GPS positioning. We often call this animal intelligence, *instinct,* a useful, shorthand term but one that also covers up the underlying reality.

And so Steiner points to the essential difference between the expression of the spirit in human and in animal. "Do the animals present themselves to us," he asks, "so that we need to speak about a special spirituality only present in man? On the contrary! It will reveal itself to closer observation that there is much more intelligence among the animal world, and that man must first gain his intelligence"—and then he adds, that "perhaps man's priority to the animal exists in the fact that he can achieve his intelligence" (Steiner 1910b). Here is the essential difference. As powerful as the animal's intelligence is, it is knitted tightly into the physical body, which is formed and guided by the group "I"-being. The human "I" by contrast is not so closely connected with the body, and, therefore, has the freedom, and necessity, to discover on its own, the wisdom pervasive in the world. Unlike the animals, the human is not born with the necessary intelligence at its disposal. This intelligence must be gained through human effort, through the exertion of the free human "I" in thinking, feeling and willing. "The difference between man and animal cannot be found in any particular detail," writes Steiner, "it has to be found entirely in the way the spirit makes use of things. For through this we behold man's relation to the spirit, how he has emancipated himself from what belongs to the body and is able to enter into direct intercourse with the spirit" (Steiner 1910a). The human being, however, does pay a price for this, for the human gives up the innate guidance granted to the animal and must find its own way uncertainly through the world. The cost is a lack of security. But it is this lack of security that forces the human to be independent and to become creative (Steiner 1910a and b; 1907).

What then is the difference in the relation of the animal group "I" to the animal group soul and that of the human individual "I" to the human soul? The animal group "I"-being, as we have just seen, is closely connected with the animal body and with the animal group soul—so much so, in fact, that Steiner will often speak of group "I" and group soul interchangeably.

Let us consider, first, the animal group "I" in relation to the group soul and the individual animal soul. Each individual animal possesses an astral body that is actually a concentrated aspect of the larger, common astrality of the group to which it belongs—the species or genus for instance. The individual soul participates in the group soul. The particular characteristics and capacities of the group soul, with its close connection with the bodily form and organization of a species, are carried from generation to generation through inheritance. Likewise, the given possibilities of the emotional—soul—experience of each species are shaped, and also limited, by the particular bodily organization of the species. The repertoire of emotions, which are available to the animal, vary, therefore, from species to species. Species have soul and emotional experiences and expressions quite different from other species. "One species can do this, another that," writes Steiner, "and this is due to differentiation of the astral body in the different animal species" (Steiner 1997). However, the same or similar emotions may be shared—find expression—across species, for example, joy, empathy, fear, and so forth. Yet each species will give its own characteristic stamp or signature to its own soul life, even to those emotions it has in common with other species. "And so," writes Steiner, "an animal is nervous, courageous or cowardly, rapacious or gentle, according to how the spirit has poured itself into its organization. The creative activity of the spirit in its organs is mirrored in the soul life and soul experience of the animal. This means that soul experience in the animal is confined within the species; it cannot go beyond the species or the genus. It expresses itself as species, as genus" (Steiner 1910b). Expressing the same thought, the distinguished modern ethologist Marc Bekoff has coined a felicitous phrase to describe the soul lives of animals as *"species specific"* (Bekoff 2007).

Here again we see a fundamental difference between the soul life of animals and of human beings. Because the human individual "I" is freed to a certain extent from the physical body, it can insert itself to a degree between the human body and soul. This ability of the "I" to intervene between body and soul means that soul experience need not be totally fixed and determined by the body, nor the "I" by the soul. The "I"-being, thus, has the possibility of guiding the soul life—the possibility even of transforming it. And a further consequence of this loosening of the "I" to an extent from soul and body is that the human has access to a much wider range of emotions available to it. In its emotional, soul life, the human is much more individual, not so "species specific"—unless, of course, one regards, as Steiner most emphatically does, each individual human as a species unto itself (Steiner 1971, 50–1). This more inclusive availability of emotional response of the human does not, however, run counter to the similarity between many human emotions and animal emotions. Both humans and animals participate in their own ways in the same cosmic, astral reality. Nor should it be forgotten, that the freedom of the human "I" with regard to the soul life has been made possible in a crucial way by the fact that certain animals, in the course of evolution, took on and thus relieved human beings of extreme emotions that would have overwhelmed the human "I"-being.

2. ANIMAL BODY, SPIRIT, AND SOUL: WOLFGANG SCHAD

In his remarkable study, *Man and Mammal*, Wolfgang Schad brings out with great insight and fascinating detail the close connection of body, soul, and spirit in the animal (Schad 1977). Schad is an accomplished biologist and a skilled practitioner of

the scientific method pioneered by Goethe and developed further by Rudolf Steiner. Employing this method of rigorous, often
painstaking, observation of nature, guided by trained, imaginative insight, Schad brings to light the close bond between the animal's body and the animal's characteristic soul life.

Central to Schad's investigation is Steiner's depiction of the
threefold organization of the human body, which Schad explores
as the key to understanding the forms and behavior of the different mammal groups. According to Steiner, the human physical form comprises three, fundamental organizational systems.
These are described as the *nerve–sense* system, the *rhythmic
respiratory–circulatory* system, and the *metabolic–limb* system.
In the healthy human these three systems work in harmony, yet
each has its center in particular parts of the body: the first in
the head, the second in the middle region of heart and lungs,
and the last in the limbs and abdominal organs. There are, thus,
three distinct organizational systems, but they are not parallel
and separate. Rather, in the human they exist and function as an
interrelated and interpenetrating whole. Schad quotes Steiner's
emphasis on the harmonious working together of the three: "It
is of utmost importance to see clearly the relationship between
the function of the nerves, the breath rhythm, and the activity of
the metabolism. These three forms of activity do not lie *beside*
one another but *in* one another" (Schad 1977, 19). While distinct,
these three systems work in the healthy human in an integrated,
remarkably coherent and harmonious whole.

Not only do these three systems work together to maintain
and enable the human body, but they are each also associated
with central functions of the human soul: thinking in the head,
feeling in the rhythmic, middle region, and will in the limbs and
abdominal region. Although the modern mind tends to attribute
all psychological, emotional activity to the brain, Schad emphasizes that the entire body with all its organic systems is the instrument of the soul. The physical correlate of thinking, Schad points
out, is, of course, the brain, which also registers and monitors
other psychological activities. It is no surprise, observes Schad,
that the head is the physical correlate of "the cold clarity of man's

unimpassioned thought." The powerful impulses of will have their physical correlates in the dark, unconscious depths of the limbs and lower body. Mediating between the upper and lower, balancing and harmonizing the two, is the rhythmic middle region of heart and lungs. It is here that feelings have their physical correlate, their organic seat. This is thoroughly in keeping also with all traditional wisdom, which, as Schad remarks, has also seen the heart as the seat of the human's emotional, soul life. "We need only recall," says Schad, "the difference in heart beat and rate of respiration caused by our experience of fear, grief, joy, or passion to understand that this is so" (Schad, 28).

The mammal also has this threefold organization, but with a fundamental difference. In the mammals, rather than being harmoniously in balance, one of the three systems tends to predominate over the other two. Schad identifies three major mammal groups according to which of the three systems is dominant: the rodents, dominated by the nerve–sense system; the carnivores, shaped preeminently by the rhythmic–respiratory system; and the ungulates (hoofed animals), formed above all by the metabolic–limb system.

Consider the mouse, exemplifying the rodent, as an animal dominated by the nerve–sense system:

> Because of its extreme sensory activity, the rodent continues (after birth) to live more in the environment than in its own small body. The animal is always more or less 'beside itself.' Whatever goes on around it is experienced intensively by the animal's soul, while its body remains unimportant, insignificant. How inadequately this animal seems to manage in its far too hastily formed body! An insatiable quest for food, constantly interrupted by terrified flight, fills its days. Frequent naps are required because of this constant nervous strain; yet these are of extremely short duration, and even in sleep shudders of excitement pass over the tiny, sleeping form. A rodent lives almost reluctantly, in a state of constant fear. (ibid., 226)

By contrast, the cow (emblematic of the ungulates) is almost completely dominated by its metabolic (digestive) system. Steiner himself writes:

> I have often spoken of how enchanting it is to contemplate a herd of cattle, replete and satisfied, lying down in a meadow; to observe this process of digestion, which here again is expressed in the position of the body, in the expression of the eyes, in every movement.... And if we further observe the animal's whole form, we see in it that what I may call an extended digestive system.... The animal is all digestion. (Steiner 1970, 23–4)

Like most hoofed animals, the cow is fully at home in its body, taken up by grazing and digestion, chewing its cud, content in itself and largely unconcerned with the world around. "Such an animal," observes Schad, "is so self-sufficient that its emotional activity can be completely absorbed in the life of its own body" (Schad 1977, 26).

The lion, our third example, emblematic of the carnivore, is dominated by the circulatory–respiratory or rhythmic system. "Picture the lion," suggests Steiner, "how he runs, how he leaps, how he holds his head, even how he looks around him. And you will see that all this leads back to a continual rhythmic interplay between coming out of balance, and again coming into balance.... The lion is all breast organ. He is the animal in which the rhythmic system is brought to perfect expression both in outer form and in way of living." (Steiner 1970b, 22–3)

Schad describes how it is this balance and tension between the carnivore's body and soul that "finds visible expression in its powerful form and striking coloration" (Schad 1977, 227). The aggressiveness of the lion (the carnivore) shows itself as a bringing together of powerful, body–will forces modulated and made effective by the balancing influences of breath and blood, by the rhythmic system.

The specialization of the animal body goes hand in hand with a specialized soul life. It is the lack of specialization in the human body, which enables the human, unlike the animal, to be at home and survive in many different environmental habitats. Likewise, it is the corresponding lack of specialization in human soul life that frees the human in ways not possible to the animal. "The science of man called 'Anthroposophy,'" writes Schad, "regards this absence of highly developed physical specialization as the necessary correlate of man's psychospiritual attributes, which so greatly surpass those in the highest animals" (Schad 1977, 15).

For the mammals, the experience of death differs according to the physical organization that is dominant in them. The mouse, exemplifying the rodent and dominated by the nerve–sense system, has never really entered deeply into its body and is always aware of the environment, scurrying about and constantly on the lookout for whatever may be threatening it from outside. Schad even suggests that the mouse may actually experience death as "a welcome release from a life filled with fear" (Schad 1977, 227). In the nerve–sense dominated animal, Schad says, there exists a tendency toward death because the senses in their constant openness to the outside world impede the animal's participation in the regenerative life processes of its whole body.

By contrast, the ungulate, the metabolically dominant animal, has a deep connection with its body. The cow is at home in its body, is contented and throughout enjoys its bodily existence, and so "dies with great reluctance" (Schad, 228). "The rodent," writes Schad "is too superficially, the ungulate, quite deeply, connected with its own body." By comparison, the carnivore lives in the tension and balance between the two poles of outer sense and inner digestion, so that life and death for the carnivore, one could say, are part of life's experience. Schad puts it nicely: "It is this inner battle of forces that makes the carnivore so aggressive in the outer world. In aggressive conflict it is equally prepared to accept either life or death" (Schad, 228).

The experience of death for any animal, however, is different from the experience of death for the human. When the single animal dies, the group soul and group "I" remain alive. They do not know death. They remain alive in the larger astral world, and the single animal, which has died, is simply replaced by another of its own species. Only at the time of its death, says Steiner, does the single animal have an experience of its "I"-being. He writes: "Anything like the beginning of an "I"-consciousness comes upon the animal only at the moment of its death...whoever is able to see what actually occurs when an animal dies has some idea of the fact that, properly speaking, what runs through the entire course of a man's life—the consciousness of its own "I"—is present in the animal only at the moment of its death" (quoted by Schad, 288). (Steiner later qualifies this blanket statement in some very significant ways. We will look at these qualifications in due course). At death, the soul of the single animal is taken up by the group soul, of which it has always been a part, and a new individual of that species is produced through inheritance, and endowed by the group "I" with the life-wisdom exemplified by that species. The human individual, unlike the animal, possesses an independent "I" during life that has the possibility of connecting the human soul directly with the spiritual world both in earthly life and after death.

3.

ANIMAL GROUP SOUL AND INDIVIDUAL SOULS

Wolfgang Schad stresses with startling clarity the importance of the animal group soul in relation to the single animal:

> We need not regard the death of an animal with cold indifference because we are beginning to understand what takes place in the animal's soul life. On the other hand, we are able to avoid the sentimentality that attributes to the single animal human individuality. The individual animal can be replaced by another of its kind, but the individual man cannot. But neither can one animal species be replaced by another. Each species is as unique as an individual man. The death of a single animal is merely the end of an unindividualized, replaceable portion of a species. Only the loss of an entire species is comparable to the death of a single man. Not the killing of the single animal, then, but the destruction of an entire species, is murder.... The death of an individual animal is often painful to us. It is the destruction of an entire species, however, that should fill us with sorrow and weigh heavily upon our consciences. (Schad, 233–4)

In this age of mass extinction of whole species, Schad's appeal to our conscience and sense of loss could not be more pressing and urgent. The mountain gorillas, the elephants, the rhinoceros, the orangutans, entire groups of whales, and many other species are in danger of disappearing forever from our world.

It is especially to the shame of the human being that most of these looming extinctions are the direct result of human greed and selfish desires: the destruction of entire animal habitats in order to extract from the earth materials—oil, metals, wood, and so forth—deemed crucial for economic growth and the comforts of civilization; the inability or unwillingness of governments to stop the poaching of elephants, rhinoceroses, and tigers, of which only a few of each are left, in order to feed a voracious market for aphrodisiacs and ivory trinkets; the felling of huge tracts of rain forests in the Amazon for the planting of soybeans, mainly for the feeding of the hapless cattle on factory farms, or for the grazing of cattle before they are off to the factory farm feedlots—and the list goes on and on. Even if we have grown up and live far from any of the great animals, once we have heard or read about them, any person of us with a healthy grasp of reality can begin to feel and sense the importance of their presence on Earth. Each species represents an entire, unique experience of the joys and pains of existence, and with their extinction this will have come to an end forever. The disappearance of these animals will leave us humans on Earth with a sense of great and inconsolable loneliness.

The words reported of Chief Seattle, even if they are apocryphal, capture well what we face with the loss of the animals:

> What is man without the beasts?
> If all the beasts were gone,
> Man would die from
>   a great loneliness of spirit.
> For whatever happens to the beasts
> Soon happens to man.
> All things are connected.
> Man did not weave the web of life
>   he is merely a strand in it,
> Whatever he does to the web,
>   he does to himself.

Schad's emphasis on the importance of the species and group soul is especially pertinent to our times. Nevertheless, I think his particular formulation and statement of that importance is one-sided and unbalanced. It writes off too easily the importance of the individual animal within the species. Is the individual animal really as unimportant and dispensable as Schad seems to assert?

Several considerations show that Steiner himself does not think so, that he does stress concern for the individual, single animal as well as for the group. That having been said, however,

Steiner is himself not altogether blameless for making it possible to dismiss too easily the importance and value of the single, individual animal. Steiner frequently employs a form of expression that by itself is misleading, if it is not balanced by other statements of his that do show concern for the individual animal. On various occasions he will make such comparisons as, "the individual animal has the same relation to the group soul as the bark of a tree has to a sprouting shoot"; or "For the group soul of lions, for example, the death of a lion here on the physical plane means as much as it means to you to cut a fingernail"; or, again, "For the group soul, the death of an animal is approximately the same as what you experience when you have your hair cut at the beginning of summer" (Steiner 1995, 145; 1978, 118; 1982, 140). Of course, in such instances, Steiner is at pains to underscore the ultimate importance of the group soul and "I"-being, in ways that Schad has described.

But such expressions by Steiner, taken by themselves, are unfortunate. One would not know that Steiner himself had the highest regard and compassionate feeling for the single animal and its importance. If the single animal is seen solely as little more than fingernail clippings, snippets of hair, or the sloughing of tree bark, then humans can relieve themselves of any reason to take the lives of individual animals seriously. These kinds of images by themselves offer humans a tempting and easy way to get off the hook: to avoid having to even think about our relationship and treatment of individual animals, whether as sources of meat, clothing, lab experiments, and entertainment, and so forth. That is why it is crucial that these images be understood along with other considerations by Steiner that affirm the importance of the single, individual animal. Let us look at four of these.

First, the consciousness, emotions, and sensations made possible by the group soul are concretely experienced and expressed only by the individual animal. We come to know the emotions contained in the group souls of the animals only through our experience of the feelings expressed by the individual, physical animals themselves. "The animal itself," writes Steiner, "experiences happiness and suffering; the astral body weaves and is active in the whole astrality of our Earth.... The being that is not only swathed by the astral element but can actually take it into itself is the animal" (1978, 23). The possibilities of the soul, which are carried—as well as limited—by the group soul find concrete experience and expression by the single, physical animal.

Second, as we shall see in more detail, some of the mammals and birds, can give a little of their own individual variations to their experience of the group soul. Yet, even these individual "soul tweaks" bear all the marks of the group soul. As Bekoff's nice phrase puts it, the individual animal's range of soul life is "species specific," yet it can also carry individual variations. Perhaps a trivial example by way of illustration: The cats, which are the companions of my wife and myself, are in every respect *all cat*— no mistaking it. Gunner and Maggie, however, are as different from one another as cats can be. They even display contradictory temperaments: Gunner, a large blue Persian Tom—phlegmatic, calm, lazy, cuddly for any available lap; Maggie, a small, red Persian female—choleric, assertive, and, yes, also cuddly, but only on her own terms and times. In all their endearing differences, however, they are always *cat*—and as true carnivores, they both spring immediately and ferociously into action at the first scent of a mouse. And in all of this, it is the single animal that expresses, and enables us to observe, the soul riches of the group soul.

A third consideration regarding the single animal is that it is the single animal that undergoes in its body the experience of pain. In Steiner's view, the individual animal not only experiences pain, but also that physical pain for the animal is much worse than for the human. The close connection between the soul and the physical body of the animal means that pain is driven deeply into and throughout the animal's entire body. Just as animals express joy with the whole body they experience pain also throughout their entire body. "The higher animal," writes Steiner, [and by higher animal he seems to be referring here primarily to mammals and to birds] "being so closely bound up with its bodily nature, feels pain with infinitely greater intensity than man" (Steiner 1910b). Moreover, the animal lacks the intellectual—the "I"—capacity of the adult human both to stand back somewhat from the physical and also come to understand conceptually something of what is going on (the child's experience in this latter respect is closer to that of the animal). "Those who maintain," Steiner emphasizes, "that human pain can be more intense than the pain felt by animals, are talking without foundation. Pain in the animal is far, far more deep-seated than purely bodily pain in man can be" (Steiner 1910a). The morally damning implication of this becomes immediately apparent when we remember that everyday our society inflicts total pain on millions of innocent and helpless animals for the entire length of their lives, with no relief whatever until the day we slaughter them, mainly because we like the taste of their flesh.

Finally, we can point to a fourth area in which Steiner shows vividly how deeply involved we are with the individual animals as well as with the group soul and "I"-being. In Steiner's account of the human experience after death, he describes how it will be necessary for every human to go through a period of soul purification. He calls this period Kamaloca, after the Sanscrit, "Region of Desire," known variously in other traditions as Purgatory, region of cleansing fire, and others. It is a period that lasts about one-third the length of a person's previous earthly life. Two primary experiences of purification must be undergone during this period. One is the "burning away" of selfish desires. The other is the necessity to experience as one's own, the suffering we have caused others during our time on Earth—to experience the suffering we have caused them as they experienced it. *Other* includes not only humans but also animals, individual animals in the flesh. We have to relive during Kamaloca the pain we have caused animals in the same way that we do for humans. It is immaterial whether we caused the pain and suffering of animals consciously or unconsciously, intentionally or thoughtlessly. Here it is clear, there is no way of evading our responsibility to the individual animals by dismissing them as mere, disposable hair clippings from the group soul (Steiner 1970, 30–31). Taking this seriously could send us back to take a new and careful look at how we stand with the individual animals in all our present dealings with them.

Perhaps there is yet a final consideration that underscores the importance of the individual animal in relation to the group soul and "I"-being. That is simply the fact that, in Schad's phrase, the "murder" of a species can occur today with the killing of the last individual animal of that species with the final shot of the poacher's gun. The poacher has access to the group soul only through the individual body and soul.

4.

ANIMAL PLAY (AGAIN)

Earlier we looked at animal play in relation to the phenomenon of emancipation—the increasing freedom from environmental constraints exhibited by successive levels of animal groups, ranging from fish to mammals and to humans. We noticed how the increase in autonomy and emancipation also involved an increase in "flexible behavior" in contrast to "fixed action patterns," which are strongly present in animal behavior (and in humans too, for that matter). This plasticity and flexible behavior provide the underpinnings for the broad learning dispositions and capacities for planning ahead that are clearly discernible in animal play. Accompanying these is a whole spectrum of emotions experienced by humans and animals alike. Animal play, indeed, offers ample evidence of what can be described as emotional and moral intelligence in individual animals, and, perhaps, also degrees of cognitive intelligence. We will first look here at animal play and at what it can reveal about animal soul life. Following this we will look further at a still wider range of emotions common to both animals and humans.

The leading authority today on animal play is the psychologist Gordon H. Burghardt, whose book, *The Genesis of Animal Play: Testing the Limits,* is regarded as the definitive treatment of the subject. Burghardt discusses five criteria for recognizing animal activity as play. The first is that the behavior does not contribute directly to survival. The second is that the activity is spontaneous and done for its own sake, that is, it does not have a purpose beyond itself. The third criterion for recognizing animal play is that it uses aspects of ordinary behavior, such as fighting, nipping, chasing, etc., but in somewhat modified form. The fourth criterion is that the behavior is performed repeatedly in similar, but not rigidly stereotyped, patterns. The fifth criterion for recognizing animal play is that it takes place when the animal is in what Burghardt calls a "relaxed field," that is, it is fed, healthy, and free from stress, such as free from the threat of predators. "All five criteria must be met in at least one respect before the play label can be confidently attached to any specific instance of behavior." He also gives an abstract, one-sentence definition: "Play is repeated, incompletely functional behavior differing from more serious versions structurally, contextually, or ontogenetically, and initiated voluntarily when the animal is in a relaxed or low-stress setting" (Burghardt 2005, 82).

Students of the field have identified three main types of play as locomotor play, object play, and social play. Among the most familiar examples of locomotor play would be dogs chasing or young deer gamboling in the meadow. Cats chasing and pawing balls of yarn is a simple example of object play. More complicated object play is that, for instance, of whales and dolphins. Beluga whales blow air bubbles that they then kick, bite, or otherwise break up. Bottlenose dolphins like to blow bubble rings (much like humans blow smoke rings, but much larger). The dolphins then catch the rings or swim up through them and manipulate them in various, frequently very creative ways (Martin, et al. 1996). Social play involves other animals in activities such as chasing, pawing, wrestling, nipping, and fighting, and it may include playing together with objects.

Almost all social play is preceded by "play signals," signs given by an animal, either to initiate play or to signal that "what we are doing—e.g., biting, is play and is not serious." The most familiar example of a play signal is probably the "play bow" of dogs. The play bow is also used by lions, baboons, rhesus monkeys, ravens, and several other birds. Other signaling examples are "play vocalizations" among squirrel monkeys and special "play faces" in primates. Pigs use play markers such as bouncing, running, or head twisting (Bekoff 2007, 97). Eye-covering play is observed among many primates in which the animals cover and open their eyes during play to experience different perspectives in the play situation. Burghardt comments that this eye-covering play "involves both imagination and representational memory, which are elements of imaginative play" (p. 102).

Placental mammals engage in all three types of play. These animals include rats and mice, squirrels, prairie dogs, cats, lions, dogs, wolves, foxes, bears, raccoons, weasels, otters, seals and seal lions, antelopes, deer, pigs, horses, elephants, and whales. Play is common in virtually all species of primates; and marine mammals, such as otters, seals, and dolphins are perhaps the most playful of all mammals. Rats, rabbits, and hares all engage in social play. Even turtles engage in object play. For a long time ethologists thought that fish do not play, but a substantial literature is appearing that says they do. Burghardt comments about these studies: "Leading fish ethologists have recently pulled together data indicating that fish can have complex social lives, cooperate, imitate, deceive, use tools, develop cognitive maps, and otherwise do 'primate' things. So why *not* play in fish?" (Burghardt, 315).

Birds, too, are extremely playful. Play of all three types has been especially observed in parrots, parakeets, macaw, and keas, and in ravens, crows, magpies, jays, and woodpeckers. "Drop catching," a form of object play in which the birds drop objects in the air and then dive to catch them, is common among hawks, eagles, owls, pelicans, cormorants, as is "aerial food-passing" among raptors. The parallels between birds and mammals in tool use, cooperative hunting, learning of motor patterns, and complex social cognition are quite striking. "Similarly, the richness of play in some birds rivals that seen in the most playful of mammals" (Burghardt, 315).

Much of the research on play supports the view that locomotor, object, and social play all have different patterns among different species. Burghardt writes:

> The nature and amount of play are not random, but are tied to a species' phylogeny, ecology, ontogeny, and normal behavior. Object play is typically predatory in carnivores and manipulative in extractive foragers (such as cebus monkeys). Social play can be composed of chasing, stalking, wrestling, and other

behavior patterns that may be derived from sexual, aggressive, or predatory behavioral systems. Many of the most playful species show all three major types of animal play, although the mix may differ. (Burghardt, 150)

This observation would seem to be in keeping with Bekoff's notion of animal emotions as "species specific" and with Steiner's account of "group soul" experience and capacities. Moreover, in both Bekoff's and Steiner's description of animal emotional life, a good deal of commonality exists across species, yet also with many variations in the expression of these commonalities.

What, then, are some of the main types of emotions that emerge in animal play, and what do they tell us further about animal soul life? In the first place is simply the experience of joy and pleasure at being alive—an emotion Steiner repeatedly underscores as central to animal life. One feels this almost immediately, and in a real way sharing the animal's joy, in watching dogs chase or deer run and jump. And two not well-known examples of animal joy point strikingly to animals' experience of pleasure in playing. As in human children, evidence shows that great apes laugh when they are tickled and played with gently. And rats, we have learned using ultrasound detection, perform a laughter-like repetitive chatter-response (giggle) when tickled, and seek out opportunities to be tickled by a familiar person.

Social Play, especially, brings out a number of dimensions of what Steiner called the "moral life" among animals. Foremost among these is a sense of fairness—fair play!—and justice. As Marc Bekoff and Jessica Pierce have written, "We want to stress that social play is firmly based on a foundation of justice" (Bekoff and Pierce 2009, 121). This can be seen in several ways. First of all, play means play. Animal social play has rules and rituals that must be followed. This does not mean, of course, that animals have a conceptual set of rules in their heads, but they do know certain behaviors that indicate play and not fighting or mating. We have mentioned the importance of play signals that indicate a desire and readiness for play—the dog play bow or the raised arm of the ape. It is especially important that the play signal be honored and obeyed because the animal is going to use, in play, actions from other contexts, such as, dominance assertion, predatory and anti-predatory behavior, and mating (Bekoff and Pierce, 122). Animals who don't follow the rules, who refuse to cooperate with the play signal, are unlikely to be chosen as play partners, or may even be excluded from the group (Bekoff 2007, 98).

A sense of egalitarianism and justice pervade animal play. This is most vividly seen in the readiness of larger or more dominant animals to self-handicap during play. Animals may not bite as hard as they otherwise could or would. Role reversal is another form of self-handicapping, for instance, a dominant wolf in the pack may roll on its back during play, something it would never do in actual fighting. Even dominant rats will usually tolerate, in play, fight-like attacks by usually submissive rats (Bekoff 2007, 121–3). Jonathon Balcombe cites a report by Cynthia Moss, known for her deep knowledge of elephants, describing how an older elephant will self-handicap when playing with a smaller one: "What is touching about these play bouts between unevenly matched individuals is how gentle the older one always is. He will be very careful not to scare or intimidate the younger one. I have seen big adult males lie down (like a dog) and then spar with a much younger male. Also older calves will lie down on their sides so that small calves can climb and play on them. It shows a remarkable ability to, in a sense, put oneself in the other's place." Larger pigs, Balcombe also reports, will self-handicap by sitting, kneeling or lying down when playing with smaller ones (Balcombe, 130).

Another very important emotion central to play is empathy. Empathy, most simply, is a sensitivity to the emotional state of the other, a feeling for the feelings of the other. Such a feeling for the other is critical from the moment of the first play signals and then throughout the entire play-time. And closely connected with empathy is the readiness for full cooperation. Play, Bekoff emphasizes, is always highly cooperative. "I can't stress enough," he writes, "how important it is that play is carefully negotiated, that it is fine-tuned on the run so that the play mood is maintained. There are social rules that must be followed" (Bekoff 2007, 82).

Robert Bellah, the eminent sociologist, has summed up his view of the importance of play:

> It is in the act of play that we can see in animals just those things that many have said only humans have and have denied that animals have: a sense of self, an ability to understand what is going on in the mind of another, a capacity for very delicate and choreographed cooperation, for example, and, if these characteristics seem to be overreaching, then certainly, at a minimum, shared intention and shared attention. (Bellah 2011, 82)

Bellah here makes clear the importance of play in revealing the soul life of animals. Whether he has, indeed, overreached in some of his statements, we will have to ask at a later point.

5.

ANIMAL EMOTIONS BEYOND PLAY

Each group of animals has its own repertoire—or suite of available sensations, feelings, and emotions. In their emotional life the animals are, again, in Bekoff's useful phrase, "species specific"; or similarly, as Steiner puts it, animals' soul capacities are set within the bounds of the group soul. But this fact needs to be carefully qualified by three other important considerations. First, the individual animals within a species can vary in the intensity or scope of the expression of emotions available to their group. As Bekoff points out, for example, "Not all dogs or chimpanzees experience and express joy, grief, or jealousy in the same way.... They can be bold, shy, playful, aggressive, sociable, curious, emotionally stable, or agreeable; they can be extroverted, introverted, dominant, or submissive" (Bekoff 2007, 44). Second, however, many emotions are shared across species and with humans. This is especially important. And, third, to complicate things further, sub-groups within the same species may have certain behaviors quite different from one another, having adopted all sorts of skills and behavior from other members of the same group. This has led ethologists to speak of "cultural variability" or of different "social cultures" within the same species. This social variability, however, seems to be limited, having to do in primates mainly with tool use and eating habits (de Waal 2005, 147).

To return to our second point, emotions are shared by animals and humans. Charles Darwin, Rudolf Steiner, and modern ethologists all maintain that animals and humans share a wide range of common feelings, while they do not necessarily concur on what exactly should be included in their respective lists. One of the major accomplishments of ethologists has been to document and provide detailed accounts and critical evaluations of the rich field of animal emotions, and in so doing have suggested hypotheses and questions for further research. Their work has been based on observation, experiments, anecdotes, and careful analysis of all of these, drawing from experience with animals both in captivity and in the wild. The ethologists, therefore, have been able to provide much concrete content to the general lists of emotions cited by Darwin, Steiner, and others. The ethological literature has become so rich and extensive that it would be beyond either my knowledge or the space available in this essay to attempt any kind of comprehensive treatment of it. Instead, what I propose is to take a look at a few key emotions, and ideas offered about them by ethologists, which might help shed important light on the whole field.

1. EMPATHY, SYMPATHY, AND COMPASSION

One such key emotion, common to animals and humans, is empathy. Empathy is the ability to feel the feelings of another; as Frans de Waal puts it, "the ability to be vicariously affected by someone else's feelings and situation" (de Waal 1996, 41). Empathy is closely related also to sympathy, compassion, and grief (Bekoff and Pierce, xiv). Empathy, says de Waal, is along with sympathy, one of "the pillars of human morality" (de Waal 1996, 41). And it seems to be central to what Steiner calls "the moral nature of animals" (Steiner 1910a).

Myriad instances of empathy, sympathy, and compassion have been observed among animals of many kinds—and expressed not only to members of their own species, but to those of other species as well. Most familiar to many of us may be how readily and quickly our cats and dogs read our emotions, and we theirs. Not so familiar, and probably a surprise to most people, are the empathic expressions of rats. One oft-cited experiment involved rats that have been trained to press a lever for food. They will stop pressing it if they see that every time they do press it another rat gets an electric shock. When that ceases to be the case, they go back to pressing the lever and continue eating. In similar experiments monkeys showed themselves to be even more averse to causing pain to other monkeys. Researchers found that rhesus monkeys refuse to pull a chain that delivers food to themselves, if doing so shocked a companion. One monkey stopped pulling for five days, and another for twelve days—starving themselves to avoid inflicting pain on another (de Waal 2006, 29). These experiments, however, are probably not conclusive because the animals may have been showing as much personal distress at the displays of pain by others as showing genuine helping desires.

With primates, however, empathy is clearly evident. A chimpanzee will put an arm around a companion who has been injured or beat up in a battle. Chimpanzees not only comfort others in need, but often come to the rescue of others, both from assaults by other chimpanzees and from threatening life situations. Many zoos, where chimpanzees are kept, have islands surrounded by water since chimpanzees can't swim. Individual chimpanzees are known to rush into the water at great risk to themselves to save drowning companions (Kazez, 72). Primates offer many examples of empathetic response to one another. The primatologist Frans de Waal comments: "And, yes, apes do show remarkable empathy, but no, they are not the only animals sensitive to the needs of others. We need only think of the incredible assistance elephants, dolphins, and lemurs offer each other to realize how widespread and well developed these tendencies are" (de Waal 1996, 70). Dolphins, for example, are well known for attempting to help rescue stranded whales, and may even beach themselves as a group because of their reluctance to abandon a stranded one of their own.

While it is true that mammals have provided most examples of empathy and sympathy this may be because they have been the most studied. Robert Bellah quotes private correspondence to him from Gordon Burghardt, the leading authority on animal play, regarding empathy in non-mammals. Burghardt wrote to him that "reptiles, snakes and iguanas are quite responsive to human behavior and that snake handlers who are confident and not antagonistic seldom get bitten" (Bellah, 74). De Waal emphasizes that "empathy is not an all-or-nothing phenomenon: it covers a wide range of emotional linkage patterns, from the very simple and automatic to the highly sophisticated" (2006, 41). And empathy is intimately related to larger configurations of emotions that make up behaviors that are cooperative, conciliatory, and reciprocal ("I'll groom you, if you'll groom me") behaviors.

2. GRIEF

An emotion closely related to empathy is grief, for it derives from a feeling for the other, but a feeling that remains hanging, unanswered. Grief, therefore, involves also the feeling of pain; indeed, it is soul pain of the deepest kind. We have many instances in which animals manifest many of the symptoms of grief as it is experienced by humans. Yet, whether the animals actually experience grief is not uncontroversial. Wolfgang Schad, the anthroposophic biologist we have already drawn upon, holds that humans alone can experience grief. Here is how he explains it: "The animal is well acquainted with the psychological experience of pain but does not know the deepening of pain to individual grief. And this is certainly connected with the fact that an animal never rebels as an individual against its fate. The question, 'Why me?' is known only to man. Even when an animal suffers a painful death we should try to avoid anthropomorphizing its experience through our sympathy, for the comparison between man and animal must encompass far more then mere sympathy" (Schad 1977). This is not altogether easy to understand—at least not for me—yet, with some trepidation I will try my hand at an attempt to get at what Schad is arguing.

Schad points to three levels of pain of which grief is the third, and deepest. Humans and animals both experience the first two levels; the human alone knows the third. The first level of pain is the actual physical experience of injury and the body's almost simultaneous reaction to it. This takes place, Schad says, on a "virtually unconscious level" and is, therefore, easily overlooked. It is, however, quickly transformed to the second level, to the psychological—the soul level—and what we know well as the conscious, bodily sensation of pain sets in almost immediately. "Man alone, however," Schad goes on, "knows yet a third form of pain, which is best—if rather inadequately—described as grief."

The crux of Schad's argument seems to be that the third level of pain is deeper even than the soul experience because it reaches the inmost core of the human Self, the I. In this respect, it is indicative that Schad uses the word *individual* twice: as in, "the deepening of pain to individual grief," and "an animal never rebels as an individual against its fate. The question, Why me? Is known only to man." Only the human being, in other words, can ask about the meaning and purpose, if any, in the injury life has dealt. This would seem to be especially true, if as Steiner and Schad hold, most animals do not have a grasp of death and the real depth of loss it can involve (I say, most, because, as we shall see later, for Steiner—if not for Schad—this does not seem to hold of all animals). Only the human being, consequently, if I am understanding Schad correctly, has the possibility of engaging the pain of loss creatively, that is, the possibility of the self working to transform the pain, to find meaning in it, and to transform itself in the process.

What then do we make of the many accounts of animals showing all the symptoms we ordinarily associate with human grief, symptoms such as depression, crying and wailing, withdrawal and listlessness, loss of appetite, even dying? Jane Goodall, for example, has described her own experience: "I have watched chimpanzee children, after the death of their mother, show behavior similar to clinical depression in grieving human children—hunched posture, rocking, dull staring eyes, lack of interest in events around them" (Bekoff and Pierce, xiv). G.A. Bradshaw, noted elephant-trauma specialist, has written, "Studies on elephants in the African and Asian wilds and those in captivity indicate that in addition to complex cognitive skills, elephants feel and express a range of emotions. Elephants are well known for showing wrenching grief when a loved one dies or somehow departs forever.... Perhaps more than any other quality, elephants show an understanding of death with their displays of grief and repeated visits to the bones of relatives" (Bradshaw, 10). Elephants are far from alone. Dogs and cats are known to become despondent and to refuse food after a companion dies and often to wail for months thereafter. Gus, one polar bear originally of two at the New York Central Park Zoo, is reported after the death of his longtime companion bear, Ida, to have become listless, slouching around, confused, and refusing to swim. And the same article adds: "Biologists tell of gorillas banging their chests with yowls of anguish during a wake for a fallen friend, of sea lions wailing when their babies have been mutilated by killer whales, of grief-stricken monkey mothers carrying dead infants around for days, of single geese singing both halves of a duet when their partners have died" (*New York Times,* July 3, 2011). All of this, as well as many other similar accounts, strikes me as being an awful lot like human grief and mourning.

Perhaps, however, it is possible to reconcile such accounts with Schad's denial of grief as such to animals. Schad has defined grief so precisely that it can only apply to the struggles of an individual self to deal with the deepest injuries of life. Schad would, presumably, strongly agree that animals deeply affected by the loss of a close companion or family member are beset by a deep and penetrating pain—the second level of soul-pain that he describes. The tragedy for the single animal, however, with only a group soul and a group "I"-being, is that their pain cannot be dealt with in any transformative way. The animal is immersed in the soul experience with no leverage over it. At the end, the surviving animal remains inconsolable, the pain festering in soul and body until it finally fades, if it does. In many cases, as witnessed especially among elephants for example, the surviving elephant is traumatized for the rest of its life (Bradshaw, passim). Schad's primary concern seems to be not to deny the real pain of the animal but to point to what is a potential for humans alone—the creative transformation of self and pain, through the individual self. He seems determined not to let go of that as a potential for every human self. This is not to say that all of us humans have developed ourselves far enough to be capable of encountering grief in a transformative way, and all persons, even those who are so developed may, nevertheless, be left with a lasting and aching wound. And, so, even in this, we are close to the animals after all, and they to us.

6.

GROUP SOUL AND GROUP "I"-BEING:
AN IMPORTANT QUALIFICATION

During the past half century, the whole field of ethology has opened up in important new directions. Students of animal behavior during recent years have begun to undertake observations and experiments that have led to some radically new possibilities for understanding animal potentials, especially with respect to a possible, nascent sense of selfhood among certain animals, advanced animal cognitive abilities, and latent animal language capacities. None of these areas is without controversy, but enough observations and suggestive evidence have been developed in these areas that serious consideration of each is imperative. At first glance, each of these new areas seems to pose a challenge to aspects of Rudolf Steiner's account of the group "I"-being, group soul, and individual animal soul.

In what ways might this seem to be so? In seeking an answer to this, let us first review the general picture given by Steiner of the individual animal in relation to the group soul and "I"-being. Two aspects of this picture are important.

In the first place, the individual animal soul experience—which includes knowing and feeling—is shaped and guided by the group soul in connection with its bodily organization. Both—individual and group souls—are coordinated by and filled with the cosmic wisdom emanating from the group "I"-being, so much so, in fact, that it is possible without too much distortion to speak interchangeably of group "I" and group soul. The animal species is immersed in, and suffused with, the wisdom, the intelligence of the cosmos, in keeping with the specie's physical and astral organization. Single animals within the same species may show some individual differences in their expression of this wisdom, but these individual differences are essentially variations on the group soul, variations owing to slight differences in bodily and astral organization. Even these are bounded, constrained by, and within the group soul. A full potential for independent control in expression of animal wisdom and feelings would require the presence in the animal of a relatively independent "I"-being.

A second, general characteristic of the relation between the group soul and the individual animal appears at death when the individual is reabsorbed into the group soul. At death, the individual animal, as such, ceases to be and merges back into the group soul and hands over its earthly experiences to the group "I"-being. The animals, in other words, mediate their earthly experiences to the group "I"-being. I take it that something like that is meant when Steiner, as quoted earlier, says that only in death does the individual animal have an "I" experience.

Rudolf Steiner, however, introduces a fundamental qualification of this general picture with respect to certain, specific animal species. I know of no anthroposophist who has taken up and explored the implications of this qualification, but that may simply reveal the limitations of my reading. If I am correct, however, and I invite correction, this qualification is of extreme importance. And if I am wrong in this, then the most recent animal research seems to me to pose a serious problem for Steiner's portrayal of the animals—a crisis for it, in fact.

The qualification goes like this. With respect to most animals, as we have seen, Steiner describes how, when the animal dies, it passes into the group soul and a new individual member of the species takes its place. But then he says, "This holds only up to a certain point." It holds for most animals, but it is different for a few of the so-called higher animals. "The ape," he says, for example, "has something that is similar to the human 'I'-being." Elsewhere he includes other kinds of animals along with the apes. At death, this "something" remains behind as a kind of spiritual entity with "I"-like characteristics. It does not pass over at death into the group soul but retains its separate identity. Here Steiner draws on traditional folklore, which has preserved in picture form important insights into the nature of things. He identifies this spiritual entity, in the language of tradition, as an elemental being of the order of the Salamander. The Salamander, this spiritual entity, is "'I'-like" (Steiner 1982, 141).

So important is this qualification of the general picture that I think it worth quoting Steiner at some length: Steiner writes:

> The group spirit is metamorphosed and its physical members merely renew themselves. That happens, however, only up to a certain stage, after which something else takes place in the animal kingdom. This is very important just when you come to the higher animals. Precisely there something occurs that no longer seems quite to fit in with what I have been describing.
>
> Let us take as a marked case the apes. The ape, for instance, brings too much from the group soul down into its own individual existence. Whereas in the relatively lower animal the whole physical form goes back into the group soul, the ape keeps something in the physical organization that cannot go back. What the ape detaches from the group spirit can no longer return. So, too, in the case of man, you have the ego ["I"] that goes from incarnation to incarnation and is capable through development of reaching different stages. Here too there is no possibility of returning into the group spirit. *The ape has something that is similar to the human ego.* (My italics)

He writes further concerning the spiritual entity designated as the salamander:

> A whole series of animals draws too much out of the group soul, others again draw something out in another way. And this remains in our evolution and works as the fourth class of elemental spirits [that is, the salamander]. They are detached group souls of animals whose individual souls cannot return into the group soul, because they have carried their development beyond the normal point. From countless animals such ego-like beings remain behind. They are called salamanders. That is the highest form, for they are ego-like. (Steiner 1982, 140–141)

Elsewhere Rudolf Steiner includes other animals with the great apes. Again I quote him at length because of the important implications:

> Now we consider the following: With the lion it is entirely as we have said, that every time a lion dies, the whole of what was sent out by the group-soul returns to it again. *It is not at all so, however, with the apes.* When an ape dies the essential part does return to the group-soul, but a part does not; a part is severed from the group-soul. There are species where the single animal tears something away from the group-soul that cannot return to it. With all the apes, fragments are detached in each case from the group-soul. It is the same with certain kinds of amphibians and birds; in the kangaroo, for example, something is kept back from the group-soul. Now everything in the warm-blooded animals that remains behind in this way becomes an elemental of the kind we call a salamander. (Steiner 1981, 302–3 italics in original)

Three reflections on these passages may be in order. First, although Steiner talks about the "'I'-like something" held back, emerging at death as a separate spiritual entity, we should be able, it seems to me, to assume that it has been present, in some form of its "I"-like existence, for some time all along, previous to the animal's death. Second, he broadens out the kinds of animals that draw this "I"-like element from the group-soul to include, besides the great apes: some birds and kangaroos. It seems to me that with reason we could extend this even further to include other animals, such as, dolphins and elephants, which exhibit capacities similar to those animals in his original listing, but that have been studied in detail only long after Steiner wrote. In this light, we may even want to go back and take another look at Schad's denial that animals can grieve, to ask whether his blanket denial actually applies to those types of animals that Steiner has said possess an "I"-like entity. It is significant, also, that Steiner did include some birds in his list because birds have become prime subjects of recent research on animal intelligence. Third, the Salamander-being that remains after the death of the animal continues to carry "I"-like characteristics, which also makes them appear, and be very active, in human–animal relationships, as in the relation historically between the rider and his steed and the shepherd and his sheep (Steiner 1981, 297). I will explore more closely this presence of the salamander in close and caring human–animal relationships when we consider our relationship to animals after death.

Let us, then, at this point, look more closely at the three areas in which evidence seems strongly to suggest that some animals appear to exhibit some "I"-like capacities: some sense of self-awareness; higher cognitive abilities; and possible language capacities.

7.

HIGHER CAPACITIES AMONG CERTAIN ANIMALS

1. SELF-RECOGNITION

One question that has occupied scientists and philosophers since Aristotle is whether animals have a sense of themselves. Most of us nonscientists probably assume at least some sense of animal "self" awareness, at least in our companion animals, or on the farm in those horses, cows, and pigs with which we have developed a special relationship. After all, when my cat, Maggie, pesters me for a petting, she is not looking for me to pet the other cat, Gunner. Maggie also distinguishes very clearly her name from Gunner's, and vice versa. There is here some basic recognition on the part of both cats of their different identities. And do not both of them recognize their own paws as belonging to them and not to the other? Still the question as to whether they have what can be called real "self recognition" is a difficult one, partly because Self can mean many things, some quite complex, and partly because self-awareness fluctuates even in humans.

Still, the scientists have not given up on animals, and one experiment they have devised has received much attention in recent years. It is called the "mirror self-recognition" test, developed by a psychologist in 1970 to see if chimpanzees could recognize themselves in a mirror. Until then it was thought by most that only humans are capable of mirror self-recognition. The chimpanzees, however, passed the test, and it has since been used in studies of human child development, as well as with animals. The heart of the test, as it has been refined for animals, consists in what is called the "mirror mark test." A visible, colored dot is placed on the animal's body in a place where it is normally out of view and can be detected only by use of a mirror. The animal passes the test if it spots the mark in the mirror and shows that it grasps that the mark is on its own body by inspecting it there, looking at it, touching it, rubbing it, or attempting to remove it. Some ethologists maintain that the importance of the test is that it demonstrates that these animals have a particular sense of self in the recognition of their bodies as their own.

So far, only a very few animals have passed the test. This select few include the four great apes, and, also, magpies, dolphins, and elephants. These seem also to belong to the types of animals Steiner described, if we include dolphins and elephants, as having an "'I'-like something" not reducible to the group soul.

However, not all scientists are convinced of "mirror self recognition," and the mirror test remains controversial as an indication of sense of self. Behaviorists, for example, have criticized the test by claiming that the relationship between self and mirror can be learned through conditioned training, much as pigeons can be trained to peck at dots on themselves in front of a mirror. Frans de Waal has responded, however, that no untrained pigeon has ever managed to use a mirror to find dots on its own body (de Waal 2008, 1621). Other critics have complained that the test is one-sidedly visual, reflecting a human bias, whereas many animal's may recognize themselves primarily by means of other senses, such as the highly developed hearing and echolocation senses of the bat, or the highly developed sense of smell of the dog, such that, as philosopher Jean Kazez has suggested, "For dogs recognizing the smell of their own urine may be a moment of self-awareness" (Kazez 2010, 64). Other critics maintain that the test doesn't tell us anything that isn't already obvious, else how could animals without some sense of their own identity move confidently through their surroundings.

Still the test has remained the main experimental standard for animal self-identity. Sometimes the animals are also inventive in finding a play possibility in viewing their image in the mirror, or are simply intrigued by the experience. Female chimpanzees have been known to drape themselves before the mirror with leaves and other parts of foliage, almost as if to say, "Look at my new jewelry." Dolphins will sometimes bring their water toys to play with in front of the mirror. And elephants will bring hay to eat while looking in the mirror.

Frans de Waal has suggested that the significance of the mirror self-recognition test may have to do not so much with self-recognition, but with deeper capacities in the animal that the test points to, such as, perspective-taking in relation to the environment, including the social environment, and the ability of the animals to meet unique opportunities or problems presented to them by their environment. De Waal writes, "Animals certainly do not need to recognize themselves to survive.... The mirror test is interesting not because it shows that an animal has the capacity for self-recognition but because of the cognitive abilities that are associated with mirror self-recognition" (de Waal 2008).

We turn, therefore, to look at some of these deeper capacities that have been observed among the types of animals successful in mirror "self-recognition." Many of these capacities and abilities are remarkable, and their accomplishment strongly smacks of something verging on, if not fully expressive of, an "I"-like independence and insight beyond the sensorially given. The examples I will briefly look at have to do with cognitive, language, and memory capacities.

2. COGNITIVE CAPACITIES

The types of animals we are especially looking at here show mental abilities that seem unmistakably to bear an individual stamp. Put another way, many of these animals demonstrate capacities that seem to go beyond the built-in wisdom of the group soul. Even when expressed within the bounds of the species, these capacities suggest intelligent flexibility, logical decision-making, and insight. The great apes, elephants, dolphins, and certain birds provide clear examples. Because the remarkable abilities of birds in these areas have only come to the fore in recent years, I will use the birds for my main examples in this section. The cognitive capacities of the other types of animals will also become evident in the following sections on language and memory, since there is considerable overlap in these areas.

Until only about fifteen or twenty years ago, it was basically assumed that the behavior of birds is largely programmed by instinct. The brain of the bird was thought to be more primitive than that of the mammal because the bird appears earlier in the evolutionary sequence, and it was thought, therefore, that the birds' cognitive abilities are inferior to those of the mammals. All of this has begun in recent years to be rethought. It has even been discovered that, when standardized for body weight, some birds' brains are much larger than earlier expected, especially the brains of ravens, crows (and corvids in general). "In fact, as a percentage of average body mass, they approach or even exceed our brains" (Marzluff and Angell 2012, 32).

Two areas of bird behavior have now emerged to be of special interest to ornithologists and other students of animal behavior. These are: 1. the musicality of song birds and 2. the problem-solving abilities of certain birds, especially ravens, crows, and jays.

Until recently, it was assumed that bird song was relatively fixed and was interpreted in terms of Darwinian utilitarianism as mainly for establishing territorial claims and for wooing mates. Bird song does serve both these purposes and at those times is fairly fixed and stereotyped, probably because of what is at stake. In more relaxed moments, however, of which there seem to be many, a great flexibility and playfulness in the musical ability of songbirds emerges. Musical variations, antiphony, improvisation, transposing to another key, imitation of others and creative responses, all are part of many a song bird's repertory. In reviewing this amazing musicality of the songbirds, Walter Streffer concludes that the songbirds, even when they are being territorial, show in their musicality a "touch of 'I'-hood" (*eine geringere Egoität*) (Streffer 2009a, 69; also Streffer 2009b). Streffer also points out that the musical abilities of songbirds is resulting in the rethinking of the nature of the avian brain. He writes that the astounding coordination of musical pitch, tone duration, and sound dynamics means that the brain of the songbird brings about achievements corresponding to those typical of the higher brain centers of the human being (Streffer 2009b, 60).

Equally impressive are many challenging cognitive achievements of ravens and crows (Heinrich 2006; Marzluff and Angell). Ravens have shown themselves able to solve in intelligent and clever ways cognitive tasks and to do so with flexibility and insightfulness, and without going through long, trial and error attempts. In one experiment, for example, pieces of meat were attached to strings hanging from a perch for the birds. The birds were unable to get the meat simply by flying directly to the piece of meat at the end of the string, simply because the meat on the ends of the hanging strings would move away from the bird when contacted. Many birds gave up after several, playful attempts to get the meat by flying directly to it; other birds, however, returned again and again, but without success. One of the birds, however, remained standing on the perch, not doing anything but simply contemplating the meat on the ends of the strings below him. Then, suddenly, he executed a logical, insightful action. He grasped the string with his beak, pulled it a little higher, then held it fast with his foot while pulling it still higher again with his beak. Repeating this, he gradually pulled the meat up until he could reach it. From the fact that the raven solved the problem without intermediate steps or without various trial and error attempts, the researchers concluded that he must have come directly to grasp the problem. There are many other examples of similar insightful problem-solving (Heinrich and Bugnyar 2007).

Crows are known to throw walnuts into the street in order to have them cracked open by passing cars. In Japan, crows have been seen to prefer streets with traffic lights so that during the red stop light they can go into the street undisturbed to collect the open nuts placed there. In America crows have been observed to place deer bones on a railroad track and then return to obtain the bone marrow after a train has come through. Researchers provide many other examples of avian intelligence (See Streffer 2009a and b).

The common titmouse is also very adaptable and ready to learn. This ability of tits to learn became famous in the middle of the nineteenth century in England. (This could have been a tip-off for scientists to begin serious study of avian learning long before only thirty or so years ago.) At that time, a titmouse had begun to open the tops on milk bottles that were customarily delivered outside the doors of houses. Other tits soon noticed and their extraordinary gift for learning quickly showed itself in how rapidly the ability to remove the bottle tops spread all over England. And then, when cardboard tops were replaced with metal ones, the tits also soon learned to open these bottles. The first tit may have opened a metal bottle top by chance, rather than by trial and error, but it soon recognized what it had done. It repeated its behavior and other tits soon learned to follow suit. This was clearly intelligent, purposive behavior. So much for the "bird brain" slander (Birch 2008).

Just to give one example of cognitive intelligence among primates, here is an instance told by primatologist Frans de Waal about an observation made at the bonobo enclosure at the San Diego Zoo (the bonobo is a small chimpanzee-like species of ape). The zoo had decided to drain the water from the surrounding moat because apes cannot swim. They did, however, hang a permanent chain into the moat so that the bonobos could visit it whenever they wanted. Here is de Waal's recounting of what would sometimes happen when the alpha, the dominant male, Vernon, would visit the moat and go down into it: "If the alpha male, Vernon, disappeared into the moat...younger male, Kalind, sometimes quickly pulled up the chain. He would then look down at Vernon with an open-mouthed play face while slapping the side of the moat. This expression is the equivalent of human laughter: Kalind was making fun of the boss. On several occasions, the only other adult, Loretta, rushed to the scene to rescue her mate by dropping the chain back down, and standing guard until he had gotten out" (de Waal 2006, 72).

This incident is relevant to our earlier exploration of empathy, and it is actually in a discussion of empathy and cooperation that de Waal tells it. However, it also says much about cognitive insight and understanding. Each of the apes understood perfectly well what the chain was, and what it was for. They also saw clearly Vernon's situation and what concrete steps they could take either to prolong his predicament or to end it. Here we see cognitive understanding serving emotional intentions, either to help or to tease. When we look at the other areas of language and memory we will see that some of these same cognitive abilities figure in them also.

3. LANGUAGE

All language is a form of communication, but not all communication is language. Animals communicate is many different ways. Apes gesture by pointing, stamping their feet, baring their teeth, holding out their arms, and so on. Birds have distinct alarm calls that signal the presence or approach of a predator, such as a hawk. Fish, cuttlefish, and frogs have all been observed using very specific forms of signaling to convey information about food, predators, and mating intentions. Elephants have extremely sensitive feet that enable them to send and pick up messages sent over very long distances by stomping on the ground. Although not well understood, thirty-four different types of calls by whales have been identified. Vervet monkeys have three predator alarm calls that convey specific information to other monkeys: one for leopards, one for eagles, and one for snakes. At the alarm signal for leopards, the monkeys climb up into trees, for eagles they stop and scan the skies, and for snakes, they stand on their hind legs and look into the grass. Chickens, also, have been shown to have thirty different calls—varieties of clucks—for communicating about food, caring for their chicks, recognition of social standing, warning of predators, and so on.

In 1960, experiments were begun to see if chimps were capable of language proper to communicate with each other and with human beings, using a system of symbols as a form of language. For instance, some investigators began to use American Sign Language (ASL), first invented for deaf people, with chimpanzees. Initially, results were disappointing. By 1972, however, one chimpanzee named Washoe achieved some notoriety by learning a vocabulary of 150 words in ASL, and had the ability to combine these in some novel sentences (Savage-Rumbaugh and Lewin 1994). Roger Fouts, who was part of the team teaching ASL to Washoe tells of some of Washoe's ability with hand signing, sometimes signing (talking) to herself by signing: "She would sign QUIET to herself when she sneaked into a forbidden room. Or when she was perched atop her willow tree she would announce to us (who couldn't see the front of the house) the name of the person about to arrive at the front door. Or she would sit on her bed and talk to her dolls spread out around her" (Fouts, 72).

A big question, posed especially by behaviorist sceptics, who maintained that the ape's apparent language was really only stimulus–response conditioning, was whether the apes could use syntax, that is, could they combine signs in such a way, not only to designate objects, but also to form a sentence of some kind (Savage-Rumbaugh and Lewin, 39, 189–191). To explore this, some investigators began to develop computer boards with keys having symbols (*lexagrams*) for communication. Using the computer lexagrams chimpanzees seemed increasingly to show some syntactical language comprehension with other chimpanzees and with humans.

The real star, however, was a young bonobo called Kanzi. Smaller than chimpanzees, bonobos were for a long time thought to be simply a variety of chimpanzee and were known as pygmy chimpanzees. It was not until the 1920s that the bonobo was determined to be a separate species of chimpanzee. The bonobo social organization is, like the chimpanzee's, hierarchical, but unlike the chimpanzee's is matriarchal rather than patriarchal. The bonobo is much less aggressive than the chimpanzee, in fact is even playful and gentle by comparison (though as some primatologists have cautioned this ought not to be overdone). The bonobos are highly intelligent, and this became especially apparent with Kanzi, much to the initial surprise of the humans working with him. Kanzi acquired a fairly sophisticated ability to communicate with symbols using the lexagram keyboard, but more than that, he showed the ability to understand words and sentences in spoken English. Kanzi was not trained in this but simply picked it up on his own, hanging around the lab while the scientists were occupied training not Kanzi, but his mother. One can picture a young child messing around, while the others (the humans) around him were seriously at work training the mother, and the child, attentively but nonchalantly, taking in everything being said. The picture is not unlike the way a human child first learns a language.

Sue Savage-Rumbaugh and Roger Lewin tell of how the investigators first became aware that Kanzi was picking up on his own an understanding of spoken English: "We first detected what seemed like spoken word comprehension when Kanzi was one and a half years old. We began to notice that often, when we talked about lights, Kanzi would run to the switch on the wall and flip it on and off. Later he simply looked at the light switch on hearing the word, apparently visually forming the pairing" (ibid., 148). Kanzi, she writes, seemed to be learning by "listening in on conversations that had nothing to do with him." Once they realized that Kanzi had acquired on his own the beginnings of language, Savage-Rumbaugh and her colleagues began building on it. Kanzi developed his language skills between 2½ months and 2½ years old, and by then had achieved a proficiency slightly superior to a 2½-year-old human child. Eventually, over 600 sentences spoken in English were used to test Kanzi. Examples of such sentences to which he responded correctly, included, "Go get a coke for Rose," "Tickle Rose with the bunny," "Take the carrots outdoors," "Go outdoors and find the carrots," and the like. He seemed to understand English word order, including word combinations and sentences that he had never heard before.

Such a symbolic–linguistic system has never developed among bonobos living in the wild. Savage-Rumbaugh and Lewin suggest two possible reasons for this, the first one having to do with anatomical limitations on the possibilities of vocalization. As we saw earlier in the evolution of the human body, the erect posture of the human made possible the unique development of the human vocal tract. The reduction of the jaws, the flattening of the face, the lowering of the tongue partially down into the throat, and the descent of the larynx—these and other changes all associated with the human erect posture—enable the human to control vocalization, especially the production of consonants, in ways impossible for the ape. Another result of erect posture, lacking in the ape, was the freeing of the arms and hands for the gestures and movement so closely connected with human language and speech (ibid., 226–227). That the bonobos speech development does not extend beyond that of the 2½-year-old human child, she also suggests, secondly, this probably also reflects the lack of an ape social culture with which Kanzi's language acquisition could have been practiced and developed further.

Whatever the limitations, the remarkable language achievements of the bonobos reveal intelligence, intention, and flexible understanding far beyond the boundaries of the group soul, and beyond "programmed instinct."

Similar capacities may also be present in the dolphin. Steiner did not mention dolphins among the animals he lists specifically as having an "'I'-like something" that does not return to the group soul at death. At the time he wrote, however, Steiner left his list fairly open-ended: He spoke of "all the apes," certain kinds of amphibians and birds, the kangaroo, and he intimated that other "warm-blooded animals" might also be included. In recent years, since Steiner wrote, we have learned much about the exceptional abilities and capacities of the dolphin, and I am assuming that we can with some confidence consider them as included with the animals that Steiner directs us to as not being at death completely absorbed back into the group soul. Of course, I have no way of knowing this for certain. In any case, the remarkable soul life and capacities of the dolphin warrant serious attention.

The size of the dolphins' brain in proportion to the body is comparable to primates. Dolphins live in complex, highly structured societies. They cooperate with great flexibility and purpose in hunting, changing tactics if the facts and situation require it. For example, they have been known to try to drive a school of fish toward the shore, but failing to do so immediately drive them out to sea toward the rest of the dolphin herd (MacIntyre, 26). Although we don't understand very well their system of communication with each other through squeals and whistles, we have learned that they have signature whistles that function as individual identifiers. So specific are these that one dolphin may mimic the signature whistle of another to get its attention. Recall also that dolphins are among that select group that has passed the mirror recognition test. They have a rich soul life of curiosity, play, affection, cooperative work together, as well as exhibiting fear and stress. They show empathy for other dolphins in need, and they can interact also with humans, helping them, as many stories attest, at sea.

It is especially the language capacities of dolphins that I focus on here. In this I rely mainly on the discussion of dolphins in relation to other animals and to human beings by the contemporary philosopher Alasdair MacIntyre. I have two main reasons for taking up MacIntyre here. First, MacIntyre tells us much about dolphins and language, or what he calls the "prelinguistic capacities" of dolphins, which he suggests may apply also to other animals, such as the great apes. Second, MacIntyre sets forth a view that is common, probably dominant, among most contemporary ethologists. This is the view that there is no sharp dividing line between animals and humans, that, as many of them like to put it, "the difference is not one of kind, but one only of degree." MacIntyre states his view clearly. We will have to evaluate later the extent to which it can be sustained. However, first I focus on his discussion of dolphins' language capacities.

MacIntyre argues against a number of philosophers who hold that animals not only do not have language, but also, because of that, cannot have thoughts, beliefs, directed action, or even perception of objects. In taking on these philosophers, MacIntyre concedes that what they say is true of many animals—moths, crabs, lizards, sea urchins, and others—in that these animals lack concepts and are mainly guided by instinctual constraints. But he maintains that this is not true of a whole group of animals that includes not only dolphins but also chimpanzees, gorillas, and maybe even dogs. These animals have shown clear evidence, he says, of having capacities that go well beyond the instinctive. It is interesting that, with the possible exception of dogs, he includes within the group just the types of animals we have been looking at primarily.

MacIntyre's argument is that animals in this group possess what he calls "prelinguistic capacities" that are prerequisite for any attainment of full-blown language. These are the same capacities, he argues, that are present in very young human children and that make it possible for them in course of development to acquire human language as such. These prelinguistic capacities are clearly evident in dolphins especially.

What are these prelinguistic capacities? They are the capacities for sensing what is the truth about a situation; the capacity to adjust should the situation change; the capacity to discriminate between what a situation calls for, and does not; the capacity for "perceptual attention," that is, to be attentive to what a situation is and to perceive and register changes in that situation and to see what these changes call for in response; the capacity to investigate the environment and in the process to recognize, distinguish and re-identify those aspects of the environment revealed in these investigations (MacIntyre, 38–39, 29–42). They are the same capacities the young human child must exercise before acquiring the powers of language itself. MacIntyre argues that the full range of these capacities in the dolphin also justify ascribing thoughts and beliefs to dolphins, and to holding that "they possess certain concepts and know how to apply them" (ibid., 27).

The presence of prelinguistic capacities in dolphins seems further confirmed by the remarkable capacity in them for "some kind of linguistic comprehension." A group of scientists has developed a simple, artificial, acoustical language, which they have taught to dolphins to understand, and to respond to sentences in that language. The dolphins, the scientists report, have learned to identify a range of different objects and respond to sentences of some syntactical difficulty. In this artificial language, the dolphins recognized the difference, for instance, between "Take the surfboard to the Frisbee" and the sentence "Take the Frisbee to the surfboard." They also showed the ability to understand new combinations of words, both in familiar and unfamiliar syntactical order" (ibid., 41). It would have been interesting had MacIntyre chosen to compare the dolphins with Kanzi.

MacIntyre's underlying concern throughout is to show the continuity between what he sees as "some aspects of the intelligent activities of nonhuman animals and the language-informed practical rationality of human beings." He wants, as he puts it, "to undermine the cultural influence of a picture of human nature according to which we are animals and in addition something else." He is intent on demolishing the view that we have in addition to an animal nature, "a distinctively human nature." Against this view, he argues, "We remain animal selves with animal identities"(ibid., 49–50). As was the case with Robert Bellah, we shall have to try and see whether or to what extent, MacIntyre seems to have overreached in this. Before that, however, we need to look at a related, important issue, the nature of memory.

4. MEMORY

Do animals have memory? This is a straightforward question and we can come up with many simple examples that seem to show that animals have some kind of memory. My cat, Gunner, as I have said, remembers his name, and so does the other cat, Maggie, and both know the difference and respond accordingly. In recent years, researchers have provided many, more complex examples, which seem to substantiate, not only that animals have memory, but also that some animals are capable of truly impressive feats of memory. Before we look at some of these later examples, let us first consider what Rudolf Steiner has to say about human and animal memory. We will then try and see how Steiner's view stacks up with the examples given by our contemporary animal researchers.

Steiner denies that animals have memory in the same sense in which we apply the term to humans. In itself, this is bound to elicit cries of protest from many sides. Before giving in to the protesters, however, we should try at first to understand what Steiner is attempting to get at in making this distinction. Memory in the human being he describes as "the perception of the past" (Steiner 1997, 42–4). We could say that it is perception of the past *as past*. Memory in this sense arises *within* human consciousness and can be directed and contemplated by that consciousness. What is called memory in the animal is triggered from without. It is, in Clopper Almon's term, a "response memory" because it is always something called forth from outside the animal's consciousness, from something within the body, like hunger, or from something in the world like, say, the animal trainer (Almon 1998). It is not under the control of the animal, but provokes a response in the animal's consciousness from outside.

Steiner's basic distinction, therefore, is that memory in humans is "*perception* of the past," whereas what we are wont to call memory in the animal is only "the *presence* of the past." The "presence of the past" Steiner describes as a process in which the past "reappears, even in a changed form, at a later time." He remarks that memory really only applies to humans, and that, if we want to persist in using the word *memory* in connection with the animals, then we should find a word other than memory for the human experience of the perception of the past, as distinct from the presence of the past (Steiner 1997, 42–3).

A couple of examples can perhaps illustrate Steiner's distinction. I will use our cats once more. For a number of years my wife and I would travel for a few hours in the car with the cats to our apartment in New York City. Once at the apartment we would let Gunner and Maggie out of their carriers and immediately they would go to their play objects by the scratch pole and start hitting and chasing them across the floor. The presence of their play objects would catapult them without more ado immediately into their play mode. It is unlikely, however, that in our car on our way to the city, they were thinking, "Why doesn't he speed up so that we can start playing sooner." No, they needed the play objects themselves—the "object prompt"—to call forth the "presence of the past" that gave them such enjoyment.

Or we can see the difference between the presence and perception of the past in our own experience. Sometimes we do have momentary experiences of the presence of the past. When, for instance, I would revisit our home farm after many years away I would climb up into the hay mow and invariably the lingering aroma of the hay would conjure up feelings from years past, but, of course, I would immediately correct this with the awareness that it was, indeed, past—nostalgia can be one side-effect of the perception of the past as past but not of presence of the past. Less benign examples of the mere presence of the past, afflicting many people today, are obsessions, neuroses, or post-traumatic stress syndromes. Many a therapist makes a living by helping people transform the presence of the past in them—which often assaults them over and over again—into a perception of the past as past, as something they can gain some control over, as something they no longer need to be victimized or driven by precisely because it is in reality no longer present but truly past.

Sometimes behavior expressive of the wisdom of the animal group soul, species specific behavior, is put forward as an example of animal memory. The migration of birds to different parts of the Earth at different times of year is, for example, occasionally cited as evidence that individual animals have a memory of where in the past they have been and when they should take flight to return (Balcome). Is this individual, conscious memory, or is it an expression of the larger, innate wisdom of the group soul that guides the species? We have little phoebe birds that return each spring to the same nest of the preceding year under the eaves of our porch to raise a new brood (whether they are last year's parents once again returning or last year's offspring, I often wonder). Is the phoebe's yearly return an example of the individual bird's memory of the right time and flight path, or a manifestation of the guidance of the inborn wisdom of the specie's group soul—which, to be sure, might employ for the individual birds, instances of the presence of the past, object prompts, providing markers along the journey's way?

In recent years, many examples of amazing animal "memory" accomplishments have been observed. One outstanding example comes from especially intelligent birds—ravens, scrub jays, and others. There are species of ravens that endeavor to survive harsh times by laying up food supplies for the future. They hide seeds and nuts, frequently in hundreds, sometimes thousands of different places—in hollow tree trunks, under the tree bark, or in the ground. The birds then return with certainty again to their hiding places, not only after days, but often after weeks and months—tits after six weeks, scrub jays and nuthatches after as much as nine months (Streffer 2009 a and b; Heinrich 2006). The question of the birds' memories becomes in these examples especially intriguing and perplexing.

We have a number of animal "memory" instances, however, that complicates the picture even more. Apes, for instance, are highly social creatures who know and distinguish over the course of many years the identities of scores of individuals, including their ranking in the group. This phenomenon could be seen as another manifestation of the species specific, soul wisdom. However, there are many instances in which individual apes seem to remember relationships that in ways that are not so much group as individual. Frans de Waal tells, for example, of having helped a childless, female chimpanzee, called Kuif, to adopt a baby chimp. "The two of us," de Waal related, "had a rather neutral relationship before, but ever since the adoption—now about three decades ago—Kuif showers me with the utmost affection whenever I show my face. No other ape in the world reacts to me as if I am a long-lost family member, wanting to hold my hands and whimpering if I try to leave" (de Waal 2005, 202). Perhaps this is a picture of memory in the service of gratitude (and it is primarily as an example of gratitude that de Waal tells the story). It is unlikely that Kuif often thinks back upon and contemplates the time when de Waal presented her with the new baby and wants to express her feeling of gratitude and affection for him whenever possible. It would seem more likely that because of the original pleasure in receiving the baby this is kindled anew whenever he appears—de Waal as object prompt. Nevertheless, it raises the kinds of questions that resist simple explanations.

To complicate things still further, the biologist Nicola S. Clayton of Cambridge University has been able to show that scrub jays can not only remember *where* they have hidden something, but at the same time also *what* and *when*. (Clayton 2008; Zimmer 2007). This has opened up a whole new dimension (and controversy) among psychologists concerning what they call *semantic memory* and *episodic memory*. These terms have at least a surface similarity to Steiner's presence of the past and perception of the past. Semantic memory in this discussion is the bare storage of facts that can be called forth as the presence of the past. Episodic memory is the ability to consciously recall an event (an episode) that can be looked at in the mind, explored, and learned from. The similarity to Steiner's "perception of the past" is that episodic memory recognizes the event as past and also seems to require some sense of self that moves from past to present and also has some sense of the future.

The scrub jays that Clayton was working with could hide thousands of pieces of food each year and return successfully much later to the location of each one. Clayton wanted to find out if this was just "semantic memory"—a filing away of the locations—or whether the birds actually met the conditions for episodic memory—a memory of the event of actually hiding the food and of what kind it was. She used two kinds of food that she knew the jays liked: peanuts and moth larva. They preferred the larva as long as it was fresh, but would settle for the peanuts when the larva turned stale after a few days. Clayton gave the jays the chance to hide both types of food. One group of birds was allowed to return to their caches after a few hours and they immediately went to dig up the larva. Often the other group was held back for five days, and when released they did not hesitate to bypass the larva, which was by then stale, and go directly to the peanuts (to control for smell, Clayton had removed the larva beforehand). The birds were able to retrieve hidden food selectively according not only to its location but also according to its tastiness based upon the birds' sense of when it had been hidden. *Where, what,* and *when!* Clayton and her team concluded that this was a prime example of episodic memory. Others have followed her experiment and found some similar results with rats, as well as with humming birds, which seem to know where and when they visited individual flowers for nectar.

The conclusion that these are instances of "episodic memory" has not gone unchallenged. The philosopher Jean Kazez has nicely summarized the main objections to the episodic interpretation by psychologists who argue that the jays could be "filing what-where-when factoids as they go about storing food. So when they encounter an old cache, recognizing it as a specific 'where' could trigger a particular 'what' and 'when'" (Kazez, 67). The results of further research and interpretation seem to be trending more and more to the episodic interpretation.

Other animal examples also seem to involve the issues of memory and perception of the past. Is it episodic memory, perception of the past, that leads chimps to gather grass and small twigs on starting out for a site hours before arriving where they will use these for fishing out ants or termites? (de Waal 2005, 38). One interpretation could be that here there is some recall of a previous successful use of these tools, some learning from that, and a sense of future time when that learning can be put to good use. It could also be, however, simply that the chimps have no memory sense of a past or of a future use for the grass and twigs, that these themselves are actually object prompts that arouse in the present a past experience of pleasure associated with an earlier use of the grass and twigs in fishing for food. This would be the presence of the past, not perception of the past (episodic memory) and projection into the future.

Another behavior witnessed among some animals raises the memory issue even more pointedly, the phenomenon, namely, of revenge. Especially chimpanzees and elephants have been noted to seek and wreak revenge on both other animals and on humans that have wronged them, psychologically or physically, in the past. Frans de Waal tells of two chimps who formed an alliance against the dominant male of their group, whom they sought to unseat because he stood in the way of their ready access to females. The dominant male was ordinarily protected by the females of the group, who, if he was attacked, would come together to his defense. The two allies, however, bided their time and waited, actually four years, until the opportunity came for them to corner their adversary alone and kill him (in a most horrific manner showing all the marks of resentment and complete vengefulness). De Waal comments, "The ape remembers and will take all the time in the world to get even" (de Waal 2005, 43–44, 204).

Similarly, elephants are notorious for identifying and seeking vengeance on individual humans who have mistreated them,
often long in the past, and whom they have not seen sometimes
for decades. Suddenly confronted by the abusive individual,
sometimes an earlier trainer, the elephant immediately recognizes and attempts to kill him, often successfully. The author of
the bestselling, nonfiction, *The Tiger*, tells a hair-raising story of
a Siberian tiger that was wounded by a hunter, whom the tiger
then stalked relentlessly, singling him out from other humans,
until the tiger was able to ambush, kill, and eat the hunter. In
such cases of revenge there is, in every instance, evidence of individual recognition and a sense of future aim, the wreaking of
revenge—and, throughout, the exercise of patience. Is it, however, the presence of the other that triggers the experience of the
presence of the past, including both the pain of abuse and recognition of the abuser? Or is more involved, a continuing sense of
injured self, recognition and remembrance of the abuser, and a
persistent yearning and planning for future retribution?

In these questions regarding episodic memory and perception
of the past, many unresolved difficulties remain. The renowned
neurologist Michael S. Gazzaniga has concluded, after doing a
comprehensive review of the existing research, that "Current evidence suggests that animals do not have episodic memory and
do not time travel [that is, anticipate the future], but," he adds,
"we are going to have to keep our eyes on Nicola Clayton and
her scrub jays" (Gazzaniga, 320). And I would add, we ought
not to turn our backs on the plotting, stalking, seething Siberian tiger. This is an area of research and interpretation much
in need of concerted attention by anthroposophic biologists and
philosophers. In my view, however, we should not lose sight of
the fact that the animals we have mainly been looking at are of
the type Steiner describes as possessing a soul–spiritual element
that, at the animal's death, does not merge back into the group
soul but persists as an independent spiritual entity having a definite, "I"-characteristic.

5. "THEORY OF MIND."

One highly disputed theory of animal behavior is what has been called "theory of mind," defined as the ability of one animal to know—or infer—the unobservable mental state of another (Gazzaniga, 48–54; de Waal 2006, 69–73; 2005, 179–186). The phrase "theory of mind" strikes me as being quasi-scientific and not a little pretentious. It does not provide adequate protection against reading a human mind-state into the animal, nor does it protect from concluding that, if the animal lacks a human mind-state, it can, therefore, have no awareness whatever of the inner mental–emotional state of another. We could perhaps avoid both these problems by simply using an old-fashioned term in place of mind and ask whether the "sensorium" of one animal can have some awareness of what is taking place in the sensorium of another, following the simple dictionary definition of sensorium as "the entire sensory system of the body."

The notion of theory of mind first arose ironically from work with chimpanzees and has since been applied to studies of human development. It seems to be widely accepted that humans do have in the full sense "theory of mind," and that the ability is well developed in human children by about age four or five (Gazzinaga, 49). When applied to animals, however, the notion remains highly controversial. Some researchers find strong evidence for it; others maintain that theory of mind has been neither proved nor disproved (ibid., 50).

We have seen especially with the apes that emotional expressions between animals, such as empathy, consolation, or reciprocity, would be difficult to understand without there being some knowledge on the part of an animal for what the other is feeling and undergoing. As Frans de Waal puts it, in the case of apes, "At emotionally meaningful moments, apes can put themselves into another's shoes" (de Waal 2005, 184).

One other pattern of animal behavior that shows strong evidence of theory of mind, if we don't anthropomorphize mind inordinately or too narrowly, is that of deceit and deception. Chimpanzees and corvids (ravens and crows) provide striking examples of how trickery reveals definite intentions and some kind of awareness of another animal's (and sometimes human's) inner emotional, sensorial state. The crafty scheming of crows and ravens to throw off others who would swipe food they have hidden is well known. Bernd Heinrich has spent his life studying ravens and crows and he does not hesitate to say of ravens that they have "personalities" within their species: "There are the bold, the meek, the curious, the nervous birds. I suspect that ravens' often unpredictable behavior resides in what we call 'mind'—something independent of programmed reactions to the immediate" (Heinrich 2006, 9).

These birds are noted for hiding—caching—food objects for retrieving later. They retain knowledge over long periods of time of hundreds of locations where they have hidden pieces of meat or other foods for retrieval. They are also very active in stealing other birds' food caches. Heinrich and his colleague, Thomas Bugnyar, devised a series of tests to study the birds' behavior in the presence of potential thieves. They started with two humans, one designated as "thief," who always stole the cached objects of the birds; the other, the "benign," non-thieving human, who examined the birds' cached objects without taking any of them. Then the two humans in the presence of the bird observed its behavior without interfering. The birds ignored the non-thieving human even when he went near their caches, but immediately retrieved the hidden food when the "thief" approached the cache. "This experiment thus showed," concluded Heinrich and Bugnyar, "not only that the birds improve their food-caching skills after experiencing others raiding their object caches but that they distinguish individuals (in this case, humans)."

Then they complicated the experiment by arranging to have two birds besides the cache-maker, one that could witness where the caching bird was hiding its food, the other able to hear the activity but was prevented from witnessing it. The caching bird was able to be aware of which bird knew and which didn't. When the birds were placed together, the cacher chased the "knower" away or immediately retrieved the hidden food before the knower could get at it. All the while the cacher simply ignored the "non-knower." At the same time the knower would try to avoid the attacks of the cacher by pretending disinterest and not going directly to the caches in the chacher's presence, but waiting till they, the cachers, were at some distance. "These results," say Heinrich and Bugnyar, "do not totally exclude the possibility that the knowers provide some subtle cues that the cacher defender may use, but such cueing is unlikely, and the finding strongly suggests that the birds engage in amazingly sophisticated behavior based on the ability either to interpret or to anticipate the actions of others." Less cautiously, Heinrich writes elsewhere, "They [the birds] *deceive* by being able to put themselves in the other's place" (Heinrich and Bugnyar 2007; ibid., "Afterward," 2006). Other researchers have shown similar behavior in crows: "Crows also appear to know what other animals (including humans) in their world are thinking, and they use this information to inform their behavior" (Marzluff and Angell, 102).

Chimpanzees are capable of a number of behaviors that show some aspect of theory of mind, or, perhaps better, some awareness of what another knows or doesn't know, feels or doesn't feel. Not all evidence of knowledge of another's inner state comes from incidents involving trickery and deception, as we have seen in the many cases of empathy and consolation. But the awareness of another chimp's sensorial state—mental state in the usual terminology—is especially apparent in situations of deceit and deception.

Chimpanzees are notorious tricksters. They will be aware themselves of what other apes know or don't know about where food is hidden and use this to get the food for themselves. Subordinate chimps will wait or hide in order to deceive a dominant member of the group in order to get the food the dominant ape would ordinarily take. Chimps are adept at outmaneuvering rivals and avoiding conflict with the dominant males. They will plot revenge on another over a long period of time, all the while concealing their real hostile intent. They will surreptitiously arrange trysts with the female mates of dominant apes. Philosopher Jean Kazez tells of a situation in which a young male chimpanzee shows his erect penis to an interested female sitting on one side of him while simultaneously hiding it with his hand from a competing—and dominant—male sitting on his other side. The subordinate male seemed to have definite intentions—to entice the female while deluding the dominant male—and to have some clear sense of the inner states of the others (the female's interest and the dominant male's hostility)—and all involving some crafty scheming (Kazez, 64).

However, whether chimpanzees have "theory of mind" as fully implied by this pretentious, quasi-scientific terminology is strongly contested. Still, it has to be said, the chimps and crows and ravens have clear and definite intentions and are fully capable of tricking rivals whose opposing intentions they seem to grasp very well.

8.

DIFFERENCE IN KIND
AND/OR DIFFERENCE IN DEGREE

One of the commonly heard rebukes against thinking about animals, let alone committing time, money, and energy for their sake, is the assertion that human beings are so much more important than animals and that concern for the animals diverts attitudes and energy, as well as material resources, otherwise needed for relieving human suffering. The assumption here is that a fundamental opposition exists between concern for humans on the one side and for animals on the other. There is something profoundly flawed in this assumption. Anyone who seriously begins to explore the place—and plight—of animals today quickly becomes aware of how interwoven the animals are with nearly every aspect and problem of modern human life, including the economy, the environment, the military, corporate power, climate warming, science, medicine, education, and so on. The animals, as we shall see in much detail, figure centrally in every aspect. Neglect of concern for the animals has already been disastrous, not only for the animals, but also ecologically, and it threatens the healthy future of even the human species. At the base of this reproach for showing care for the animals is a still deeper assumption that care is a limited quantity, and must be rationed lest it be used up. But care, like love, grows the more— and only if—it is exercised. The theologian John Cobb has stated well the nature of caring:

> We should not suppose that caring for other animals reduces caring for people. On the contrary, those persons who are most sensitive to others are often sensitive to *all* others, and those

who restrict the range of their caring often care less for any. It is a mistake to restrict 'the least of these' to the human in the interest of ensuring concern for human 'least ones'. To harden oneself against the suffering of other animals does not heighten sensitivity to fellow human beings. (Cobb 1998)

Many animal advocates, among them leading philosophers and ethologists, have attempted to combat this assumption that care for animals hinders care for humans by maintaining that there is no fundamental difference between humans and animals, only difference in degree. This was the philosopher MacIntyre's main effort to undermine the idea that we are animals but also with a second, "distinctively human nature."

1. SPECIESISM

This desire to level entirely the differences between humans and animals has acquired in recent years a kind of battle cry in the word *speciesism*. This somewhat awkward expression was first coined by a psychologist in 1970 and then was brought to widespread attention by philosopher Peter Singer in his 1975 publication of *Animal Liberation*. It has since gained considerable currency among champions of animal welfare.

The essence of the concept of speciesism is that no species can claim special consideration or special treatment over any other species. In his book Singer defined *speciesism* as "a prejudice or attitude of bias toward the interest of members of one's own species and against those of members of other species" (Singer 2009, 6). Singer later tried to refine this definition, and others have sought to draw it even tighter, as does Joan Dunayer in her book by that title, as "a failure in attitude or practice, to accord any nonhuman being equal consideration and respect" (Dunayer 2004, 5). Most clear perhaps is the *Oxford English Dictionary* definition of speciesism as "discrimination against or exploitation of certain animal species by human beings, based on an assumption of mankind's superiority." For anyone sensitive to the human mistreatment and exploitation of animals over the centuries, an attitude of speciesism on the part of humans can easily be seen to have been a major cause of this mistreatment. The possibility of undercutting the presence and practice of speciesism by leveling the differences between humans and animals, showing that all differences are simply those of degree and not of kind, can, therefore, have a strong appeal to animal advocates.

But the term *speciesism* warrants closer examination than it has ordinarily been given. The attitude of speciesism itself has deeper causes that have both given rise to it and have reinforced it further. These deeper roots are both religious and scientific. Very influential has been a common, often main, interpretation of the passage in the Book of Genesis in which God is said to have given humans "domination" over all the other creatures on Earth. Dominion, then, has a long history of being interpreted to mean that the animals were placed on Earth by God explicitly for human use and pleasure. Concern for the animals as such has little or no standing in this interpretation. The rise of the mechanical philosophy and its wholesale incorporation into modern science further eliminated all protection for animals from anything humans might choose to do to them, and for whatever reasons—curiosity, profit, supposed medical progress, or sadism. Since the animals were now, on the grounds of science and philosophy, regarded as unfeeling mechanisms, anything was allowed, especially if it could be promoted as serving human purposes. This was convenient since, in dealing with non-feeling automatons, bothersome ethical questions, such as, "Does might make right?" or, "Are there limits to what can be done to living beings?" need not intrude as they are irrelevant. In popular culture the notion of human "dominion" as might and right has melded with the mechanistic claims of science, both pervaded by a general indifference to the life and suffering of animals.

So speciesism, with its assumption of unchecked human superiority and entitlement does capture a widespread attitude toward animals in today's world. One favorite major way of combating speciesism is to level the differences between human and other species by maintaining that the differences between them are in degree only, not in kind. This effort to eliminate significant differences between the species is cast as the mark of a truly open and enquiring mind. Marc Bekoff has said that speciesism is a form of anti-intellectualism because it seems to deny any recognition of the many commonalities between the animal and human. But applied indiscriminately and in broadside fashion, the blanket charge of speciesism itself can be anti-intellectual in stifling at the outset any attempt to ask whether there might, indeed, be some serious differences worth taking into account. Still, speciesism does capture a widespread, popular attitude toward animals in today's world, and exposing its presence and harmful consequences in our treatment of the animals can be essential. If, perhaps, at the same time, it can be shown that difference does not have to mean despotic dominance, then paying attention precisely to the most crucial question of "kind" and/or "degree" of difference need not close off, but, rather, heighten rigorous inquiry and understanding.

In Steiner's view, the human–animal relationship contains many commonalities and similarities, and *both* differences of degree and differences of kind. Moreover, for Steiner, neither similarities nor differences are grounds for misconceived and misapplied notions of superiority. For Steiner, human differences of kind from the animals entail ever-greater responsibility on the part of the human, while similarities simultaneously serve to reinforce our human–animal kinship.

For Steiner, the fundamental difference in kind between humans and animals is that the human possesses a "self-conscious 'I'-being," a self, and an animal, for the most part, does not. Again, this is bound to raise hackles, for do not the animals show many signs of some kind of self-identity and self-direction. It is very important, therefore, that we be as clear as possible about what Steiner is saying.

Steiner affirms that animals have experiences as single animals, as well as members of a group soul. As we have seen repeatedly, for Steiner as for the ethologists, animals feel a range of emotions, many of them in common with humans. For Steiner, as for the others, the experience of these feelings is centered within the being of the single animal. The single animal feels pain, joy, anger, empathy, and so on. At one point, he writes,

Here we are coming ever nearer to individuation; the higher the evolution of nature ascends, the nearer we come to beings whose center is within themselves.... The animal has a soul and admittedly feels happiness and suffering within the limits of its skin. We do not actually see this soul because it is in the realm we call the astral world. The animals are creatures that have a center in themselves, and themselves and their souls live in the astral realm...the animal has its center in itself, in the realm that is invisible. (Steiner 1978, 21)

I take this to mean that the single animal incorporates within itself that portion and organization of the astral-feeling reality of the cosmos, in accordance with its particular species—its particular body and soul—nature. And within this there exists a kind of focal point of experience, a "center" of experience, agency, and direction. This would not mean, however, that the single animal can stand back and reflect conceptually upon its experience. It does not reflect conceptually, either on what it has done or experienced in the past,or forward on what it will do, or feel, in the future. In a useful phrase from the American philosopher John Dewey, it is given to the animal "to suffer and to undergo," and this can range from the simple to the complex, from the exhilarating to the excruciating. Perhaps, among certain types of animals, it can even take on an "I"-like potential.

What, then, of the human "I"? How can we see it as different in kind from the astrally-focused center of the animal? Let us briefly review some of the major areas that we have already explored in part, but now with an eye to how they might reveal the presence and potential of a human, self-conscious "I"-being. These areas in brief review will include again: the human and animal body, memory, and thinking. In each of these areas a fundamental difference in kind—the presence of an independent "I"—reveals itself.

2. THE "I" AND THE BODY: REVIEWED

Having an "I" and being conscious of the "I" are not the same. Once humans received an "I"-being as they began to assume bodily form on Earth, the "I" worked with the assistance of high spiritual beings unconsciously into the body to make it increasingly fitted for the emergence and exercise of independent, self-consciousness. We have seen that one of the first developments necessary to, and indicative of, the beginnings of "I"-consciousness, was the raising of the human physical body to an erect posture. We have noted how the erect bearing of the human preceded the development of a large brain, and how subsequently then the brain developed to become the largest of all mammals in proportion to body size. Erect posture also lifted the human out of the horizontal, and freed it significantly, unlike the animal, from the downward pull of earthly forces. The arms were freed for gesture, the larynx and facial structures settled to make speech possible, and other bodily structures and organs unique to humans developed accordingly (Verlust; Kipp). The generalized nature of the human body freed the human, relatively, from determination by any particular environment. This unspecialized human was free to roam and settle the Earth from environment to environment, unlike the animals whose highly specialized bodies limit them to only certain kinds of environments and make them too fixed to serve as the vehicle of an independent, individual "I"-being.

3. The "I" and Memory: Revisited

In our earlier exploration of human and animal memory we discussed Steiner's distinction between memory in animals as presence of the past and memory in humans as perception of the past. We also looked at some animal research that speaks of semantic memory—the storage of facts—and episodic memory—the memory of an event involving a sense of time—past, presence, and future. We saw these categories (semantic and episodic) as similar, or even identical to Steiner's "presence of the past" and "perception of the past." We also saw that the evidence of episodic memory, or perception of the past, in animals is ambiguous and not solidly established. However, we did see that in certain lines of recent animal research—as, for example, with the scrub jays, the elephants, the dolphins, and the great apes—the question still remains decidedly open. These are of the types of animals, we also observed, that Steiner identifies as having "I"-like qualities, and so the question with them especially should remain open.

Let us look a little closer, then, at Steiner's depiction of the role of the "I" in human memory. We can see the importance of the "I"-being, or self, in relation to memory in at least three ways. First, it is the "I" itself that makes possible the perception of the past as past. The "I" takes up the event, now in the past, and recognizes it as past. The "I" can now move freely with the past event. It can examine it, contemplate it, learn from it, be perplexed by it, or regret it—among other things. The "I" makes it possible to live freely with the past—free from the past and free for the future. It is the "I" working freely with the perception of the past as past that is essential to the reality and exercise of freedom.

Second, we can see the "I" in relation to memory as what gives permanence, continuity, and coherence to our life experience. The "I"-being, the self, is the ground of a relatively permanent sense of ongoing self-hood through change. This sense of permanence and cohesion of the self is given, not by past events and experiences themselves, but by the "I"-being, which takes up the past experiences, connects and holds them together, moves among them, and is the permanent element within them. Were the "I" not to hold past events together in a coherent relationship, we would have only disconnected, dissociated fragments of experience. We would only experience, in the words of the American philosopher, William James, "one damned thing after another." And when the "I" weakens and loses its grip, our lives, to that extent do come apart. The single animal, however, does have a permanence of experience and behavior by virtue of its participation in the group soul and group "I"-being.

Third, the "I" links memory with the idea and experience of time. As the I develops and works with memory, it moves through time. The "I," moving through time with its memories, can look back almost to the time of birth, or to that time when memory begins, and forward to the time of death. Working with memory, the I is even able to imagine *alternative futures.* It is unlikely that this is a possibility for animals.

Some suggest that animals seem to understand time and to plan ahead, as, for examples, when birds fly south for the winter, when squirrels hide acorns for future consumption, or when bears fatten up in summer and fall in preparation for hibernating through the winter. All of this kind of activity, however, seems to be not so much planning by individual animals as guidance by the group wisdom conferred on the animal body by the group "I" and soul. If we wished we could probably also describe the working of this wisdom at the level of internal cues, glandular processes, bodily clocks, and other life rhythms. Michael Gazzaniga probably has it right when he comments: "A bear that hibernates for the first time cannot be planning ahead for the long cold winter. It doesn't even know that there *are* long cold winters" (Gazzaniga, 314).

4. The "I" in Thinking, Feeling, and Willing

When Steiner talks of *spirit,* he is pointing to the objective reality of the cosmic intelligence that is the creative source of all that is. The modern, materialistic mind-set has difficulty with this since it tends to assume that the universe is void of meaning and intelligence, and that these exist only in the minds of humans, preeminently in the heads of scientists and philosophers. The eminent quantum physicist, Steven Weinberg, gave expression to the modern mind-set when, not long ago, he famously said, "The more the universe seems comprehensible, the more it also seems pointless." Hearsay has it, however, that Weinberg later did voice his puzzlement about the fact that scientists like himself are able to use their intelligence to comprehend a universe regarded by them as unintelligible and meaningless.

Against the modern view represented by Weinberg, Steiner put it this way: "Man would find himself involved in a strange self-contradiction were he not to take for granted the presence of spirit in all the phenomena of existence around.... When human beings need wisdom in order to understand things—that is, when we extract wisdom from them—this shows that wisdom is inherent in the things themselves, for no matter how hard we might try to understand things with wisdom-filled ideas, we would not be able to extract wisdom from these things if it were not present in them to begin with" (Steiner 1910a and 1997, 192–3). The difficulty of the modern mind to conceive of intelligence—wisdom—as constituent of the world may help explain the scientists' tremor of excitement and confused surprise when they first began to discover the intelligence and wisdom actually present in the animal world, and expressed by the animals.

Wisdom, as Steiner emphasizes, is "present in all beings" (Steiner 1987, 111). Our central question at this point is, "In what ways is wisdom—intelligence—present similarly in animals and humans, and in what ways differently?" A fundamental difference between the human and the animal is that there are certain areas of intelligence that are given to the animal from birth, which the human lacks and must gain on his or her own. The wisdom of the animal can be quite extensive and complex. The papermaking capacities of the wasp, and the engineering abilities of the beaver, we have seen to be among Steiner's favorite examples. The human lacks this inborn wisdom and has to win, through the exercise of independent human intelligence, what is given to the animal through inheritance.

Steiner writes: "Man is so ready to ask in infinite pride: 'Am I not greatly superior to the animal?' But he would also do well to ask: 'In what respect have I remained behind the animal?' Then he would find that he has remained behind the animal in respect of many faculties—faculties that are innate in the animal, but that man, if he is to develop them himself, has to acquire and master by dint of effort" (Steiner 1910b). These include, as we saw in an earlier context, capacities specific to the human being that are not given by heredity but that have to be acquired *de novo* by the human in childhood; such as, acquiring a sense of balance in the world through the struggle to stand and walk; learning to speak through listening and imitating the speech of other human beings; developing the ability to think conceptually through the experience of language; and, through all of these, eventually developing a consciousness of self. Most of the wider intelligence of the world, which is not given in inheritance, has to be wrestled out of the world by the independent exercise of human intelligence. Central to all of these capacities is the independent human "I"-being.

Essential differences between human and animal intelligence become still clearer when looking more closely at the relation of the human "I" to body, soul, and spirit. In the animal, the soul is intimately connected and bound up with the animal body, which carries the creative wisdom and power of the group soul and group "I"-being. The creative activity of the spirit in the animal body is, in Steiner's words, "mirrored" in the life and soul experiences of the animal. In other words, in the animal an immediate and direct connection exists between spirit, soul, and body. In the human it is different.

In the human we find something that breaks, to an important extent, the close connection between soul and body, and between soul and spirit. This something is the human "I"-being. Steiner expresses this in various ways. In the human, "the living 'I'-being, which is found in the soul, pushes its way between spirit and bodily organization" (Steiner 1910a). Or, he says, the human soul is "emancipated" from the immediate influences of the body. The "I" "intervenes" between body and spirit, "loosening" the tight connection as it exists in the animal between the two. (Steiner cautions here that this is to be understood as relatively so.)

This emancipation of the soul from body and from spirit has at least three, crucial consequences. The first we have just looked at; namely, that important capacities essential to the human are not inherited but must be won, starting with the growing young human. A second consequence of the emancipation of the human soul from the "wise" determination by the body is not an entirely positive one for the human: "The human being becomes insecure" (Steiner 1910b). This is not to say that the animals do not experience insecurities, fears, anxieties stemming from the threat of predation, shortage of food, lack of shelter, and so forth. But the human insecurity is more fundamental, more existential. For one thing, the human, in being set free from the kind of bodily, group soul wisdom enjoyed by the animal, cannot know directly either what is good or bad and is unable without further ado to adhere firmly to the good. The human being must make decisions without certain guidance, and, moreover, must be able to bring strength of will to hold fast to them. "The animal," writes Steiner, "has a certain security in its instincts; it knows which food is harmful and which is good for it." In fact, animal insecurity is at its height when threatened and mistreated by the likes of human beings. "The animal," stresses Steiner, "injures itself very much less than it is injured by man. Animals are injured most of all when man keeps them in captivity." (An observation that will acquire added relevance when we consider zoos, circuses, and high-density animal confinement in factory farming.)

Furthermore, human beings must engage their soul directly. This is not set for us. We must make decisions about our own feelings, a requirement spared the animal. The passions and emotions of the animal, even ferocious ones, are appropriate to the nature of the animal soul and body and are even ennobled by the integrity of the animal's being. Because they are not contained and channeled by the group wisdom, passions and desires can be unleashed in the human being that have to be directly checked or guided, lest they degrade and obliterate the full human potential. The insecurity of the human being reaches deep, far beyond our ordinary cares and anxieties, beyond even our anxieties about death, because it is an anxiety that involves our identity itself. This insecurity is not a problem for the animals. *It involves, indeed, a fundamental difference in kind.* Human soul life, writes Steiner, "has emancipated itself from its bodily nature, but at a cost" (Steiner 1910b).

At the same time, on the positive side, this emancipation of the individual human soul from the body, this insecurity, can become a major source and impetus for human creativity. This creativity can be practical, moral, and spiritual. Practically, the human is forced to develop new powers of intelligence and to use these in creative ways. "Whereas the spider spins its web with unerring certainty, and it would be absurd to talk of it reasoning, man is obliged to think a great deal before he can perfect any handiwork" (Steiner 1910b). Moral creativity and courage are demanded of human beings in our having to examine and reflect on pressing or consuming desires. Moral creativity and courage are also required by the fact that human beings must constantly decide between the good and the bad and, still more difficult, between the good and the good. These are decisions that the animal, being moral by nature, is not confronted with. The emancipation of the human soul from the body has the potential, furthermore, for enabling the human to turn outward to enrich the human soul ever more and more from what comes into it from without, from the world and from the spirit. Ideas, artistic qualities and beauty, conversation, fellowship, and so forth, all can become outer sources for infinite, inward soul growth and enrichment. The animal, to be sure, can experience and enjoy all the feelings made possible by its group soul and associated astral body, with a freshness and purity sometimes denied to the human soul by a dry and overweening intellectuality.

Finally, the freeing of the human soul from direct and overpowering bodily and group soul influences makes possible a direct connection between the human soul and the spirit. The human soul now has the potential for direct enrichment from the spiritual world—the ability—to incorporate, and to unite the soul directly, and ever increasingly, with the spiritual qualities of truth, beauty, goodness, meaning, purpose, and value. The reality of the spirit is directly present to the animals within their particular bodily organization and group soul, but individual spiritual development is not possible for the animal, nor need it be, for in their own way and within the boundaries of their own group soul and astral body, the animals are spiritually complete.

Steiner makes an exceedingly interesting observation in relation to the place of the concept in the human and in the animal. He makes a distinction between the "realization," or, we can say, between "experience of the concept" and "understanding of the concept." They are not the same. Concept experience in itself is very different from concept understanding. Concept experience is immediate; concept understanding requires the further engagement of the human intelligence. As we have seen, both the human and the animal are shaped by "laws of the spirit"—the creative concepts or formative principles in all creation. The animal has immediate access to the spirit in the wisdom (the formative concepts) written directly into its body–soul organization. The human can also have immediate access to the spirit as a result of the "I" having intervened between body and spirit, thus making the spirit itself directly available to the human soul. Steiner describes how, in the experience of the gifted artist, the intellectual capacities of the human can be bypassed and the spirit in its formative power grasped directly. The human artistic experience of the spirit and that of the animal living in the spirit in its body are basically similar. Both are direct, both make available an experience of the formative powers of the concept, and both are without initial conceptual understanding.

Steiner illustrates this with the examples of two near contemporaries, Michelangelo and Galileo. Michelangelo died the same year, 1564, in which Galileo was born. Galileo had a deep understanding of the laws of mechanics—the laws of oscillation, of the motion of projectiles, of the velocity of falling bodies, of equilibrium, etc. These same laws had been given actual, external expression by Michelangelo in his great work, the dome of St. Peter's in Rome. Michelangelo had grasped the laws artistically and directly without Galileo's conceptual understanding of them. Steiner points out that in Michelangelo we can see how the human can enter into a perception of and direct relationship with the spirit and the creative, formative forces of the world, but without conceptual understanding—"not through the intellect at all." But for one, such as Galileo, who brings concepts to bear, the laws of the spirit can not only be experienced but also understood. Steiner pictures it this way:

> Through an ennobled and purified instinct, man creates what he discovers only later. As animals create instinctively, the way bees, for example, organize their wonderful bee community, so man creates directly out of the spiritual world...Through instinct the animal arrives even in its feeling life at reflecting into its intelligence what it puts into its buildings, and so on. Take, for example, the beaver and what it builds. Among

beavers a Michelangelo will always be found, but never a Galileo who understood the same laws to which the beaver gives form in its construction. (Steiner 1910a)

The laws of the spirit—the creative, formative principles and forces—can be grasped directly by the animal and by human artistic genius alike, apart from intellectual, conceptual understanding. The presence of self-conscious "I"-being working intelligently in the laws of the spirit can lead to the next step of conceptual understanding in the human mind. In Michelangelo and Galileo we have instances of both difference of degree and difference of kind in the human–animal relationship.

5. ALISDAIR MACINTYRE: A FURTHER EVALUATION

Having just looked at Steiner's description of the unique role and importance of the "I" in the human being, I want at this juncture to return to review the position of Alisdair MacIntyre, who is determined to reject any suggestion that "we have first an animal nature and in addition a second distinctively human nature." MacIntyre presents a carefully argued case for the view that animals and humans differ only in degree, and that a fundamental, unbroken continuity exists between the animal and the human. MacIntyre finds in certain animals—dolphins and chimpanzees particularly—the strongest evidence for this view. These animals especially exhibit what he calls clear "prelinguistic abilities" that demonstrate their essential continuity with language-using, concept-capable human beings. As full-blown language users, humans can do important things, which even the prelinguistic animals cannot, but the prelinguistic abilities and accomplishments of these animas, MacIntyre argues, show their essential continuity with the human.

In his analysis, MacIntyre maintains, we can even speak of these prelinguistic animals as having "beliefs" and reasons for acting in certain ways, and for altering an already set-upon course of action, if the perceived need (reason) for doing so presents itself. MacIntyre suggests a scale reflecting different levels of animal capacities. At the lower end of the scale are animals that simply receive imprints from outside and instinctively respond. Moving up the scale to animal types such as dolphins and the great apes are those that have, as he puts it, "perceptions, beliefs, reasons for action, and intentions" (MacIntyre, 58). "Dolphins, gorillas, and members of some other species," writes MacIntyre, "are no more merely responsive to the imprints of their senses than we are" (ibid., 60). These non-instinctual abilities, MacIntyre argues, are similar enough to those of humans to enable many animals at their level to form relations, intelligently and purposely, with one another, and, also with animals of other species and with human beings.

It should be noted again that MacIntyre focuses almost entirely on animals belonging to the type depicted by Steiner as having an "I"-like, human-like, element that does not merge back into the group soul and group "I" at death but, rather, continues at the death of the animal in the form of an independent, "I"-like spiritual entity. Recall that Steiner includes in this type of animal all the great apes, certain birds and amphibians, some kangaroos, and certain other warm-blooded animals. I have suggested that, from what we have learned since Steiner, we can reasonably include in this list also the dolphin and the elephant.

MacIntyre describes one capacity that the human must necessarily possess in order to function fruitfully as human in the world. This is the ability to stand back and get some distance and leverage on our present desires. Standing back from them is necessary if we are to be able to evaluate our desires and act accordingly. If we cannot do this, then we are bound to be driven unwittingly by our immediate desires, and in ways and directions often to our detriment.

Using the dolphins as his main example, MacIntyre makes this significant observation. Dolphins do develop and change, and orient themselves toward different kinds of goods to be pursued, "goods of sociable hunting and play, for example." On this level according to MacIntyre, if I understand him correctly, these animals do make some inner-directed changes—in goals and methods, but these changes are part of their natural development. "They do not have to go through a stage in which they separate themselves from their desires, as humans do, a separation that involves recognition of goods other than the pleasures of satisfied bodily wants" (ibid., 68). From Steiner's perspective, it should be emphasized, the animals do not have to separate themselves from their desires because their bodily wants are intimately enwoven with the given wisdom of their body, and there is, thus, no need to stand back and evaluate.

Another significant point touched upon by MacIntyre here has to do with the kind of desires and wants that are involved. In his statement just quoted, it is bodily desires that are the focus. Humans in addition, however, have to stand back and evaluate desire on a wholly other level. It is given to the human being, not only to have the ability to choose between bodily wants and satisfactions—which, to be sure, is hard enough—but also to evaluate and act at the level of truth, meaning, purpose, values, and a host of other forms of qualitative reality and distinctions. These are moral and spiritual evaluations that confront the human. The animal does not have to deal with these, for the moral and the spiritual are written into the animal's physical body and soul being. The human, of course, can occupy himself or herself mainly with the satisfaction of immediate desires and, thus, remain at an animal-like level, without the given moral and spiritual connection and reality of the animal (Steiner 1971, 21–22).

Another capacity of the human, related to being able to stand back and evaluate immediate desires, is being able to move from an awareness of the present to a grasp of time past and time future. This ability is not given to the animals, and, curiously, MacIntyre, indirectly, helps make this especially clear. (This, of course, is related to our earlier discussion of the presence of the past and the perception of the past.)

Stressing again that dolphins and humans both have animal identities, MacIntyre goes on to add, however, that humans, unlike dolphins, "have the possibility of understanding their animal identity through time from conception to death..." (MacIntyre, 83). And with this movement through time, humans have the possibility of *imagining alternative futures*. MacIntyre quotes Wittgenstein: "One can imagine an animal, angry, frightened, unhappy, startled. But hopeful? And why not?" And then MacIntyre comments on Wittgenstein's further statement: "And he [Wittgenstein] goes on to point out that a dog may believe that its master is at the door, but not that its master will come the day after tomorrow" (ibid., 74).

In the end, MacIntyre does not explain or discuss how it is that without a self-conscious "I"-being, the transition from prelinguistic to full-fledged language and concept use is accomplished, just as he does not discuss the transition from the ability to evaluate bodily desires to the evaluation of moral and spiritual desires and goals. Something is missing. Desires do not evaluate desires, and alternative futures in themselves have no future. The connecting link—an "I"-being—is missing. It is as though MacIntyre introduces and takes account of major "I" evaluative functions while denying throughout the existence or presence of an "I"-being. A neat slight of hand. The gaps that dog so much of Darwinian theory appear at this level, as well as at other levels, to remain un-bridged.

9.

EVIL

We now come to a realm in which the difference in kind between the human and the animal is seen to be stark and pronounced: The realm of evil. In Steiner's view the animals are not evil; the human being alone is capable of evil, and of the worst kind. Steiner is very clear on this, and before attempting to analyze the issue in the light of Steiner, it is worth quoting him at length:

> In the animal kingdom one can speak of ferocity and cruelty, but one cannot apply the concept of evil to animals. Evil is confined to the human kingdom. But modern natural science tries to derive knowledge of human beings from investigations of animals, and as all differences are glossed over, evil is ignored. One has to enter deeply into human characteristics in order to discover the origin of evil. One must above all recognize that humanity constitutes a kingdom by itself. (Steiner 1987b, 67)

Elsewhere Steiner writes in a similar vein: "Whatever fury may be exhibited by a lion, for example, we shall not say of a lion as we might say of a human being: he can be evil, he can sin, he can commit immoral deeds. We shall never speak of immorality in connection with the actions of an animal" (Steiner 2003, 52–3).

In reading some of the students of animal behavior who want "to gloss over differences," one does, indeed, get the sense that the larger question of evil is also "glossed over." One exception to this, however, are those ethologists who see the aggressiveness and violence sometimes exhibited by chimpanzees, one of the closest of the apes to the human being, as the evolutionary source of violence and aggression in the human being. A popularized version of this is the one-time best seller, *The Naked Ape* by Desmond Morris. It is the case that the early pioneer of ethology, Konrad Lorenz, is a scientist who has analyzed carefully the expression of aggression in animals and humans (Lorenz 1963). The renowned student and friend of chimpanzees, Jane Goodall, has been among the few scientists of animal life to deal directly with the question of evil. She was the first to become aware of and call attention to instances of extreme patterns of aggression, often very brutal, among chimpanzees, and she has not hesitated to take up the question of evil in relation to the animals and humans. Interestingly, her conclusions regarding the animals and evil are, in at least one respect, very close to those of Steiner.

As a young scientist, Jane Goodall was sent to Gombe in the Congo, which was to be her primary research center. Living for many years among the chimpanzees she experienced firsthand the compassion, empathy, caring, and quick reconciliation after fights that largely characterize chimpanzee life together. "During the first ten years of the study [at Gombe], I had believed.... that the Gombe chimpanzees were, for the most part, rather nicer than human beings" (Goodall 1999, 117). Then she made a shocking discovery. She became aware of outbreaks of extreme aggression by chimpanzees against other chimpanzees. The first incident came as a report by a colleague who had witnessed a brutal attack on an infant chimpanzee and its mother, both from a neighboring community. The infant was eaten and the mother died of her wounds from the attack. "Sadly," Goodall writes, "the 'noble ape' was as mythical as the noble savage." After that she witnessed many more such incidents. Some were within the ape community and involved infanticide and cannibalism on newborn infants of females of the attackers' own community. Others were between neighboring communities. One series of hostilities, which she dubbed the Four Year War, was between an original community and a breakaway, neighboring community. The Four Year War eventually ended with the brutal and total extermination of the breakaway community.

Goodall's attempts to publish these accounts of Chimpanzee aggression met initially with much resistance from many in the ethological community who felt that all aggression is learned and is not innate. Others who held that violence and aggression are embedded deep in our genes and are inherited by human beings from our primate ancestors encouraged publication of her observations. As a good Darwinist, Goodall accepts the notion that humans have innate aggressive and violent tendencies "rooted in our ancient past," meaning animal past. But, here, Goodall makes some important distinctions.

Apes and humans she points out have many aggressive behaviors in common that are triggered in the same kind of contexts—"jealousy, competition for food or sex or territory, fear, revenge and so on." Humans and apes, she also observes, share similar postures and gestures associated with aggressive behavior: "swaggering, scowling, hitting, punching, kicking, scratching, pulling out hair, chasing," hurling rocks and sticks. She comments that if the apes had guns and knives they would use them as humans do. But she goes farther to draw much the same conclusion on this particular issue as Rudolf Steiner:

> In some respects, however, human aggressive behavior was, indeed, unique. Thus while it seemed that chimpanzees had *some* awareness of the pain they inflicted on their victims, they were surely not capable of cruelty in the human sense. Only we humans inflict physical or mental pain on living creatures *deliberately* despite—or even *because of*—our knowledge of the suffering involved. Only we, I concluded, are capable of evil.... Thus I could see that human wickedness is immeasurably worse than the worst aggression of the chimpanzee. (Goodall, 134)

Later, however, she goes on to affirm, as Steiner does also, that evil is not the final reality of the human being, that it can be transformed and redeemed: "and just as it appears that our wicked deeds can be far, far, worse than the aggressive behavior of chimpanzees, so too our acts of altruism and self-sacrifice involve greater heroism than those performed by apes" (Goodall, 146).

Here we face a whole cluster of interrelated and difficult questions: What is the origin and nature of human evil? Is it, as many

Darwinists maintain, an inheritance from animal ancestors? If not, how do we account for the similarity between animal and human aggression? How deeply rooted is human evil? Is it the last word about human nature? Or can evil be confronted, transformed, and redeemed? Does evil have an indispensable role to play in human and animal destiny?

In trying to approach these questions from Steiner's perspective, we have to do with at least three concepts anathema to the dominant modern, materialistic mind-set. We have dealt with these earlier, but somewhat differently. We have first, to see the evolving human being as existing in a spiritual state long before appearing as a physical being in the material world. Furthermore, we have to see the animals as having descended from the human rather than the reverse. And, finally, we have to see that higher spiritual beings other than the human and animal have been intimately involved in the evolutionary process.

The arrival of evil—described in various Western forms as "the fall of man"—occurred at the moment higher spiritual beings had endowed the developing human being with an independent "I"-being. At just this point, other spiritual beings, with different goals and attributes than those of the guiding beings, intruded into the human astral body. The result was to give the human astral body a certain independence from the guiding beings, while stirring up and unleashing powerful astral forces in the human soul, forces much too strong at first for the young human "I" to control. As the evolving, successive beings of the animals—especially from the reptiles through the mammals—took up for themselves premature forms of the human body, they also absorbed into their own being aspects of this unleashed astrality, in degrees corresponding to their particular animal forms (Steiner, 1987). The animals, thus, relieved the developing human of an excessive astrality that threatened to overwhelm the developing human "I"-being. "This astrality run wild," the science writer, John Davy, has commented, "is reflected right down into the Mesozoic reptiles, with their often terrifying and stormy aspects" (Davy, 103). While some of this astrality was, indeed, ferocious and violent, it was contained in ways fitted to the corresponding animal bodies, and became characteristics of the various animal group souls and species. In the animals, even the ferocious emotions have their rightful place, and so, for example, frightening as it can be, we stand in awe and wonder at the roar of the lion.

The effect of this stirred up, and still potentially out-of-control, astrality in the human was to give rise to desires that drew the young human "I" itself into the orbit of their influence. The human soul and "I" were pulled more and more into the physical body and material world as an alluring means of satisfying those desires. The strong temptation arose to identify with the physical body itself and to be governed by its desires. Eventually, however, it was possible for the human to resist this downward pull to an important degree and to achieve a kind of inner balance so that only the possibility of the worst passions remains within the human being (Steiner 1987, 95).

But the possibility does remain, and surfaces in different ways at various periods of time. Rudolf Steiner has said concerning the human being in what he designates as the *fifth post-Atlantean epoch,* his term for our current modern age beginning about 1400 CE:

> Since the beginning of the fifth post-Atlantean epoch, evil tendencies are subconsciously present in *all* men. It is precisely this influx of evil tendencies into men that marks his entrance into the fifth post-Atlantean epoch [the age of modern consciousness]. Expressed somewhat radically one could say with every justification: he who crosses the threshold of the spiritual world discovers that there is not a crime in the calendar to which every man, in so far as he belongs to the fifth post-Atlantean epoch, is not subconsciously prone. Whether in a particular case this tendency leads to an evil action depends upon wholly different circumstances and not upon the tendency itself. (Steiner 1976, 118)

(The twentieth-century theologian, Reinhold Niebuhr, is said to have once remarked to the effect that the Christian doctrine of Original Sin is the only one supported by abundant empirical evidence.)

Too often in our time, the worst comes to the fore. To deny the human capacity for the worst kinds of evil, in face of the horrors of the twentieth- and twenty-first centuries, is to be oblivious of events or in outright denial. Much the same can be said of the treatment of animals by humans, beginning especially with the advent of the modern age. All nature, it should be reemphasized, is innocent and without guilt. Attempting to see the human beings in all respects as simply a product of this innocent nature can only make it exceedingly difficult to recognize and deal with the capacities for evil in the human being.

While the extremes of passion, which would threaten to overwhelm the human, have been taken up by the animals, Steiner cautions that we should not, however, suppose that all the animal forms around us, which are representative of specific emotional patterns in the animal body and soul, "are derived from wicked human passions" (Steiner 1987, 95). Indeed, we know from common experience that many animals close to us are among the most gentle of creatures, and it is, perhaps because of this—they can't fight back—that we mistreat them the worst (think: cows, pigs, sheep, chickens and turkeys, and rodents). Nor, as we have seen in much detail, does the entire emotional life of, say, the most aggressive of carnivores consist entirely of violent and ferocious passions.

The human I, however, always confronts the possibility of choice—the choice among various desires, the choice of whether to stand back, evaluate them, and transform them, or to give in to them entirely, wherever they may lead. If the "I" identifies with the soul's desires without standing back and evaluating, the result can be an unbridled egoism running rampant over everything and everyone. It is the human "I" having to choose between good and bad—and, even more excruciatingly, between good and good—that alone makes possible human good and evil alike. The animal *is* good. The passions, which in the human can lead directly to evil, are in the animal integrated coherently with the wisdom of the animal body and group soul.

Throughout, however, the animal is not without suffering. The human suffers and is guilty; the animal suffers but is not guilty. When we grasp this, that the animals suffer but are not guilty, we become aware, says Steiner, of "a great world tragedy":

> The world tragedy consists of the fact that we have bound the animal world to us. The animals must suffer with us in spite of their not becoming guilty. Thus we come to the tragic thought that animals are there because of human beings; they must suffer with us, even though they cannot commit error. Enter into this concept with your feeling. Feel this reality, that the animal world suffers evil, even though it cannot do evil. (Steiner 2010, 127)

The suffering of our astral body, which arises from our own guilt, has been entwined with the astral body of the animal, which must now suffer, because of us, without guilt. When we grasp this tragedy, we realize that our debt to the animals is great. They have taken on and ennobled bodily forms of no use to the developing human, thus enabling the human archetype to develop further; they have absorbed excess passions that would overwhelm the human I; and they suffer innocently through the evil we have brought into the world. Our great responsibility, therefore, is to redeem the animals, but this we will be capable of only in the far, far distant future when world conditions are different. In the meantime, however, our responsibility to the animals is to provide them with every love and kindness of which we are capable in order to relieve their present suffering.

The mystery of evil in the human being is enwoven with the mystery of human freedom. It was the intrusion of, shall we call them, contrary beings to give the human "I" a certain independence from the spiritual world itself that introduced the possibility of genuine human freedom. Without the possibility of breaking free, at least to a certain extent, from the strictures of the emotions, on the one side, and from a potentially suffocating embrace by the guiding spiritual beings, on the other side, human freedom would never be possible. Having the capacity of free choice, however, does not in itself make us free. It is only a necessary first condition. The human being could not be created free from scratch. That would be almost a contradiction in terms. Freedom must be experienced by the "I" as its own; that is, freedom must be won by the Self. So, as Steiner has often said in various ways, the human being is *on the way* to freedom—that is, the potential for freedom increases with every incremental achievement of true freedom. And the achievement of freedom means transforming the evil that otherwise constrains and corrupts the self. So the evil that makes possible the potential for freedom, must also be confronted and transformed by that freedom.

All depends upon the Self. The Self now has possibilities for both enormous good and enormous evil. The Self can turn in upon itself, becoming an enemy of everything other than itself—becoming rapacious and predatory—or fall back into itself in despair at its own loneliness. Or, the Self can turn outward to the world and to others, fulfilling its true potential in opening to and joining with the other in freedom and love. So evil is not destined necessarily to be the last word about the human being. The potential of the "I" for freedom and love has critical consequences for understanding our relation to the animals. It means that the human being is capable of self-transformation and taking action in the world accordingly in a way that the single animal is not.

This capacity for self-transformation means that the human carries an immense responsibility toward other humans, and toward the animals and toward the Earth itself. I understand that part of the driving concern of those who want to erase all significant differences between the human and the animal is the conviction that doing so might increase our sensitivity to them as fellow creatures and sufferers. And to an important extent there is an undeniable truth and hope in this. The knowledge gained especially by animal researchers in our time of the rich feeling, emotional, and moral lives of animals raises the most serious questions for those who think we can continue to use the animals for human purposes in any way we want without taking into account what our actions mean for the experience of the animals and for *their purposes*. But I fear that this leveling drive, if taken to its extreme, can have the dire consequence of sapping the sense of urgency demanded, especially in our time, by our unique, human responsibility, which, in turn, exists only because of our unique capabilities.

We are more responsible to the animals than they can be responsible for themselves. The whales will not, and cannot, save the whales. The elephants cannot save the elephants. The Earth cannot save the Earth. The future of the Earth, along with all its creatures, has been put in jeopardy by the irresponsibility and hard-heartedness of the human being. This same human being alone has the capability to reclaim its responsibility, and to exercise it in love for the future of all. It is critical at this time that, while we acknowledge and are sensitized by the similarities and the kinship between humans and animals, we not flag in recognizing and exercising our unique responsibility for the animals.

PART III

ANIMAL RIGHTS

INTRODUCTION

Throughout his work Rudolf Steiner stresses that basic to all progress in spiritual/moral knowledge is an underlying attitude of compassion and sympathy for all creatures of the Earth and for nature itself. In one of his basic books, for example, he sets forth a path of discipline and practice for developing "knowledge of higher worlds," that is, knowledge of non-sensory realities, such as truth, beauty, goodness, being and beings, meaning, value, purpose, and many others. As the underlying attitude for the entire path of development he writes early in the book:

> During the elementary exercises for Enlightenment the pupil must take care to ensure that his compassion for the human and animal world and his response to the beauty of nature are constantly increasing. (Steiner 1986, 59–60)

In many other places, he speaks similarly of the importance of "reverence for life." The German word, often translated as reverence, is *Ehrfurcht*, which also carries suggestions of respect and even of awe.

This was an attitude that pervaded the consciousness and life patterns of many ancient peoples whose wisdom traditions valued the kinship of human and animal. Steiner has commented that in those parts of the Earth where people have preserved the ancient, sacred wisdom "there is a deeply sympathetic and loving treatment of animals." The compassion and respect toward animals, once central to these ancient traditions, has become seriously eroded by their contact with materialistic Western thought and practice. Early in the twentieth century, Rudolf Steiner wrote, "conceptions of the world that still contain elements of the primordial spiritual truths, the ancient wisdom of humanity, preserved a kind of knowledge of what exists spiritually in the animal kingdom; and in spite of all misunderstanding, in spite of all that has crept into their views of the world and destroyed their purity, they have not been able to forget that spiritual activities and spiritual laws are active in the life and development of the animal kingdom" (Steiner 2000, 29). Since Steiner wrote these words more than a century ago, the compassion toward animals so strong in these ancient traditions has been undercut even further by modern science and technology, global economic forces, and spreading cultural and philosophical materialism, among other influences.

One consequence has been a palpable weakening and laxity within the traditions of their original spiritual and moral insights and commitments. For example, the American Buddhist, Norm Phelps, has recently written a spirited critique of American Buddhists for their watering down of the First Precept of the Buddha, "Don't Kill," and for their alacrity in developing rationalizations "to justify their addiction to meat, eggs, and dairy." Phelps is particularly concerned because he sees Western Buddhism as "the next great Buddhist manifestation" and already in danger of fatally compromising its essential nature. "Buddhism cannot be true to itself," he writes, "until Buddhists resolve their ambivalence toward nonhuman animals and extend the full protection of their compassion to the most harmless and helpless of those who live at our mercy in the visible realm" (Phelps 2004, xiv). Still, that Western Buddhism can produce such forceful self-criticism as that of Phelps is some indication that the original fires of compassion continue to smolder, and even on occasion to flare up.

The three Abrahamic religious traditions—Judaism, Christianity, and Islam—have always affirmed the goodness of God's creation and its inherent value. As far as the animals specifically are concerned, however, two opposing views have long vied with each other in each of these traditions. One way of describing these contrasting views is to see them as deriving from different interpretations of the meaning of the passage in the first chapter of the Book of Genesis in which God gives to humankind *dominion* over every being: "Be fruitful and multiply, and fill the Earth and subdue it; and have dominion over the fish of the sea and over the birds of the air and over every living thing that moves upon the Earth" (Gen. 1:28). "Dominion" has been interpreted in two contrasting ways. On the one hand, dominion has been taken to mean mastery and rulership, and this has tended to be the dominant interpretation. On the other hand, it has also been taken by some to mean guardianship and protector-ship, stewardship. The first interpretation has undergirded the notion that the animals were created by God explicitly for human use, and this could quickly be understood as giving humans free rein to exploit and treat animals as they please. Against this, the other interpretation has affirmed human responsibility and care for the animals.

In the Hebrew scriptures we find both interpretations. The Jewish people have many traditions in which care of the animals is commanded by God. In the Ten Commandments, and elsewhere, it is instructed that animals be allowed to rest on the Sabbath. Elsewhere it is commanded that, if the donkey of one's enemy even has collapsed under its burden, the animal is not to be kept lying but freed from its load. Every seventh year fields are to be kept fallow, and portions of the seeds and fruit of the vineyards be kept as food for the poor and wild animals. And there are many other such commandments in the scriptures (Norm Phelps provides a convenient summary of Biblical attitudes toward animals—Phelps 2002, 180–192).

At the same time, there are a number of incidents that enjoin the Israelites to kill their enemies ruthlessly along with their animals, and in at least one passage, right down to "infants, ox and sheep, camel and donkey" (I Sam. 15:3). And in other incidents God commands the total extermination of entire peoples along with their animals (See Phelps 2002). This represents an expanded interpretation of "dominion" as supremacy and mastery with a vengeance. But the interpretation of dominion as guardian and stewardship, nevertheless, remains strong throughout the Jewish traditions. This is expressed, for example, in the accounts of the covenants God made with the Jewish people, which in some passages also included the animals. After the flood, for instance: "Then God spoke to Noah and to his sons with him, saying, 'Now behold, I Myself also establish My covenant with you, and with your descendants after you; and with every living creature that is with you, the birds, the cattle, and every beast of the Earth with you" (Gen. 9:8–17). And, elsewhere, when the city of Ninevah repents and God chooses not to punish it, Jonah complains to God that God should destroy it anyway in punishment for its sins, God replies, "And should I not pity Ninevah that great city, in which there are more than a hundred and twenty thousand persons who do not know their right hand from their left, and also much cattle?" That "also much cattle" stands out conspicuously. One can find other examples in the Jewish tradition of God's ongoing concern and love for the animals. Also in Islam, there are traditions in which Mohammed promises that, "Kindness to any living creature will be rewarded."

With Christianity, however, the picture has been quite other. The two contrasting interpretations of dominion have both been present, but the dominant tendency has been toward dominion as human superiority over animals and the denial that animals have any intrinsic value in their own right. This has been the dominant view of both Roman Catholic and Protestant theology. It is easy to find statements by the great Catholic, Aristotelian theologian, St. Thomas Aquinas, as well as by the leading Protestant reformers, John Calvin and Martin Luther, holding that animals are given by God primarily for human use. For Aquinas, humans alone possess reason, unlike the animals, and humans, therefore, are entitled to exercise mastery over them "in making use of them without hindrance" (Linzey and Regan 1988, 17–20). In similar fashion John Calvin commented on the passage from Genesis, "Let them have dominion": "Here he [God] commemorates that part of dignity with which he decreed to honor man, namely that he should have authority over all living creatures...that he expressly subjects the animals to him...and hence we may infer that what was the end for which all things were created; namely, that none of the conveniences and necessaries of life might be wanting to men" (ibid., 21–22). And Luther: "The beasts of the field and the birds of the heavens were created for mankind; these are the wealth and possessions of men."

Scholars have pointed out that a close reading of these theologians, Catholic and Protestant, shows that they were much more nuanced in their views of the human–animal relationship than such isolated quotes suggest (see, for instance, the essays on Aquinas and Luther in, Deane-Drummond and Clough). Nevertheless, the main effect of the theologians on Western cultural attitudes and actions toward the animals has been more one-sided than their full theologies may actually have been. Their influence has tended overwhelmingly to reinforce dominion as mastery over the animals and the right to use them at will for human purposes.

As we have seen, adding further to the plight of animals in the modern world has been the rise of the mechanical worldview in which animals are seen as machines, without feeling and with no value in their own right. Especially significant was the involvement of major voices in Western Christian theology in encouraging the rise of the mechanical philosophy. This is often not recognized or acknowledged even by many historians of science. For starters, the views on "dominion" held by most Christians offered little, if anything, in the way of resistance to a mechanistic view of animals. Beyond this, however, the mechanistic model of the natural world was actually promoted by many of its most influential, early proponents precisely because they thought, among other things, that it strengthened the case for the church and Christian theology. This was true of most of the early, major supporters of the mechanical philosophy, including the scientists and philosophers, such as Newton, Boyle, Descartes, Locke, Bishop Mersennes, and others.

Descartes, for example, so important in the formulation of the mechanistic model, argued, like the others, that if the world is a machine then there must be a creator deity to bring it into being and to keep it going. The alternative view, which the mechanists were mainly opposing, was that associated with alchemy and the Hermetic tradition. The alchemists held that there is a principle of life and motion—in short, of soul—inherent in all natural beings. The mechanists opposed the alchemists for two main reasons. For one, alchemy threatened at first to make official religious authority unnecessary because the presence of divine life in all things would in principle be accessible to anyone without the mediation of the church or other religious authorities. For this reason the mechanical philosophy received the backing of important church figures, such as Bishop Mersennes. It is true that Newton spent much of his life pursuing alchemical experiments, but eventually he joined the British Royal Society, which had as one of its main aims the promotion of mechanistic science. A second reason the mechanists opposed the Hermeticists and alchemists was that the Hermetic–alchemist emphasis on the presence of the soul in all creaturely beings threatened to place religious and ethical limits on unrestrained scientific curiosity, and especially on commercial exploitation of the earth's riches, such as, in mining (Griffin 1988, 10–13, 102–104).

The almost immediate rise of vivisection in the scientific community and the rapid growth of mining and logging in the commercial realm (in which the scientist and government official, Robert Boyle, was deeply involved), demonstrate how quickly the mechanical view eliminated any semblance of ethical constraints on either science or commerce, both of which were intricately entwined. Eventually, of course, many scientists and other thinkers came to deem the view of the world as a machine as sufficient unto itself, without the need for an attending creator God. The coming together of Western theology and the mechanical philosophy is one of the important turns in Western history.

In a brief, and very astute observation, describing the joining of Christian theology and the mechanical philosophy, Rudolf Steiner wrote:

> It is remarkable that the idea of the animal as a nonsentient being with no soul life, the idea of the animal as a kind of automaton, should have emerged in the course of the Middle Ages right until our day in those countries where the Christian worldview was spreading.... this idea expressed by a great body of Western philosophy, that animals are automatons and possess no actual soul, has trickled down into those parts of the population where there is no compassion for the animal

and where there is often no limit, either, to the cruelty meted out to the animals. (Steiner 1995, 27)

Another obstacle to religious concern for the animals has been the tendency in Christian theology to emphasize mainly what Christ has done for humans in his saving work, to the large neglect of the animals, and the wider creation. The theologian John Cobb has commented that "When Christology is understood in this way, the question of the relation of Christ to animals other than human beings can hardly arise." Cobb also points out that the New Testament view in actuality goes well beyond a narrow interpretation of Christology as solely human-oriented. Cobb refers, for instance, to Jesus' affirmation that God cares about the flowers of the field and the sparrow. "His point, it is true," observes Cobb, "is that God cares even more for us human beings. But the way he formulates his message would be meaningless if God did not also care for the plants and animals for their own sake." Key to the importance of the Earth and the animals along with the human in the New Testament message is the Prologue to the Gospel of John, which affirms at the outset that the Word that became flesh in Jesus is the power in all God's creative activity. "All things were made through him," which includes all creaturely life. And the heart of Jesus' message is the proclamation of the Kingdom of God, which is the announcement of a future, whole new world order, in which it would be incomprehensible if cruelty to animals continued to be part of it. St. Paul also envisages a transformation of the Earth, in which the whole creation, which "now groans in travail," will be set free from its bondage to decay and suffering. The whole creation can include only earth, plants, animals, and human beings (Cobb 1998, 173–180).

Nevertheless, one still has to dig for these deeper implications of Christology, and the whole history of Christianity has tended to be decidedly human-focused, with little attention to the animals, and with explicit teachings directly detrimental to the animals. In this regard, Cobb observes, "Those Christians who insist on the importance of other animals and connect their interest with their understanding of Christ have usually been viewed as eccentric or worse. St. Francis, John Woolman, and Albert Schweitzer have been loved, but they have not been followed. Their ideas have been treated with charitable condescension, and are rarely studied in theological schools" (ibid.). In very recent years this has begun to change somewhat as a few theological schools here and there have started to include some courses on animals and ecology in their curricula (Deane-Drummond and Clough; Linzey 1994; Linzey and Yamamoto 1998).

It should not be overlooked, however, that, as Cobb notes, a kind of undercurrent of concern for the animal has always run throughout the Christian tradition. Early Church fathers maintained a sense of the essential kinship of humans and animals. "Surely we ought to show kindness and gentleness to animals for various reasons," wrote St. Chrysostom, to take one example, "and chiefly because they are of the same origin as ourselves" (Linzey 1994, 11). The iconic figure in Christianity exemplifying an active Christian affirmation of our kinship with the animals is, of course, St. Francis of Assissi. St. Bonaventura wrote of St. Francis, "When he considered the primordial source of all things, he was filled with ever more abundant piety calling all creatures no matter how small by the name of brothers and sisters because he knew that they had the same source as himself" (Linzey and Regan, 12).

The great nineteenth-century Catholic convert and theologian, John Henry Newman, in an 1842 Good Friday sermon on "the suffering of the Lamb of God," compared the suffering of "the inoffensive and unprotected animal" as an image of the suffering of Christ. In his sermon Newman said:

> I mean how very horrible it is to read the accounts that sometimes meet us of cruelty inflicted upon brute animals. For what was this but the very cruelty inflicted upon our Lord...What should move our hearts and sicken us is that the animals are mostly innocent, that they have done no harm. Next that they have no power whatever of resisting; it is the cowardice and tyranny of which they are the victims that makes their suffering so especially touching...there is something so very dreadful, so satanic in tormenting those who have never harmed us and

who cannot defend themselves, who are utterly in our power, who have weapons neither of offense nor defense, that none but very hardened persons can endure the thought of it....

He concluded, "Think then, my brethren, of your feelings at cruelty practiced on brute animals, and you will gain one sort of feeling that the history of Christ's cross and passion ought to excite in you" (quoted in Linzey 2000, 65). While small in numbers and largely unheeded, a few religious leaders like Newman continued to keep alive, out of their own Christian convictions, a lively concern for animals and the prevention of cruelty toward them.

In the eighteenth century, Enlightenment views of human rights, nature, education, and abolition also began to inspire reform efforts on behalf of animals. Art historian and philosopher, Stephen Eisenman has also explored the early role of artists, beginning especially also in the eighteenth century, in taking a leading part in exposing the horrors of cruelty to animals (Eisenman). In fact, during these years, and extending well into the twentieth century, Enlightenment and liberal Christian, humanitarian reform often merged as, together, the main impetus for the defense of animals. In 1824, for example, a small group of clergymen, led by the Reverend Arthur Broome, met in a London coffee house to found the first Society for the Prevention of Cruelty to Animals (SPCA—later changed to RSPCA, the Royal Society). These clergymen were also joined by a small group of evangelical solicitors and members of Parliament, including William Wilberforce, a convert to evangelical Christianity and a leading opponent of the slave trade.

In England in 1876, the first anti-vivisection society in the world, the Victoria Street Society, was founded by important and religiously inspired persons in the church and society. Cardinal Manning, Lord Shaftsbury, as well as a number of women reformers and other Christian social leaders championed the anti-vivisectionist cause. A few years later, following the English example, a group of similar, religiously inspired and reform-minded men and women founded the first American anti-vivisection society. During the late nineteenth century a number of interconnected reform movements, including care for the poor, women's rights, and, to a lesser extent, animal welfare, together constituted what came to be known as "The Social Gospel" of the nineteenth-century progressive reform movement.

During the twentieth century, efforts and organizations for animal welfare began to proliferate in increasing numbers. The emergence and growth of these groups, such as, the Humane Society, the World Wildlife Fund, the International Fund for Animal Welfare, and many, many others, including myriads of small and dedicated animal shelters and sanctuaries, have resulted, especially since World War II, in something of a sea-change in organized efforts to come to the aid of the animals. Most of these movements, it seems safe to say, have shed explicit religious connections and motives, and understand themselves mainly in secular terms; but their driving compassion for the animals links them, nevertheless, with the older spiritual traditions that preceded them, and still exist to an extent.

Much of the concern and movement on behalf of animals today turns on the concept of "animal rights." This concept has the advantage of being able to enlist all persons, for whom the religious origins and inspiration for care of the animals has lost meaning, but who, for whatever reason, are moved to action by the animals' suffering. Marshaled against the movement for animal rights are all the powers of corporate profit, industrial agriculture, numerous university and other animal research centers, large sectors of the medical and pharmaceutical industries, influential sectors of the military, and hunting, fishing, and fur interests. Undergirding all this resistance is the massive force of popular indifference and lack of interest.

2.

DO ANIMALS HAVE RIGHTS?

"The range of our use of animals is enormous: we hunt, ride, shoot, fish, wear, eat, exhibit, factory farm, and experiment on millions, if not billions, every year. None of us are untouched by our use of animals and all of us, directly or indirectly, benefit from it." —ANDREW LINZEY, Oxford University

"We kill nonhuman animals, and sometimes inflict pain on them, because we want to eat them, because we can make useful products out of them, because we can learn from experimenting on them, and because they interfere with agriculture or gardening or in other ways are pests. We also kill them, and sometimes inflict pain on them, for sport in hunting, fishing, cockfighting, dog fighting, and bull fighting. We may even kill them because having done some sort of useful work for us, they have outlived their usefulness and are now costing us money." —CHRISTINE M. KORSGAARD, Yale University

Where in all this are the animals' rights, if they have any? One anthroposophist, noted for his astute analyses of politics and culture has recently cast his aspersions on the whole idea of animal rights. He regards talk of animal rights as symptomatic of a larger moral relativism and philosophical materialism that sees no difference between humans and animals and that seeks at bottom to reduce human morality to animal behavior. The situation has come, he writes disapprovingly, "to a point where today our scientists and media pundits can soberly discuss or eagerly enthuse about the prospects for civil rights for animals" (Boardman, 48). Unfortunately, this puts him as a serious student of Rudolf Steiner in a somewhat awkward position, since Steiner himself speaks affirmatively of animal rights. Steiner writes:

We see strongly marked a certain life of rights, a moral life among animals. But we *understand* [my italics] the life of rights, the life of the state, and the whole course of world history, only when we see in man the emancipation of the spirit from the bodily nature by the intervention of the ego ["I"] between spirit and bodily nature, through which the ego enters into immediate intercourse with the spirit. (Steiner 1910a)

The animals have rights, Steiner affirms, because they are moral beings. It is the human alone, however, who brings concepts to bear in understanding, not only the animal's life of rights, but also the nature of rights in the larger context of human history and culture, from whence the whole concept of rights originates. The individual animal is too closely bound to the wisdom incorporated in its bodily nature by the group soul and group "I" to have the distance necessary to access the spirit—the realm of concepts—consciously. To the extent that the human can free its "I" from determination by the body, including the astral body— not easy as a matter of course—the human can enter the realm of spirit consciously, that is, into the realm of creative thinking and formative concepts that make possible true understanding. This does not, however, for Steiner, obviate the animal's moral nature nor the animal's rights based on that moral nature.

1. Two Approaches:
Frans de Waal and Rudolf Steiner

It might be useful to compare Steiner's statement on animal rights with a similar statement by the primatologist, Frans de Waal, especially since I draw extensively on de Waal's animal research. In one of his major books, *Good Nature: The Origins of Right and Wrong in Human and other Animals*, de Waal writes:

Even if animals other than ourselves act in ways tantamount to moral behavior, their behavior does not necessarily rest on deliberations of the kind we engage in. It is hard to believe that animals weigh their own interests against the rights of others, that they develop a vision of the greater good of society, or that they feel lifelong guilt about something they should not have done.... Animals are no moral philosophers. But then how many *people* are? (1996, 209)

The similarity here with Steiner is clear. Of course, they differ on many things, most importantly in that for de Waal human morality is an evolutionary product handed down (or is it "up") in some way through inheritance after having first developed in previous animal species. On one level, Steiner could agree with de Waal's statement that "many of the sentiments and cognitive abilities underlying human morality antedate the appearance of our species on this planet" (de Waal 1996, 210). But for Steiner this would not be because of a continuous evolutionary development from earlier animals to humans but because humans and animals both share in various, common aspects of the astral, the feeling and consciousness reality of the wider cosmos. The "sentiments and cognitive" abilities common to humans and animals do make their appearance on Earth in animals first because the animals appear first on Earth as premature forms of the human archetype, which remains in a spiritual state until entering last into the sense world of Earth.

Interestingly, de Waal does express doubts about animal rights as such. He resists expansive animal rights talk because he fears it may result in the ascription of rights to animals of low consciousness, such as cockroaches, which would have very unfortunate consequences. He does favor, however, giving the great apes special consideration because of their high level of social awareness and emotional–cognitive complexity. He urges that we should either phase out experimentation on the apes or take steps "to enrich their lives in captivity and reduce their suffering" (de Waal 1996, 216). In this, de Waal begins to reveal some of the complexity involved in consideration of animal rights. We will return to both Steiner and de Waal in due course.

First, however, I propose we look at some of the major issues involved in conceptions of animal welfare and animal rights. Champions of *animal welfare* generally and *animal rights* more specifically may actually differ from one another in certain respects. Those who emphasize animal welfare stress preventing cruelty to animals and treating them humanely, although a variety of uses of animals might still be permitted. Animal rights advocates tend to be against any and all human use of animals. In the efforts to reduce animal cruelty and suffering, animal welfare and animal rights supporters often cooperate. As the philosopher Cass Sunstein has pointed out, if we define animal rights to mean "protection against suffering," then animal welfare advocates also believe in animal rights. But, if suffering is the focus, then animal welfare advocates might accept some scientific experimentation and meat eating, if the suffering is held to the minimum. This would not be the case, as a rule, for animal rights advocates (Sunstein and Nussbaum, 5).

Before turning to Steiner's full view of the moral life and rights of animals, and where he might or might not fit into the wider contemporary discussion, it might be helpful to look at some of the main issues dealt with by today's leading animal advocates.

2. BACKGROUND: IMMANUEL KANT AND JEREMY BENTHAM

Two major figures writing at the end of the eighteenth century, whose influence in the development of the idea of rights is still felt strongly today, were the German Enlightenment philosopher, Immanuel Kant, and the English philosopher, Jeremy Bentham. Although Kant was concerned almost entirely with human rights, his thinking and its formulation, were instrumental in shaping the concept and language of rights, and remains so today. Kant's ethics turned on his view that every human being is "an end-in-himself," who is never to be used as a mere means to another person's end. Did this apply to animals? No, said Kant, animals lack reason and are guided purely by instinct and necessity, and, so, also lack the autonomy—the capacity for free choice—essential to moral beings. Only moral beings command our respect; animals, therefore, cannot. Kant, however, did seem to have a soft spot for animals. He found it disgusting that a man would shoot his dog because the dog was no longer useful to him. And he wrote, "The more we come in contact with animals and observe their behavior, the more we love them, for we see how great is their care for their young. It is then difficult for us to be cruel in thought even to a wolf" (Quoted by Kazez, 31). Still, for Kant, only human beings are ends in themselves and it is to them alone that we owe moral respect and moral duties. He did make a concession to his tender feeling for animals since he recognized that they are sentient beings and should not be cruelly treated. Still, however, he held to his position of putting humans first by maintaining only that the main cost of being cruel to animals is that as a result we will more likely also be cruel to human beings. (Kant does seem to have been on to something important here since there is much solid evidence that people who treat animals badly are more liable to treat people badly (Linzey 2013; Linzey forthcoming).

A further aspect of Kant's ethic that is important with regard to animals is that in confining moral respect to humans only he was also seeking to break any link between moral judgments and unfettered, scientific investigation of nature. His larger philosophy really aimed to provide a conceptual foundation for the Newtonian and mechanical worldview. Moral judgments out of their proper sphere were liable to inhibit unhampered scientific investigation of the natural world. Since animals are part of that world, one consequence of Kant's breaking the link between ethics and science was that it left the animal ever more vulnerable to being treated in all respects as means to human ends. (Since then, we have also begun to learn that failing to bring value judgments to bear on scientific pursuits and discoveries has also failed to protect humans from being instrumentalized and treated as mere means for other's ends, especially for those others who have become powerful in part through science (Rollin 1989; Lederer; Goliszek).

In England the development, beginning also in the eighteenth century, of the school of philosophy known as "Utilitarianism" took a very different direction from that of Kant. The leading utilitarian at the time was the philosopher Jeremy Bentham, who made the phrase, "the greatest happiness of the greatest number" the watchword of the utilitarian school. It is our moral duty as human beings to do all we can to maximize happiness and to diminish suffering in the world. This holds also in our treatment of animals. We have moral duties to animals because like us they are sentient creatures, like us they can feel pleasure and pain. Bentham famously put it this way regarding animals: "The question is not, Can they reason? nor Can they talk? but Can they suffer?" And his answer was, of course, yes, and he denounced the mistreatment of animals and saw it as the result of human prejudice and sense of superiority.

But as Gary Steiner has pointed out, and this seems to be seldom noted, Bentham did allow for humans to kill and eat animals on the grounds that death is not as great an evil for animals as it is for humans. Animals lack a sense of time, he thought, and cannot, therefore, experience anxiety about their future death, and, suffer less when we kill them than when they die a "natural death" (G. Steiner, 97–98).

3.

MODERN APPROACHES TO ANIMAL RIGHTS AND ANIMAL WELFARE

1. UTILITARIANISM: PETER SINGER

In the contemporary scene, probably the main representative of the utilitarian stream of philosophy in relation to animals is the professor of philosophy, Peter Singer, formerly of Australia and now at Princeton University. Since the publication in 1975 of the first edition of his book, *Animal Liberation*, Singer has come to be regarded by many as the preeminent champion of animal welfare and animal rights. Singer is a major spokesperson for the utilitarian school of ethics, and he follows, in more ways than one, in the footsteps of Jeremy Bentham. As a utilitarian, Singer's primary concern is with pain and suffering, pleasure and happiness.

Basic to Singer's approach is the concept, first popularized by him, of "Speciesism." For him, Speciesism describes the tendency in Western culture (for Singer, especially Western, Christian culture) to assume the superiority of the human species over all other species, and, therefore, to justify the use of animals in nearly every way possible to satisfy human desires. As a prejudice or attitude in favor of the interests of one's own group over and against those of other groups, speciesism for Singer is in the same class as racism and sexism. In many respects the concept of speciesism is a modern refurbishing of the interpretation of human dominion as mastery and superiority over the natural and animal worlds. Singer presents utilitarianism as the best way to undermine speciesism and the mistreatment of animals that it entails.

Utilitarianism requires, according to Singer, that we take into account, as he puts it, the interests of all beings, and that we do everything to maximize the interests of all beings we are involved with. What does this mean? He explains, especially in a chapter in *Animal Liberation*, with the provocative title, "All Animals Are Equal." Clearly, all humans are not equal in every respect, nor are all animals. But we and the animals are all equal in possessing one common property; namely, sentience and consciousness, the capacity to experience suffering and pleasure. All sentient creatures have the capacity to feel pain and, therefore, have an interest in avoiding pain. Accordingly, this common capacity for pain and suffering requires in Singer's utilitarianism that the interests—the desire to avoid pain and suffering—of all beings, human and animal alike, be given "equal consideration." Only in this way can we overcome Speciesism and its unjustified—immoral—infliction of pain and suffering on sentient beings. In two central chapters of *Animal Liberation* Singer presents vivid and harrowing accounts of the pain and suffering we mete out to animals in factory farming and animal experimentation in order to satisfy our Speciesist desires and claims to entitlement.

Singer's *Animal Liberation* has been responsible, as perhaps no other writing, for exposing and awakening people to the intense suffering undergone by animals at our hands in modern agriculture and in much of modern science. It may even be that *Animal Liberation* has been the one most important, recent inspiration for animal welfare and rights organizations to actively take on the powerful agricultural and scientific/medical interests responsible for the painful deaths of millions of animals every day and year. Exposing the mistreatment of animals, however, remains extremely difficult and must be undertaken often at great risk by members of the animal organizations, since they usually have to go incognito and undercover to reveal what actually takes place in factory farms, slaughterhouses, and animal laboratories, places usually forbidden to public inspection.

Singer's utilitarian calculus of weighing and balancing pain and pleasure has not been without its critics. A number of animal rights proponents have put forward alternatives as a more satisfactory basis for grounding and promoting animal rights. One main point of controversy has to do with the fact that, despite a major chapter in *Animal Liberation* entitled "All Animals Are Equal," it turns out on closer scrutiny that actually, for Singer, all animals are not equal. Singer invokes the classical utilitarian view, following Bentham closely, that animals with a degree of self-awareness count more in the utilitarian calculus than animals without self-awareness. For Singer, self-awareness means having a consciousness of time, and, therefore, an interest in life going into the future. Humans have this self-awareness; animals as a rule do not. Humans are individual moral agents because they have self-consciousness and the ability to anticipate the future. To the extent that animals lack this self-awareness, when they die they no longer have interests that need to be considered. At death the individual animals are simply replaceable. When an animal is killed, argues Singer, "it is not easy to explain why the loss of the animal killed is not, from an impartial point of view, made good by the creation of a new animal who will lead an equally pleasant life" (Singer 2009, 229). If some animals can be shown to be more self-aware than others, say, one of the great apes compared to a mouse, the mouse is not equal in value, or equally deserving of protection. The ape would possess interests deserving protection, while the mouse would not. As a utilitarian, Singer is not, strictly speaking, primarily an animal rights champion, or rather, more accurately, perhaps, he is a proponent of rights with some leeway, which sterner rights people would not permit. For example, he would allow some animal experimentation, if it can be shown that, in accordance with the utilitarian cost–benefit analysis, the benefits—the pleasure—outweigh the costs—the cruelty involved.

A second point of controversy in Singer's utilitarianism is his applying the criterion of self-awareness over time to differences in value among human beings. This leads him to maintain that only infants who are at least one month old should be included in the moral community. A baby less than a month old is inferior in self-awareness to many animals and it is not, therefore, wrong to kill such a baby if it is born with severe disabilities. "A week-old baby is not a rational and self-conscious being, and there are many nonhuman animals whose rationality, self-consciousness, aware-ness, capacity to feel, and so on, exceed that of a human baby a week or a month old...and the life of a newborn baby is of less value to it than the life of a pig, a dog, or a chimpanzee is to the nonhuman animal" (Singer 2000, 160–66). This self-awareness criterion—the demand that a being possess a self-aware existence and be able to look forward into the future to a meaningful life—supports, in Singer's view, infanticide (to be sure, within the one-month time limit).

A third point of controversy is that utilitarianism can mean different things, depending on who is employing it, and what kind of cost–benefit calculations they are favoring. Intensive factory farming and the attendant suffering of massive numbers of ani-mals can be justified by utilitarianism, as it usually is, if the ben-efits in efficient food production are deemed more valuable than the suffering of the animals. This is the kind of utilitarianism espoused regularly by the animal industry and usually accorded public approval by the media. The ethical questions don't have to be raised when utilitarianism is used in this way because ques-tions of right and wrong are pushed aside by the question, "Does it benefit us?"

Another problem with the utilitarian ethic has to do with the pleasure and desires themselves as the sole interests that have to be considered. Are all pleasures and desires good? Is not the sole emphasis on pleasure and desire itself problematic? An empha-sis on pleasures and desires, in and by themselves, can make for a rather shallow estimation of the meaning of life. Human life would seem to be much more complicated than to be fit neatly into a mere pleasure–pain calculation. Human life is replete with all manner of complex relations with self and others, with differ-ent goals and aspirations, with different soul capacities. Do we not need to consider all these in assigning worth to people? And similarly with animals, is the worth of their lives to be assessed merely in terms of pleasure and pain? Do the animals' wisdom, emotional capacities, and beauty count for nothing? In fact, is the significance of the very presence of the animal world to be understood merely in terms of a balance of pleasure and pain?

In this sense, while clearly affirming the importance of animal rights, Rudolf Steiner, nevertheless, strongly emphasizes that "there are responsibilities that go beyond the realm of rights and law" (Steiner 2010, 127). He makes this statement in a discussion of the great human responsibility in the course of Earth evolution "to redeem the animals," to lift them up to the higher stage of acquiring their own individual, independent "I"-being. This is a responsibility humans cannot fulfill now, for it can only take place in the far distant future when Earth conditions and human spiritual development will have both radically changed. But it is a responsibility that extends into the present, placing upon humans the responsibility to be guardians and stewards of the animals now, and in preparation for the future. This entails taking animal rights seriously, but also taking seriously our responsibilities to them in relation to the full life, capacities, and value of the animals now. While affirming the importance of rights, the Anglican theologian, Andrew Linzey, at whose views I will look at presently, has also stressed the importance of not being limited only to rights considerations, whether utilitarian-based or other. "Rights talk," says Linzey, "should not obliterate other kinds of language, such as generosity, love, respect, and care—all of whom have their place. It is a mistake to think that rights language is, as it were, the philosopher's stone in terms of correct argumentation, so that no argument can be valid unless it somehow issues in rights claims" (Linzey 2013, 127). This appears to me to be very much in keeping with Rudolf Steiner's urging that "there are responsibilities that go beyond the realm of rights and laws."

2. Rights Theory: Tom Regan

A more thoroughgoing champion of animal rights than is Singer as such is Tom Regan (Regan 1983). Regan differs from Singer in maintaining that sentience—the ability to feel pain—is not a sufficient basis for grounding animal rights. Sentience is important, but equally or more important is what Regan calls "subjecthood." To be a subject means experiencing a life that has its own inherent value. This for Regan is true of many animals in that "they want and prefer things, believe and feel things, recall and expect things"—they have preferences, emotions, will, and an orientation toward the fulfillment of life (Regan and Singer 1989, 111). To have inherent value as a subject means that the animal has the moral right to have that value honored and protected. Animal rights would seem to apply for Regan to all mammals and birds.

Regan's criterion of animal rights has a number of implications. It requires that animals have rights against the infliction of cruel and needless pain. Beyond this, however, valuing subjecthood involves respecting the rights of animals to fulfill their positive capacities and preferences—freedom of movement, freedom from boredom, freedom to live out their preferences and inborn capacities; in short, the right to live. Animal rights, in this view, carries a strong claim of equality—that is, that animals that possess inherent value as subjects have equal rights, regardless of what species they belong to. In this sense, Regan, like Singer, is strictly opposed to attitudes of speciesism. Both are opposed to factory farming, hunting and trapping, most animal experimentation, and meat-eating as morally unjustified. Regan does differ from Singer's willingness to sum up the balance between pleasures and pains, insisting that individual animals not be sacrificed for the common good. In other words he rejects the utilitarian logic that would override individual animal rights for the sake of the greatest number. Despite their differences on utilitarianism, Regan and Singer agree on a number of things, and have cooperated in making the case for animals (Regan and Singer).

3. THEOS-RIGHTS: ANDREW LINZEY

We will look at other animal welfare advocates who also say that the animals have many qualities, which must be considered along with their rights. First, however, I want to take a closer look at the views of Andrew Linzey, who is an important figure fighting for animal welfare, an Anglican priest, member of the faculty of theology at Oxford University, and Director of the Oxford Centre for Animal Ethics. Linzey comes to the question of animals and of animal rights from a theological perspective quite different from Singer's naturalistic utilitarianism. Linzey is probably the most important, and certainly the most prolific, writer on animals from a theological perspective. To date he has authored and edited more than twenty books and written countless articles on animal welfare and animal rights.

Linzey can be almost as critical as Singer of Christianity's history of speciesist "dominionist" attitudes toward animals. Linzey, however, not only points also to the continuous sequence of Christian individuals who have over the centuries worked for the welfare of animals, he insists, too, that the Christian message, if rightly understood and heeded by Christians, provides the strongest of support for animals. At the center of Linzey's approach is his understanding of the incarnation of Christ, which for him has manifold significance. First, it establishes the entering of God into the suffering and future possibilities of his created world. Animals, therefore, like all creatures, possess intrinsic value because they are of value to God. Humans do not grant rights to animals, rather, God does. Humans must recognize that animal rights are given by God. Linzey has coined the term *Theos-Rights* to describe animal rights as grounded in "God's own rights in creation," "Theos-Rights," "God's Rights." "Christians," Linzey says, "are precluded from a purely humanistic, utilitarian view of animals" (Linzey 2000, 37). The whole debate about animals, he insists, "is precisely about the rights of the Creator...and to recognize animal rights is to recognize the intrinsic value of God-given life" (ibid., 40–1).

Central to this conception of God's rights is the idea of "generosity." God expresses his generosity in Christ's suffering in and for creation. In his suffering Christ reveals God's special concern for the weak, the powerless, the innocent. Animals, like children, therefore, have more than equal claim for consideration; they have greater claim, "precisely because of their vulnerability and relative powerlessness." Linzey argues that Singer is led to permit infanticide because he does not allow innocence and vulnerability to enter into his pleasure–pain calculus (Linzey 2013, 152).

Here, however, Linzey takes an interesting turn: Humans are uniquely different from animals and morally superior to them. This moral superiority, he argues "is actually central to good animal rights theory" (Linzey 1994, 45). This superiority consists in the capacity for service and self-sacrifice. Drawing upon the suffering of Christ on behalf of the weak, the oppressed, the vulnerable, and powerless, among whom animals and human infants stand foremost, Linzey calls upon the human to follow Christ in this sacrificial service. "The uniqueness of humanity," he says, "consists in the ability to become the servant species" (Linzey 1994, 57). Linzey is adamant in rejecting animal experimentation, meat eating, hunting, fur farming, commercial sealing, and all else that infringes on the animals' rights as creatures of God. As for the attitude of the general public toward animal rights, including the general Christian public, Linzey has this to say:

> Part of the reason rights language is so controversial is that people sense from the very outset that recognizing animal rights must involve personal and social change. Whatever else animal rights means it cannot mean that we can go on consuming their flesh, destroying their habitats, and inflicting suffering. Quite disingenuously some church people say that they do not "know" what "animal rights" are. Meanwhile, by steadfastly refusing to change their lifestyles, they show a precise understanding of what those rights are. (Linzey 2000, 40)

Other animal defenders have in recent years striven to take a wider view other than an exclusive emphasis on rights. Space does not permit, even if I were capable of it, to give a comprehensive account of several different perspectives now represented in the wider discussion. Here I will simply point to a few selected types of main perspectives and arguments that seek a larger context than merely that of rights, but almost all are agreed that the concept of animal rights is and has been very important, in alerting us to the suffering of animals and in establishing moral limits in our treatment of them.

4. The Capabilities Approach: Martha C. Nussbaum

Martha C. Nussbaum, who teaches in the philosophy department, the law school, and the school of divinity of the University of Chicago, puts forward what she calls the "capabilities approach" to our relationship with animals (Nussbaum). The capabilities approach stresses the need to go beyond humanitarian compassion, as important as that is, to include also a firm sense of justice for animals. The capabilities approach means that living beings have goods in their lives and abilities (capabilities) to pursue them. When these capabilities and the flourishing of life they make possible are denied or thwarted by human beings, then an injustice is being done the animals. These capabilities are to be honored and seen as giving the animal "entitlement" to their exercise. This recognition of animal entitlement warrants both an attitude of humanitarian sensitivity and responsibility toward the animals, but whenever possible also legal and constitutional protection for them.

Nussbaum argues that the capabilities approach enables us to bring into our consideration of animals many things left out by exclusively utilitarian and narrowly focused rights approaches. She does give credit to utilitarianism for having contributed "more than any other ethical theory to the recognition of animal entitlements." By itself, however, utilitarianism is deficient in important ways. Pain and pleasure, for example, are not the only things we ought to be looking for. Many things in an animal's life are just as important as mere pleasure; for examples, freedom of movement, care of the young, sacrifice for kin and group, emotional attachment to other animals and humans, and so on. Yet, the wider extension of justice to animals requires as basic the utilitarian emphasis on sentience and the capacity for suffering.

The capabilities approach honors important differences between species and among individuals of the same species.

Species differences are important. Here Nussbaum is clearly challenging the broadside use of the concept of speciesism by some
animal rights people to demand a leveling out and ignoring of
real differences between species. It is true, she acknowledges, that
humans through the centuries have often arrogantly claimed for
themselves alone what other species in fact also possess. "But it
seems wrong," she adds, "to conclude from such facts that species membership is morally and politically irrelevant." She gives
as an example of the importance of species differences the case
of a mentally disabled human child who is still enabled to flourish meaningfully as a human being through the care and help of
other human beings." That is so," she emphasizes, "because he
[the child] can only flourish as a human being. He has no option
of flourishing as a happy chimpanzee.... " The species category
gives us a "benchmark" for "judging whether a given creature
has decent opportunities for flourishing. With the example of the
human child, she gives a parallel example of the chimpanzee: "For
a chimpanzee," she says, "it seems to me that expensive efforts to
teach language, while interesting and revealing, are not matters
of basic justice. A chimpanzee flourishes in its own way, communicating with its own community in a perfectly adequate way
that has gone on for ages." Without a clear concept, or at least
acknowledgement, of species differences, not only the particular
differences but also distinct needs and potentials of a given species get smudged over and erased.

Nussbaum lists ten capabilities that animals require for their
flourishing. Without attempting a detailed look, we can briefly
get a sense of what is included in each:

1. *Life:* Whether they have conscious interests or not, all animals are entitled to continue their lives. Gratuitous killing such
as hunting for sport or killing for luxury items such as fur should
not be permitted. And the torture and the early curtailment of
life involved in factory farming should be prohibited. And she
touches on other issues. 2. *Bodily Health:* Animals are entitled
to a healthy life. Laws banning cruel treatment and unhealthy
confinement are required. 3. *Bodily Integrity:* This is related
to the preceding. Animals are entitled to be spared violence,

injury, abuse and other forms of treatment harmful to the body. 4. *Senses, Imagination, and Thought:* Animals have an entitlement to opportunities and environments that support their own needs and abilities for expression. 5. *Emotions:* Animals have a wide range of emotional needs that should be taken into consideration. 6. *Practical Reason:* Animals that have a capability to frame goals and projects need to be enabled. From Steiner's point of view this would seem to apply especially to the ability of animals to follow and realize the inherent wisdom of their own group soul and body. 7. *Affiliation:* Animals are entitled to fulfill their own appropriate forms of relationships and attachments, and in their relations with humans should be treated with respect as dignified beings. 8. *Play:* Play and opportunities for play, are important for almost all sentient beings. 9. *Control over One's Environment:* Animals require respect and support for the integrity of their habitat, a need especially in jeopardy today. 10. *Other Species:* Animals are entitled to live in "cooperative and supportive" relationships with others.

This last capability, *Other Species*, deserves a bit of special attention. This capability she describes as "calling for the gradual formation of an interdependent world in which all species will enjoy cooperative and mutually supportive relations with one another.... Nature is not that way and never has been. So it [this capability] calls, in a very general way, for the gradual supplanting of the natural by the just." It may not be too much to see Nussbaum, unlike almost all other writers on behalf of animals, edging toward hope for a future world, however far distant, in which pain, suffering, and predation are no more—an eschatological hope.

Nussbaum's capability approach is more flexible than many more stringent rights advocates would permit. For example, she leaves open the question whether a complete ban on all killing for food is required, especially if done painlessly. That, of course, avoids the further question about the premature ending of animals' lives and the cutting short their flourishing. And while she maintains that a good deal of animal research is to be opposed, some, she thinks may be permitted if it can be shown to be absolutely necessary for human benefit. But, even then, she acknowledges that all animal research violates basic animal entitlements to justice. We will look at the actualities and ethics of animal research again.

We have not dealt by any means with all the voices speaking out on animal welfare and animal rights. Two further approaches, however, do need to be briefly noted. One can be called the "environmental approach," and the other the "process approach," based on the "process philosophy" of Alfred North Whitehead.

5. THE ENVIRONMENTALIST APPROACH

The environmental approach to animal rights considers care for the animals in the larger context of concern for the whole environment. This approach holds that what is of most importance ethically is not the individual animal but whole species and the Earth's environment, which supports the life of the species. The primary focus of this approach, then, is the animal species, the animal habitats, and the wider biosphere. Moral consideration, in other words, is concerned not so much with the rights of single animals, as with nurturing and preserving life itself and, with that, protecting the survival of whole species. The wholesale destruction of the environment and of animal habitats by humans constitutes the major moral crisis of our time.

Many environmentalists do not hesitate to endorse the killing of large numbers of individual animals—say, of deer, kangaroo, or rabbits—if their numbers are such as to threaten the surrounding environment and with it the species itself. They also tend not to concern themselves much with domestic animals and farm animals. They can even be hostile to humane societies and animal welfare and rights groups for, as they see it, siphoning off energy and resources needed for the larger and more pressing task of preserving the Earth with its many creatures. As they stress, rightly it seems to me, that if humans don't succeed in this larger task, then all talk about animal rights goes by the board in any case.

An extreme version of the environmental approach, which its champions sometimes refer to as "deep ecology," even speaks of a "democracy of values," in which the human being has no more rights than any others. Deep ecologists sometimes look back to the early hunter–gatherer stage of human history. They see this as an epoch in human history in which ecological balance and harmony among animals, humans, and the wider Earth environment, made up the underlying conditions of Earth existence. The hunting and gathering communities helped maintain this harmony and balance, while showing deep reverence and respect for nature and a vital sense of oneness with the animal world. Even the killing of animals necessary for human survival was done out of a religious sense of reverence and gratitude—and guilt—in relation to the animals, their fellow creatures. The radical environmentalists see this natural balance and harmony as having been upset by the rise of human civilization, especially by the development of agriculture. Thus began, in their view, the long and intensifying exploitation and destruction of the Earth and its nonhuman inhabitants. Thus also came about the disruption of the supposed original "democracy of values,' as humans came more and more to see themselves as the only beings of value, entitled to use all the rest of nature and its creatures for the satisfying of human desires and purposes.

There would seem to be much truth in this picture, which ought not to be dismissed. If Jared Diamond is right, however, there is an irony in the environmentalists' picture of an almost Edenic ideal of hunter–gatherer culture. According to Diamond, the rise of human civilization itself depended on the massive (and probably brutal) exploitation of animals for food, clothing, and work (Diamond 1998). Compounding the irony is that still today some impoverished societies are forced to depend on wild animals to feed their families, such that, for example, the reliance on "bushmeat" in impoverished places of Africa threatens the extinction of many species of apes and monkeys. Yet, it should also be pointed out that many hunter–gatherers sometimes maintained for centuries a sense of the relatedness and interconnectedness of all things, and a sense of reverence and gratitude toward, especially, the animals they killed.

The environmentalist-oriented animal rights advocates, including the extreme, have, nevertheless, been in the forefront of those alerting us to the endangered fragility and tenuous balance of the biosphere, and to the dire threat it is under from continuous human encroachment and exploitation. We are left, however, with two crucial questions raised by an exclusively environmentalist approach. One is whether radical concern for the environment must always be at the neglect and expense of individual animal suffering. The other second, related question is whether the extreme environmentalist tendency to level out all differences of worth and value among the different species, including especially differences of value between humans and animals, actually works to the benefit of the animals.

A further perspective on human and animal relations, which I want to briefly note, answers "No!" to both these questions. This perspective maintains that concern for the group and for the individual, concern for sustainability of the system and for nurturing the individual animal and relieving its suffering, must be held together. This can only be done in the long run, according to this view, if important differences of value among species and between humans and animals, are recognized and honored in the right way. This is the view of the great, twentieth-century philosopher and logician, Alfred North Whitehead.[*]

6. THE INTRINSIC VALUE APPROACH: ALFRED NORTH WHITEHEAD

Central to Whitehead's philosophy with respect to living beings are two realities especially: subjectivity and intrinsic value. Subjectivity, or feeling experience, is a fundamental attribute of all organisms. Different organisms have different degrees of subjectivity or feeling. Feeling is the means of connection and interaction among beings—all beings feel the feelings of others. Subjectivity—consciousness and feeling—also includes the capacity for pain and suffering, for joy and pleasure. That

---

[*] I rely here particularly on the work of John B. Cobb and David Ray Griffin, two outstanding authorities on the thought of Whitehead.

animals have feelings is the ground for endowing them with moral standing and rights.

Whiteheadians also connect subjectivity with value and worth. They distinguish between intrinsic value and extrinsic value. Intrinsic value of any being is for it to have value in itself for itself. Extrinsic value is what value it may have for others—instrumental value, for example. The ground or locus of intrinsic value is subjectivity. There exist among living beings different grades or degrees of subjectivity and, hence, different gradations of intrinsic value. The higher the degree of subjectivity—consciousness and feeling—the higher the degree of intrinsic worth. John Cobb and David Griffin write, "Everything else being equal, those with a greater intrinsic value are to be preferred, when a choice must be made" (Cobb and Griffin, 79). It is on this point that most other advocates of animal rights differ from the followers of Whitehead. They argue, against Whitehead, that all beings—human and animal—must be given equal consideration, that is, equal rights, based on their common capacity for pain and suffering. Against them, the followers of Whitehead are firm in their insistence that difference in subjectivity and the ensuing difference in intrinsic value must be considered in assessing animal rights.

Whitehead and his followers push this further to maintain that the human being probably has an intrinsic value greater than that of any other being on the planet, and that this has a crucial role to play not only in thinking about rights and human responsibilities, but in all human–animal relationships. Strict animal rights advocates along with many environmental ethicists object that it is human beings who are making this judgment, and that it smacks, therefore, of just another anthropocentric, speciesist prejudice. The Whiteheadian response to this is that this objection vastly underestimates the important consequences of affirming that other creatures besides the human do, indeed, have their own intrinsic value, and, therefore their own ends, purposes, and life projects to pursue—and that this must never be lost sight of in thinking about animal rights. John Cobb writes:

Their [the animals'] own ends must be considered as well. We have the responsibility to work for a world in which both they and we have a habitat and opportunity to flourish. This is not just a slightly modified anthropocentrism. It involves a drastic rejection of the now dominant world system.... One of the highest expressions of human intrinsic value is the exercise of responsibility for the well-being of other creatures—human and animal—out of a real concern for them. (Cobb 2001)

It is on this basis, the Whiteheadians insist, that a solid foundation for human and animal rights alike can be built.

7. THE GREAT APE PROJECT: PETER SINGER AGAIN

A recent attempt to introduce a new perspective and impulse in animal rights advocacy, is "The Great Ape Project," organized by a group of thirty-four scientists and philosophers. Especially prominent in the movement are Peter Singer and Paola Cavalieri. The Great Ape Project does deserve some special attention because it seemingly deviates more radically from other animal rights positions we have looked at. It is accordingly controversial in a way that reveals important, central issues in the rights discussion. The Great Ape Project seeks to extend *civil rights* to all the great apes of a single genus (chimpanzees, bonobos, gorillas, and orangutans). The initiative wants to include the great apes within "the community of equals," which is conceived to include the sphere of the human. The basic argument of the movement is that the great apes ought to be given the same rights as humans and be treated as moral equals with humans. Three basic rights are to be extended to the apes: the right to life, to individual liberty, and to protection from torture. The Project is campaigning to have the United Nations endorse these rights in a Declaration on Great Apes. While tactically the movement focuses on the great apes as a start, the hope is to extend human legal rights beyond the great apes to embrace elephants, dolphins, and whales.

Two sets of arguments are given for including the apes within the "community of equals." One is the argument that the apes are our closest biological relatives. This is based on a particular interpretation of genetic research, which shows that chimpanzees (and also other apes) have 96 to 98 percent of the same genetic material (DNA) as humans. This argument seems to me to be the weaker of the two, given advances in genetic research that show that the potential of the genetic material is expressed differently over time and also interacts differently with epigenetic cellular influences as well as with environmental influences (Talbot). Furthermore, despite any similarity in genetics, physiological and organic differences between the ape and the human are pronounced. This shows itself, to take one example, in the fact that in medical research the apes can be considered reasonable candidates for certain kinds of human disease and totally useless and unpredictable for others (Greek and Shanks).

The second argument given to support the Great Apes Project, however, appears much stronger. This is the argument based on the rich data of ethological research showing that the great apes are intelligent beings with a multifaceted emotional and social life, and in these areas are very close to human beings. Jane Goodall, a member of the original Project group, has expressed the argument vividly and attractively, based on her lifetime of work and companionship with chimpanzees:

> The postures and gestures with which chimpanzees communicate—such as kissing, embracing...hair-pulling, tickling—are not only uncannily like many of our own, but are used in similar contexts and clearly have similar meanings. Two friends may greet with an embrace and a fearful individual may be calmed by a touch, whether they be chimpanzees or humans. Chimpanzees are capable of sophisticated cooperation and complex social manifestations. Like us, they have a dark side to their nature: they can be brutal, they are aggressively territorial, sometimes they engage in a primitive type of warfare. But they also show a variety of helping and care-giving behaviours and are capable of true altruism. (Cavalieri and Singer, 13)

The Project organizers maintain that ethological research has shown that the chimpanzees have rationality and complex abstract thought, highly developed emotions, the ability to communicate in a symbolic language, and are autonomous, that is, capable of freedom of choice. The Project argues, therefore, that the apes should be included among the moral "community of equals," and should be accorded the status of personhood and the legal rights that apply to human persons. The "community of equals" means something other in the Great Ape Project than it does for the "deep ecologists." For the deep ecologists, the Community of Equals includes all living organisms; whereas, for the Great Ape Project it is a community limited to the animals with human characteristics, primarily cognitive complexity and self-awareness over time. If other animals can be shown also to qualify, such as dolphins and elephants, the community of equals would be extended to them as well.

The Great Ape Project has arisen primarily from a keen sense of what chimpanzees have endured for nearly a half century in laboratory experimentation. Their lifespan in captivity can range from 40 to 60 years. In the lab they live for years on end during much of that time in small, cramped, barren cages, whereas in the wild they cover two to three kilometers a day. Repeatedly in the lab they experience anesthetization by dart guns ("knockdowns"), which they come to fear, perhaps anticipating something of what is to follow, and desperately try to avoid, screaming, pressing themselves against the back bars of their cage, sometimes vomiting and defecating in terror. The experimental procedures performed on them routinely include liver punches, wedge and lymph node biopsies, and infection with HIV and various forms of hepatitis virus. Their life of pain and terror is exhibited in a diversity of symptoms, described by one observer as: "self-injury, seizure-like episodes, screaming, panic attacks, trance states, acute anxiety, depression, hyper-aggression, anorexia, dysphoria." The observer concludes, "Given the unrelenting horror of their experiences, the most straightforward diagnosis is Complex Post-traumatic Stress Disorder" (Gay Bradshaw). Since the animals cannot give meaningful consent to any of these experiments—consent being required for any such experiments on humans—the advocates of the apes argue they must be represented and given protection from human society.

Against this background, animal welfare and rights groups, including the Great Ape Project, have had some success in gaining legal protection for the apes. Great Britain, Sweden, Austria, Belgium, and the Netherlands ban research on apes for ethical reasons. In 1999, New Zealand's Parliament passed a bill, inspired by the Great Ape Project, conferring "rights" on Chimpanzees and other primates with legal protection from experimentation. In 2008 the Spanish Parliament approved resolutions urging the country to comply with the Great Ape Project (Glendinning). The U.S. is the only Western, industrialized country that continues to experiment on apes, but here too some progress has been made in lessoning the amount of ape experimentation. The National Institutes of Health, under intense pressure from animal advocates, has decided to retire 90 percent of its chimpanzees (about 300) to Chimp Haven, a chimpanzee sanctuary in Florida, but still intends to keep 50 in reserve should "research needs" arise in the future. Many chimpanzees (approximately 500 by one count) are owned by pharmaceutical companies and private research centers, and most of their research takes place in the dark. The pharmaceutical industry, along with more than ten universities, has spent enormous sums opposing bills in Congress seeking to provide protection for primates against invasive experimentation. In 2011/12, the pharmaceutical industry alone spent more than $475 million lobbying against legislation that would restrict animal experimentation. Animal welfare groups have been decisively outmatched in terms of money (Steinbach).

In spite of this opposition, a major step in the protection of chimpanzees has just recently been taken. The Fish and Wildlife Service has announced (May 2015) that all chimpanzees, captive and wild, will be designated as endangered under the Endangered Species Act. Chimpanzees held in captivity in the United States will receive the same protections as wild chimps under the Endangered Species Act. This means, summarizes the *New York Times,* that "biomedical research, interstate trade, and export and import of captive chimpanzees will now require permits.... There are 730 chimpanzees in the custody of biomedical laboratories...and the changes require that any research that might harm or harass chimpanzees requires a permit" (St. Fleur). In light of the drastic decline in the number of chimpanzees in the last few decades—their current numbers are estimated between 172,000 and 300,000 worldwide, down from a million in the early 1900s—and given the horrific experimental procedures regularly practiced on chimpanzees, this new policy promises to be a major breakthrough for these intelligent and sensitive animals.

Another group of animal rights proponents, probably inspired in part by the Great Ape Project, and very active at the present time, is the Nonhuman Rights Project (Nh,R.P.), lead by a prominent lawyer, Steven M. Wise and Jane Goodall (Siebert). The NhRP has gone further than all others in working toward actual legal rights and protection as "persons" for any species that can be scientifically proven to be self-aware and autonomous. They claim this includes the great apes as well as elephants, dolphins, and whales. Currently (October 2014), the Nonhuman Rights Project has three court cases being heard in New York State arguing for the rights of four chimpanzees, two cruelly caged alone in two New York towns, and two used for invasive biomedical research in the Anatomy Department of Stony Brook University. The larger aim of the Nonhuman Rights Project is to gain momentum beyond New York State for animal legal rights nationally (McKinley).

The Great Ape and Nonhuman Rights Projects have not been without their critics, even from within animal welfare circles. Two of these critics, Gary L. Francione and Frans de Waal, are of special interest. Francione, lawyer and well known as a devoted animal rights advocate, was an original backer and signer of the Declaration on Great Apes, only later to see it as ill-conceived and to regret his original participation. Frans de Waal, we have known already as one of the world's leading primatologists who has perhaps done as much as anyone to bring to light the rich emotional and social life of the great apes. He too is a foremost critic of the Great Ape Project. We will look at Francione first.

Francione is in many ways an absolutist among animal rights proponents. He is against humans claiming property rights over animals, and, hence, against all use of animals for human purposes, including keeping them as pets. He is against all experimentation on animals and is a strict vegan. He thinks that it is wrong to use great apes in research or in circuses, or to confine them in zoos, and so forth. Perhaps these views make it all the more surprising to find him as a leading opponent of the Great Ape Project.

His criticism of the Great Ape Project turns on his rejection of what he calls its "similar minds" approach that links the moral standing of nonhumans to their possession of humanlike cognitive capacities. Basic to Francione's rights position is his view that sentience, the capacity to suffer, is all that is required for animals to have rights. "No characteristic other than sentience," he says, "is required for personhood." To say that some animals are entitled to more rights than others based on their similarity to humans is wrong in at least two ways. The first is that it assumes, without evidence, that the animals with less intelligence than primates suffer less. This is certainly without evidence, and, in fact, flies in the face of much evidence, which demonstrates that, for example, rats suffer greatly in a laboratory setting. Furthermore, there exists considerable evidence, to take the same example again, that rats have their own kind of intelligence, are emotional, even show empathy for other less fortunate, experimented-upon rats, and form complex social relationships. No evidence exists that their suffering is any less than that of the great apes, or of humans for that matter. It would seem, to speculate a bit, that Rudolf Steiner's view that animal suffering is, in general, greater than that of human beings, would lend support to Francione on this score.

The second point in his criticism is that the Great Ape Project endows those with greater self-awareness and rationality with greater moral value, thus, qualifying them alone for legal personhood. This, Francione rejects, giving the example of a mentally disabled human who may possess less cognitive ability than a chimpanzee, but to whom we grant equal, if not higher moral value and standing (Francione 2006).

This is also a criticism made by some others, but in even starker terms. These critics suggest that the Great Ape Project is really harkening back to Immanuel Kant. Recall that for Kant only human beings have the rational ability to make moral choices. Only humans, therefore, can command our respect for their moral dignity as "ends in themselves." For Kant, because animals lack this rationality they do not have moral standing and exist, not as ends in themselves, but only as a "means to other ends," usually to human ends. The hope of the Great Ape Project is that animals that can be shown to have the requisite rationality can be drawn into and counted as members of, essentially, the Kantian "community of ends"; that is, to be accounted legal persons. This means drawing a line between those who possess the requisite rationality and those who do not. But, then, where to draw the line? And what happens to those who are left on the other side, who don't make the cut? Some critics have gone further to suggest that the Great Ape Project's rationality criterion is a reinstatement, not simply of Kant, but also of the old Cartesian split between rational, autonomous beings as persons and animals as unfeeling machines, things. And, if the Great Ape Project were to apply the rationality criterion to bring more animals into the circle of autonomous persons, would that mean that all those left out would be mere things, to be treated as such? I have not found that the Great Ape Project's supporters have responded satisfactorily to these criticisms, though a satisfactory response might be possible.

Another kind of criticism of the Great Ape Project specifically, and of animal rights in general, is that of Frans de Waal. Because he does have a high regard for the apes' intelligence and rich emotional life, de Waals' criticisms are especially interesting and significant. De Waal is dubious about animal rights talk in general. While he is firm in his insistence that we cannot do with animals anything we please, he expresses deep discomfort in framing the issues in terms of rights. He thinks animal rights talk is abstract and absolutist. He argues that it cannot deal with the real complexities of human morality, which he is adamant should be the central focus, and that it leads ultimately to a call for the abolition of *all* use of *all* animals under *all* circumstances, whether for meat, medical research, or entertainment. De Waal clearly is no absolutist on the proper use of animals. Our first obligation, he insists, "is to fellow human beings" (de Waal 1996, 214).

De Waal takes on the Great Ape Project for advocating a "community of equals" consisting of apes and humans. He points out that concepts of rights are empty if they do not go hand in hand with responsibilities. He rejects Singer's and the other Great Ape Project members' rejoinder that since mentally retarded people are unable to carry out duties and responsibilities, why not apes. This, de Waal thinks is profoundly condescending. "Have we really reached the point," he asks, "at which respect for apes is most effectively advocated by depicting them as retarded people in furry suits?" (de Waal 1996, 214–5). And once we grant apes equal status with humans, again, where do we draw the line, why keep out cockroaches, and others? Nevertheless, he does think apes warrant special respect and consideration. We should either phase out research on certain species altogether, out of kindness and respect for their "beauty and dignity," or if humanity cannot forego the benefits derived from them, we must at least enrich and enhance their lives in captivity and reduce their suffering." Such decisions should be made out of human responsibility for other life forms. He does emphasize that this all involves difficult ethical dilemmas for which there is no easy solution (de Waal 1996, 214–5). He does fail to observe that a mark of the human "I" is that it alone can recognize the presence of an ethical dilemma.

And this points to a basic problem of de Waal's own in his approach to human morality. For de Waal human morality is a product of Darwinian evolution working through natural selection. For de Waal, the empathy, sympathy, cooperation, group loyalty, reciprocity, reconciliation, consolation, and so forth, exhibited by the animals and investigated so creatively by de Waal himself, constitute the evolutionary building blocks of full-blown human morality. These evolutionary building blocks, he thinks, make up a firm evolutionary foundation from which human morality emerges. This evolutionary development presents a picture of unbroken evolutionary continuity in which the moral difference between human and animals is, again, one only of degree, not of kind. As a consequence, de Waal maintains, human beings are moral "to the core," presumably because this human morality is rooted in eons of biological evolution through natural selection. As human beings we are naturally good, and this is the product of biology just as the future of human morality is guaranteed by our biology. We are born, he writes, with a moral capacity produced by natural selection that "has provided us with the psychological makeup, tendencies, and abilities to develop a compass for life choices that take the interests of human community into account, which is the essence of human morality" (de Waal 2006, 58).

A problem here is that the purely material, mechanistic principles of Darwinian evolution and natural selection provide no basis for the origins of the emotions as such, much less for the ability to make "life choices." It is true that for de Waal and Rudolf Steiner alike, the animals and humans share many common emotions, but for Steiner this is because they both participate in aspects of the common feeling soul of the universe, not because with ever greater complexity the emotions have arisen gradually from lower to higher forms of life through the mechanisms of Darwinian evolution. The difference from de Waal is that for Steiner the human has the possibility—not always realized—of being able to stand back from the emotions in evaluating and choosing among them. These "life choices" made by humans between good and evil, and sometimes between good and good, betoken the presence of a self, an "I"-being, capable of making such choices in its thinking, feeling, and willing. De Waal, however, relies upon his faith in Darwinian, biological determinism. He writes, "Biology constitutes our greatest hope; one can only shudder at the thought that the humanness of our societies will depend on the *whims of politics, culture, or* religion. Ideologies come and go, but human nature is here to stay" (ibid.). Yes, it is true that the whims of politics, culture, and religion have large ideological, biological, and epiphenomenal components, but at a deeper level they are also the outcome of "life choices" made by human selves, individually and collectively. De Waal's ultimate biological determinism obviates the moral nature of life choices he otherwise values so highly.

8. AN ARTIST'S APPROACH: JOSEPH BEUYS

The German artist, Joseph Beuys, was very different in his engagement with animals—and more direct and unsettling—than anyone we have looked at. Regarded by many as one of the most influential artists of the second half of the twentieth century, Beuys was a sculptor, graphic artist, and art and social theorist. He is especially known for his dramatic action art—artistic happening and installations. Beuys was a deep student of Rudolf Steiner and Anthroposophy. This influence played a central role in his efforts to redefine and extend art to enable it to play a major role in the renewal of thinking and of society. These concerns were very pressing for him in light of his own experiences of having been shot down as an airman on the Eastern front and his subsequent experiences in the aftermath of the war. For Beuys, the renewal of art and society both depended on a renewal of creative thinking, the basis for which he found in the work of Rudolf Steiner. He described Steiner's approach to thinking as one "that refers to reality in a direct and practical way, and that by comparison, all forms of epistemological discourse remain without direct relevance to current trends and movements" (quoted, Wickepedia).

Beuys had had a fascination with nature since childhood, but with the beginning of his artistic career in 1950, he began what was to be a lifelong engagement with the animal world. Beuys assumed a shamanistic attitude in relation to the animals, which in many traditional cultures served as guardians and spirit guides for the shaman in his spiritual journeys. In his first solo exhibition in 1965, *How to Explain Pictures to a Dead Hare*, he cradled a dead hare in his arms, mumbling into its ears, and with his own face covered with honey and gold leaf. Honey is the product of bees, and bees for Beuys, following Rudolf Steiner, manifest a highly developed wisdom, and maintain a warm, complex social existence (Steiner 1998). He explained his performance with the hare in this way: "In putting honey on my head I am clearly doing something that has to do with human thinking. Human ability is not to produce honey, but to think, to produce ideas. In this way the deathlike character of thinking becomes lifelike again. For honey is undoubtedly a living substance. Human thinking can be lively too. But it can also be intellectualized to a deadly degree, and dead, and to express its deadness in, say, the political and pedagogic fields. Even a dead animal possesses more powers of intuition than some human beings with their stubborn rationality" (Rothfuss). Beuys identified closely with several animals, the hare being special. He always carried a rabbit's foot as a talisman. He also had a deep affinity for the horse, and for the stag, animals with deep ties to Germanic myth and legend. He sometimes called himself "Stagman."

In 1974, in the Rene Block Gallery in New York City, Beuys spent three days, eight hours a day, in a room with a wild coyote, watching the coyote as the coyote watched him, and as both were watched by the gallery visitors. At the end of the three days, he hugged the coyote, which had grown used to him, and was taken to the airport. As art historian, Stephen Eisenman observes, Beuys had asserted his own marginal (liminal) status as an artist in the modern world, along with other marginalized beings such as concentration camp inmates, "by associating himself with two of the world's most hated and despised animals." Hares are widely regarded as pests, but "they are also objects of affection and pity." "They shed real tears when hurt, and their outcries recall those of children." Eisenman also observes that Beuy's choice of the coyote revealed his "new shamanic wish to erase the barrier between human and animal' (Eisenman, 238). The U.S. Fish and Wildlife Service set out to exterminate all coyotes in the U.S. between 1937 and 1981, shooting, poisoning, trapping and otherwise killing some 6 million of them, mainly at the behest of the ranching industry. (This was based on a false conception of the coyotes ecological importance, and since then the coyote has begun to stage a comeback). An outcaste everywhere in the U.S, the coyote, Eisenman notes, is at the same time sacred to Native American communities in the Southwest, "who see it as a trickster and an heroic figure." Eisenman writes: "Beuys himself was a notable trickster, fabulist, mythmaker and fraud. He employed animals— from his early drawing of elk, goats, foxes and rabbits to his rabbit and coyote appearances—to pose a challenge to an economic and political order that denied animals autonomy and divorced humans from nature and their own animal being" (Eisenman).

In 1969 he drew up a proposal for the first ever, *A Political Party of Animals.* He identified with the animals by including his own name on the list of "active members," who included Elk, Wolf, Beaver, Horse, Stork, and many others. When asked whether he had a lot of members in his party, he answered, "It's the largest party in the world." Beuys identified with the animals because he saw himself, like many of them, as marginalized in the modern world; and, just as important, he hoped to learn from what he considered their superior wisdom (Eisenman; Rothfuss).

4.

CONCLUDING THOUGHTS ON ANIMAL RIGHTS

As we have seen, Rudolf Steiner agrees with those who attribute to the animals a life of rights. Indeed, he says, we see "strongly marked" a life of rights among animals precisely because we recognize their having a "moral life." He goes on to say that they do not have a concept of rights, much less a conceptual understanding of these rights. Because they are moral beings, however, and because we do have the necessary concepts we can recognize their entitlement to rights and justice, and act accordingly, if we will (Steiner 1910a).

We can also distinguish, at least theoretically, negative rights and positive rights. The idea of rights based primarily on the avoidance of pain and suffering can deal well with negative rights. For examples, animals have a right not to be confined for life on a concrete floor and caged so as to be unable to turn around as happens for millions of factory-farmed pigs; animals have a right not be clubbed and skinned alive as happens each year to thousands of pup seals; animals have the right not to be electrocuted through the anus so as to preserve their pelt from damage in the killing, as is the case for thousands of small animals in the fur industry; animals have the right not to be subjected to excruciatingly painful laboratory procedures without anesthetics, as happens to millions of rats and mice each year—and the list seems endless.

Positive rights, however, point beyond the avoidance of pain and suffering to the realization of life aims and joys—to the animals' desire for life and wellbeing, to their desire to enjoy life and to flourish. With positive rights we begin to see that we have to look at other things besides the avoidance of pain and suffering, as essential as that is, for a full grasp of all that is involved in the animals' welfare. Martha Nussbaum made a substantial beginning in this with her identification of a number of animal capabilities—positive capacities—that ought to be honored and taken into account along with a narrower focus on rights. An example of a beginning attempt to formulate a positive rights approach was that made as early as 1970 in England by the British Farm Animal Advisory Committee: "The fact that an animal has limbs should give it the right to spread them; the fact that both animals and birds are mobile should give them the right to turn around; and the fact that they have eyes should give them the right to see" (Linzey 2013, 52). This is a beginning list of positive rights, all of them totally denied animals in the factory farm or in the lab. It was a beginning, minimal statement based on a perception of both animal pain and suffering and animals' need to express and enjoy their own intrinsic worth, starting with their animal bodies.

Rudolf Steiner, however, rejects a focus on rights alone. He says that when we grasp that animals are innocent, but, nonetheless, suffer on account of us, we will also begin to realize that rights concepts, however important they may be, are not enough. More is needed. "There are responsibilities that go beyond the ream of rights and the law" (Steiner 2010, 127). These are the responsibilities that humans have toward the animals. We are responsible both to honor and to protect those rights, and the animals' welfare in general.

The unpleasant question, then, cannot be avoided. How do we in actuality treat the animals in our time?

PART IV

ANIMALS IN THE MODERN WORLD

Biomedical Research and Testing

In just the last half-century, human attitudes and actions toward the animals have become better in many important ways. Scores of new animal advocacy groups have appeared, such as the Humane Society, The Physicians Committee for Responsible Medicine, the International Fund for Animal Welfare, and many others. They have joined and broadened the work of older societies founded in the nineteenth century, which are still vital, such as the original anti-vivisection societies and societies for the prevention of cruelty to animals. Increasing numbers of people have become sensitive to the needs and suffering of animals. And more and more people have begun to recognize the rich emotional and social lives of animals, and our kinship with them. Courses on "teaching the animal" and "animal studies" have begun to appear in the regular curricula of colleges and universities (Demello). These and other positive advances ought not to be ignored or downplayed. They provide support, and encouragement for not flagging in our efforts to work for the animals. It should not be overlooked, however, that this increased concern for the animals has still taken place only among a relatively small number of people in the larger human community.

And still, it must be said, the plight of animals is in some ways even worse than before. As the ethologist Marc Bekoff has stressed: "In nearly every area—whether it be science, education, industrial farming, clothing, zoos, rodeos, the wildlife trade, and so on—we are abusing animas, sometimes horrifically, and we are doing so by choice" (Bekoff 2010, 128). The number of animals killed in the millions and billions every year for food, medical research, product testing, and hunting should alone by its sheer magnitude give us pause and signal that something is seriously amiss.

The use of animals to gain insights about humans began eons ago. One of the earliest, and perhaps most famous, in using animals to study humans was the first-century Greek physician, Galen. Known today by the somewhat dubious honorific as "the father of vivisection," Galen examined the anatomy of animals and attempted to apply his observations and resulting theories to humans. In 1543 the study of anatomy through dissection and autopsies came into its own with the publication of the book by the Belgian anatomist and physician, Andreas Versalius, *Structure of the Human Body*. The modern use of animals in science was pioneered by the French physiologist, Claude Bernard, who is sometimes credited with the founding of modern, experimental physiology. Bernard used human autopsies and animal vivisection—on a scale far exceeding that of Galen centuries earlier—to try to learn basic facts about major organs and in doing so helped lay the foundation for the practice of modern biomedical research. Bernard is a favorite target of critics of animal experimentation. His work revealed from the beginning the ethical issues lying at the heart of animal medical research and experimentation. It is said that when his wife and daughter discovered him vivisecting the family dog, they founded one of the early anti-vivisection societies in Europe (Greek and Shanks, 6). After Bernard, animal dissection, vivisection, and various other medical procedures on animals soon became ensconced in the curricula of all modern medical schools.

Oversimplifying somewhat, we can distinguish two main types or orientations in biomedical research in general, although they do overlap at points: basic research and clinical or applied research. Basic research aims to discover medical and biological knowledge whether it has any practical application or not. Clinical research is the attempt to see if any such discoveries have actual, practical application for human health, and in veterinary schools, animal health. The undergirding assumption of biomedical research is that experimentation on animals is essential in understanding human disease and in the search for cures.

Clinical research is itself specifically of two main kinds. One is to develop an animal model that simulates a particular human disease as closely as possible with the purpose of better understanding and to test potential therapies. The other related use of animals in biomedical research is to test medical procedures or drugs, as well as potentially harmful chemical products, such as pesticides, toxic chemicals in the environment, and even cosmetic products for the market.

Biomedical research and experimentation with animals raise two central—and difficult—questions: 1. Scientifically, is it valid? Does it produce important and applicable results? 2. Ethically, is it justified? Is it necessary in the light of the animal suffering involved, and are there other alternatives? Each of these questions is interwoven with the other: there is no value-free science, and there is no ethics that does not have practical consequences.

1. Ethics

The central ethical question is, at bottom, what the leading laboratory veterinarian, Larry Carbone, calls "The Big Question: Do we have a right to use animals in research at all?" (Carbone, 18). Now, in response to this question, we again have two main answers. On one side are the animal advocates like Peter Singer, Tom Regan, Gary Francione and others who, with some variations, oppose animal experimentation for human medical purposes on the grounds that the pain inflicted on animals in the lab is too great, and that the animals have interests in their own right that warrant equal consideration with humans. They see testing and experimentation on animals for human purposes as yet another expression of the speciesism that regards the human as superior to the animals and, therefore, entitled to experiment on them at will. These critics also see the justification of animal experimentation for human purposes as resting on an ethic of "might makes right"; we can experiment on the vulnerable and helpless because we have the power to do so.

On the other side, is a majority of the medical profession. Many compassionate medical researchers defend animal biomedical research and experimentation for human benefit, but are also concerned to mitigate as much as possible the animal suffering involved (Redmond). This is relative, of course, because many lab procedures are unavoidably painful and prolonged, often in the extreme. Nevertheless, these researchers maintain that the human benefits justify the animal pain and suffering involved.

From this side, however, the entire situation becomes more complicated because many vested interests stand to benefit financially and in organizational power from animal biomedical research and experimentation. A number of medical organizations exist for the main purpose of promoting animal research and experimentation, lobbying Congress and appealing to the general public through various public relations efforts. More important are the many organizations that stand to gain huge financial rewards and organizational prestige through their involvement in biomedical research. These include, among others: universities, private research facilities, animal breeding firms that supply millions of animals to the labs, pharmaceutical companies, lab equipment manufacturers, and others. All of this is massively supported by the general population, which assumes from the start that anything that even promises medical progress trumps all, whatever the animal suffering involved. On this side, both scientific and ethical questions are very difficult to be identified and properly weighed.

A middle position between these two extremes does exist and in the last few decades has been gaining some ground. A major step in this direction has been the establishment since the 1960s of important government agencies to regulate animal research in the attempt to put some limits on animal suffering in laboratories receiving federal funding. The passage of the Animal Welfare Act in 1960 was largely a response at first to public outrage at articles in *Life Magazine* and *Sports Illustrated* describing how lost pets and dogs from pet dealers were ending up in laboratories under no restrictions as to what could be done to them. The 1966 version of the Act put some minimal restrictions on labs that experiment on cats and dogs, required licenses by dealers selling animals to labs, and set up some basic standards for the housing and feeding of animals before and after experimentation, though as philosopher Jean Kazez has pointed out, "nothing was said about their treatment during experimentation" (Kazez 148). The law was amended seven times between 1966 and 2008, expanding much coverage of animals.

In 1985, following reports of horrific mistreatment of animals in a number of laboratories, the law was amended to require each research facility to establish at least one animal care committee (Institutional Animal Care and Use Committee—IACUC), to review and approve, or not, proposals and protocols for animal experimentation. The law mandates that each animal care committee (IACUC) include among its members a veterinarian, who will also be present on site to look after the needs of the animals, an expert in the scientific use of lab animals, a nonscientist, and one member of the wider community who is not affiliated with the research facility being reviewed. A number of other members are permitted as well, often themselves related in one way or another to animal research and experimentation. The U.S. Department of Agriculture is charged with overseeing the Animal Welfare Act and ensuring that its provisions are followed. The animal care committees are responsible for reviewing proposals, and, among other things, the procedures to be used to limit the animals' discomfort and pain to what is unavoidable for the research being proposed, as well as the euthanasia procedures to be used (Latham 2012).

Another aspect of animal research in which some appreciable improvement can be seen in the alleviation of animal pain and suffering is that of product testing, a practice that has involved the suffering and subsequent killing of millions of animals, mainly mice and rabbits, each year. No law in this country requires that cosmetic products be tested on animals, but historically most cosmetic companies have, nevertheless, conducted such testing to protect themselves from possible lawsuits. By contrast the law does require that fertilizers, farm chemicals, weed killers, household cleansers, and pesticides be tested on animals. The FDA has similar testing requirements for drugs and various chemicals. These testing procedures are by any definition cruel and result in the deaths—usually through prolonged suffering—again of millions of animals every year.

Two forms of toxicity testing are the most prevalent. One is the "lethal dose 50 percent test" (LD50 test). In this test groups—often very large groups—of animals are force-fed, through the mouth, anus, or vagina, increasing amounts of a substance until 50 percent of the animals die. In the process animals suffer horribly and without relief. The accuracy of the tests has never been scientifically validated. One medical opponent of the LD50 Test has called it "the loathsome LD50 Test." The other main method for product testing, the "Draize eye-and-skin-irritation test" dates back to the 1940s, and for years was the major procedure for testing cosmetic products. During the test, rabbits usually are strapped down or otherwise rendered unable to move, and, held in the unmovable positions for long periods of time, have cosmetic substances dripped into their eyes or smeared on their shaved skin, while lab technicians record the damage (painfully irritated eyes, blindness, ulcers, bleeding skin, and so forth).

Hopeful developments in product and toxicity testing, however, have begun to appear. The Draize test has been increasingly rejected by a number of countries and even by some household product companies themselves, as a result mainly of pressure and publicity generated by animal advocate groups. Perhaps a certain awareness of the ethical issues involved in torturing millions of little animals—which are killed afterward, in order to market, without fear of lawsuits, a better-selling mascara, skin cream, botox applications, etc.—has played some part. Also, the development of alternatives to the use of animals have become more and more available, for example, cell and tissue cultures, other forms of in vitro testing, computerized models, and so forth. The Draize test, or variations of it, is still used around the world, and has not been completely abandoned by U.S. companies (such as, Estee Lauder, and others). However, cosmetic testing is no longer permitted in the United Kingdom, and, as of March 2013, the European Union banned the sale of any cosmetic or cosmetic ingredients that have been tested on animals. This means that companies around the world will have to abandon cosmetic testing on animals if they want to sell in the EU (Zurlo).

Still, the basic ethical questions are rarely asked within the regulatory framework. The Animal Welfare Act (AWA) is itself a prime example. In spite of efforts by animal advocacy groups, or most likely as a backlash against them, the 2002 amendment to the AWA legally formalized the longtime AWA practice of excluding rats, mice, birds, reptiles and amphibians from protection by the act, essentially denying them even being accorded the status of animals. These "non-animals," "things" for all practical purposes, are the most commonly used animals in laboratory experiments. It has been estimated that some 800 U.S. laboratories are not subject to federal law because they experiment exclusively on animals not covered by the AWA. A small bright spot for the animals in this is that the National Institutes of Health's *Guide for the Care and Use of Laboratory Animals* fills in some of the gaps left by the AWA, since it covers the treatment of rats, mice, and birds, and also cold-blooded vertebrates like Zebra fish—a current favorite for laboratory studies of pain and nerve function. The NIH *Guide* standards have become mandatory for all research facilities receiving federal funds.

It should also be noted that neither the AWA nor the NIH *Guide* counts farm animals as "animals" to be protected by some standards of treatment. This has been disastrous for the animals in factory farming and in agricultural experiments. We shall return to this.

Nor do the animal care committees (the IACUCs) offer the kind of protection and guidance one might have expected of them. The conceptual scheme that is often appealed to as a guide for animal research is commonly referred to as "the Three Rs": refinement of the methods to reduce pain, suffering, or distress; reduction of the number of animals used; and replacement of animals with non-animal alternatives. The IACUCs almost never raise questions of animal suffering—certainly never Larry Carbone's Big Question. The emphasis is almost exclusively on refinement, the technical details of how the experiment will be conducted and to make it more humane, not to raise questions about the need for the research proposal as such. Rarely is a proposal rejected outright for other than purely technical reasons. Whatever ethical perspectives may be raised they tend almost always to come from the committee's community member who is often a lone, and out-voted, voice on the committee. Too often, the care committee serves as a legitimizing cover for whatever experimental proposal is being reviewed (Mak 2009; Latham 2012).

Another major obstacle to looking at the ethical question is the nature and institutional functions of the funding process itself. Because the university receives a sizable chunk of the funding—frequently 50 percent in overhead—university administrators are not likely to turn down grants because of ethical scruples of some of their colleagues. And, although the university researchers themselves must use their share of the grant for the research and not for personal remuneration, they have to "publish or perish" and their careers turn on the publications produced by the completion of the research. In an analysis of the use of animals in research, scientists Ray Greek and Neall Shanks observe rather acidly: "Conducting animal studies is the most efficient way to generate a large number of papers in the shortest amount of time. It is far easier and faster to crank out five papers using animals than to conduct human-based research. The five papers may contribute nothing to ease human suffering, but that has never been a requirement for promotion" (Greek and Shanks, 96). The researchers are the last to want to endanger their funding.

In addition, there is often more than a little touch of fraud involved in the writing and submission of the research proposals themselves. The researchers are well aware of how the public, and with them Congress, are above all interested in new medical discoveries and cures. They are also aware that NIH primarily gives money for basic research with, on the face of it, no apparent health or medical applications. To enhance the appeal of their basic science proposals to Congress and the grant funding agencies, a constant temptation exists for researchers to suggest, hint strongly at, the potential of their basic science project to also have practical payoff for the advancement of health and medical science. Greek and Shanks comment: "Connecting basic research on animals to possible cures for humans is stock and trade for many researchers," and they quote two well-known researchers who wrote in 2008: "Many scientists who work on model organisms, including both of us, have been known to contrive a connection to human disease to boost a paper" (Greek and Shanks, 15).

Added to the drive for animal research funding from within the universities and research facilities themselves, is the huge influence of the multi-billion-dollar industry involving universities, entrepreneurs, pharmaceutical companies, animal breeders and suppliers of research equipment, and others. It is difficult not to see the entire interlocking, animal-research industry as a nearly unstoppable juggernaut—certainly not one in which ethical questions raised by individuals will be readily entertained.

The exact numbers of animals used, and in the end destroyed, in animal research are hard to come by—transparency is not a strong virtue of the animal research and experimentation industry. From what is known and can be reliably estimated, the numbers are staggering. Reports of animals used for research and testing in the United States alone for the year 2010, according to one tally, total more than 26 million. Mice, rats, fish, and birds—mostly mice and rats—make up about 96 percent of the total. The number for guinea pigs, rabbits, and hamsters for the same year is over 600,000. The number of primates, dogs, pigs, cats, and sheep is down somewhat from previous years but still is in the tens of thousands for each species. These are all low numbers since mandatory, self-reporting only applies to Animal Welfare Act, US Department of Agriculture, regulated species. So the total figures reported do not include large numbers of rats, mice, birds, or frogs. Moreover, some scientists count only the animals left in the final stages of the experiment, neglecting to report failures and discards along the way, or animals that have to be euthanized because the experiment was too invasive. In 2004, the laboratory veterinarian Larry Carbone, probably one of the most knowledgeable persons regarding laboratory research, wrote: "I believe my own observations are as accurate an estimate as any, and I believe that there were nearly 80 to 100 million laboratory rats and mice bred for research in the United States in 2002, and that number will continue to increase for several years" (Carbone, 25–27; Greek and Shanks, 11–12; United States Department of Agriculture, *Annual Report Animal Usage by Fiscal Year,* 2011). These figures are for the United States only, and similar numbers hold also for Canada and the United Kingdom, to say nothing about figures for the rest of the world. Carbone adds: "Of more concern than the raw numbers, of course, is what happens to those animals in the laboratories: their confinement, their pain and distress, their suffering, their deaths." Nearly all of these animals, when their ordeal is over, are killed.

2. SCIENCE

Along with ethical questions, serious scientific questions have been raised about one of the main reasons given for the use of animals in medical research: the use of animals as predictive models for human drug and disease response. In detailed analyses, the scientists Ray Greek and Niall Shanks have argued that the use of animals as predictive models for human drug and disease response is scientifically unreliable. As a result, they further conclude, billions of dollars of the public's tax dollars and charity gifts are being wasted on biomedical research models that have been shown to be futile. Other investigators concur with them (Greek and Shanks, passim; Pound et al., 514–7). Greek and Shanks are careful to point out that they are addressing one specific use of animals in biomedical research, to be sure a main one, but are not denying that some experimental use of animals can be validated scientifically—if not necessarily ethically; for instances, the use of animals as heuristic (interpretive) models for devising explanatory hypotheses, as a source of spare parts, as bioreactors, and so forth. Animal use, however, as predictive models for human medical responses is not scientifically valid because animals differ in many unpredictable ways from humans and from each other in their responses. Despite genome similarities to humans—and in the case of primates, it is quite high, with 95 percent to 99 percent similarity to the human genome, and often cited as justification for using animals as predictors—differences in physiology, biochemistry, organ functions and responses, all override any genomic similarities and make the animals extremely unreliable models for humans. These differences can result in wildly variant reactions to both illness and hoped-for treatments.

Greek and Shank give a number of examples. AIDS research provides a glaring example. During the past twenty-five years or so more than 85 HIV vaccines were developed that showed results in chimpanzees but failed in 200 human trials, and in one instance an HIV vaccine that proved effective in chimpanzees turned out to increase the likelihood of HIV infection in humans. In 2007, an HIV vaccine developed by Merck, using rhesus macaque monkeys, failed to protect against HIV in humans.

Another major example has to do with the history of the discovery of penicillin, which has actually been a matter of controversy since its discovery by Alexander Fleming in 1928. Fleming tested it *in vitro* first. The *in vitro* results showed promise so Fleming tried it on rabbits (the rabbits being mentioned specifically in his original paper). He found, however, that the rabbits metabolized it too quickly and was led to believe it would be useless for humans when administered systemically. In 1942 in a last desperate effort Fleming administered penicillin to a friend dying of streptococcal meningitis who dramatically recovered. The British scientist Howard Florey, friend of Fleming and later co-winner of the Nobel Prize for penicillin, administered penicillin to his sick cat at the same time Fleming was giving it to his sick friend. Florey's cat died. Greek and Shanks also observe that penicillin kills guinea pigs. They ask, "If you had been Fleming or Florey, or one of the other scientists, which species would you have believed? The dead cat? The rabbit that metabolized penicillin so rapidly? The guinea pigs or hamsters it would have killed had it been tested on them? Or the mice on which it worked?" Animals, Greek and Shanks conclude, could not then, nor can they now, be used to accurately and safely predict human responses to drugs and disease (Greek and Shanks, 70–71).

Thalidomide is another example of how differences in underlying biology make the predictive power of animal tests unreliable. Rats are highly resistant to exposure to thalidomide, while humans are extremely sensitive (Greek and Shanks, 92).

An example, often trotted out by defenders of the animal model is the development of the polio vaccine in the 1950s as prime evidence of the importance of animals in medical research. Since the early 1900s monkeys were used as the major animal for the study of polio. They showed the same lesions in the spinal cord as humans, and they could be infected by other monkeys, which ensured a steady supply of the virus. By the 1950s various vaccines had been tested on human children and monkeys with repeatedly unsuccessful results. But in the 1950s, however, Doctor Jonas Salk developed an injected vaccine and a co-scientist, Albert Sabine, developed an oral vaccine. An estimated 100,000 rhesus and macaques monkeys died in the process of developing Salk's vaccine.*

When the vaccine was developed it was tried out, first, on the monkeys and then on children living in homes for the mentally and physically disabled. After that it was tried on students of a Pittsburgh prep school and on Salk's own sons. The 100,000 monkeys involved died horrible deaths. When one thinks, however, of the millions of children worldwide, who have been spared the ravages of polio, was not the death of the monkey's well worth it? The development of the vaccine is often trumpeted as a prime example of the importance of animals in medical research.

The actual picture, however, is not so clear; in fact, it is much cloudier than commonly supposed. Greek and Shanks point out that, while the animals did provide a constant source of the virus

---

* A personal note: I grew up in a rural community in the 1950s. When summer arrived a certain atmosphere of background terror settled over the whole community—the fear of coming down with polio, especially when the local public swimming pool opened, which was thought to be one of the main breeding grounds for the polio virus. The fear of polio was a constant, especially among mothers who found it difficult to resist their children's clamoring to go swimming in the 100 degree plus Kansas summer. A further personal note: my wife grew up during these years in a small western Kansas town by the name of Protection. The pharmaceutical companies marketing the polio vaccine chose to launch their nationwide introduction of the vaccine at Protection, Kansas, under the slogan, "100 percent Protection!"

for research, the monkeys failed in many ways to accurately reflect human responses and were responsible for several major delays in the development of the vaccine. "But the worst thing to come out of animal studies," write Greek and Shanks, "was that scientists ignored human-based studies." This, they add was the climate at the time, and unfortunately still is (Greek and Shanks, 68). A final touch to this drama was that in 1984, about 30 years after he developed the oral vaccine, Dr. Albert Sabin testified under oath before the U.S. House of Representative that misleading animal models had actually delayed progress in the development of the polio vaccine (Greek and Shanks, 68).

Another shocking failure of the animal model was the prediction that cigarette smoking is safe, animal models having failed to provide evidence to the contrary. For decades, the tobacco industry was able to use the lack of prediction from animal models as justification of their claim that smoking did not cause cancer—despite overwhelming epidemiological evidence that it did (Greek and Shanks, 72).

Many drugs and substances, such as asbestos, Vioxx, Hormone Replacement Therapies, and others, tested safe in animals, but killed human beings. In 1998, the *Journal for the American Medical Association* estimated that at that time 106,000 people die in U.S. hospitals from reaction to drugs that had previously been tested on animals and approved by the Food and Drug Administration. This may have been a low figure because adverse drug reactions are underreported, and there is no reason to suppose that the number has declined significantly since then (Bekoff 2007, 141–2).

Animal modeling has also resulted in a whole new biomedical industry; namely, the use of genetic engineering to produce animals with certain diseases or disease tendencies to facilitate research. The extension of genetic engineering in the breeding of specially designed laboratory animals, especially rodents, has not been good news for the animals. Genetic engineering of mice and rats now takes a number of new directions. The aim is to develop animals as models for specific disease forms. *Transgenic* mice are genetically engineered to carry genes from another species.

So-called *knock-out* mice may have one or more of their genes removed to create a specific defect or disease proclivity in them. Correspondingly, *knock-in* mice have human genes, bone marrow, or stem cells introduced into them. One of the first steps taken in this field was to genetically engineer a line of mice with a special genetic predisposition to develop cancer. "Onco-mouse" was the name given to the first European patented model. Patenting animals adds another sticky layer to an already problematic enterprise. Transgenic rodents are now bred for a number of specific purposes, some selected not only for cancer, but also for immune system failure, cystic fibroses, gland tumors, obesity, and other assorted disorders.

The development of genetic engineering in designing animals for specific research purposes has meant, as Larry Carbone has noted, that any possible trend toward decreasing the number of animals has been drastically reduced, as universities and research institutions vie to increase their stocks of specially disease-designed rodents and mice. Genetic engineering has also meant that the animals' suffering has been heightened beyond measure. Their suffering, sometimes extreme, has been built into them from birth on.

We can wonder whether these genetically engineered creatures will be any more reliable predictors for human purposes than the non-engineered kind. Here I want simply to point to one issue raised by the creation of transgenic animals. Genetic engineering of rodents, especially, will lead not only to an increase in the number of laboratory animals, but also to a substantial expansion of the animals' suffering. In short, it means an enormous expansion in the meaning of *vivisection*. Animal researchers do not like to be known as vivisectionists. By any definition of the term, however, they are vivisectionists. Traditionally, vivisection has tended to be associated with cutting into the living flesh of animals, but even the ordinary dictionary definition broadens this definition. Vivisection, according to the American Heritage College Dictionary is, "The act or practice of cutting into or otherwise injuring living animals, especially for the purpose of scientific research." Nearly everything done in the laboratory involving the animals falls within this definition.

Now, with genetic engineering of lab animals, the scope of vivisection has been broadened beyond bounds. Vivisection now includes not only injuring an already-living body, but also ensuring that the body will, from its beginning, be a living injury. These transgenic rodents are fated to a double vivisection. First, they are condemned to a physical body intended *by design* to be a body of lifelong pain and suffering. And, second, while suffering in that body, they are fated to undergo countless intentional experimental injuries until the moment of their euthanasia. The deepest integrity of their bodies has been invaded and damaged before birth. Then, during their short lives they are further subjected to various experimental invasions, often again and again. Until the laboratory researchers are finished with him, getting cancer may be the least of "onco-mouse's" worries.

To be sure, many medical researchers are sensitive to the suffering they must inflict on large numbers of animals in order to carry out their experiments. Many of them are careful to alleviate as much of the animals' unavoidable suffering as possible. Even for them, however, the larger question is seldom asked, whether the amount and degree of animal suffering involved is worth whatever benefits may result from it. This is a question that remains pressing in light of the unreliability of the animal model for human drug and diseases responses. Many scientists, moreover, are conditioned by their professional training and culture to be agnostic about animal pain and suffering, or to deny it outright. Even if a researcher is fully cognizant of an animal's pain, he or she may feel it to be an essential sign of professional seriousness and objectivity to remain unmoved by it. The assumption that to show empathy or concern for an animal under experiment is unprofessional, anthropocentric, or simply sentimental, is deeply engrained in the institutional and professional culture, and difficult to transform (Rollin 1989).

Although it is nearly impossible for the interested and serious, ordinary citizen to gain access to animal research facilities, evidence, nevertheless, emerges regularly of the kind and extent of experiments being conducted within them. In many cases, the animal pain revealed is almost unbearable to contemplate. And in many experiments, as Singer observes, "despite the suffering the animal has gone through, the results obtained, even as reported by the experimenters themselves, are trivial, obvious, or meaningless" (Singer 2009, 49). And some of the examples we will look at betray more than a tinge of sadism, and sometimes even a kind of erotic frisson of pleasure in the exercise of power over the powerless.

Biomedical research is also conducted on larger animals. Texas A and M University conducts "alcohol research" on sheep and lambs. During these experiments, pregnant sheep are injected with alcohol—to a dosage of 9 to 10 shots of hard liquor—over the course of an hour. This is repeated to simulate weekend binge drinking in humans. Near the end of the pregnancies, the sheep with their babies are killed and the lamb's brains dissected to determine how maternal alcohol consumption affects fetal brain development. Critics have pointed out that the effects of alcohol on human fetal development are already well documented and that, furthermore, the animal models used are oversimplified and cannot adequately mimic "fetal alcohol disorder" in humans. A Dallas cardiologist has, therefore, asked, "After 17 years, can you give me an example of anything that has come from these experiments that has actually made an impact?" (Physicians Committee for Responsible Medicine [PCRM] 2014, 15). These alcohol experiments on sheep and lambs are also being carried out at Brown University, Loyola University, and more than 150 other university research facilities (PCRM, May 2014).

For two decades, Wayne State University has carried out "heart failure" experiments on dogs, collecting about $400,000 in funding every year. The dogs are subjected to various surgeries, and have multiple medical devices implanted in them. Then they are forced to run all the while on treadmills, and by other means have heart failure induced in them artificially. At the end of this ordeal the dogs are killed. "There's nothing to say for these experiments," comments cardiologist John Pippin, "except a pile of dead dogs... Modeling heart failure in animals has not proved its worth" (PCRM June 1913, 9; summer 2014, 16).

Ivy League universities are among the most culpable in the mistreatment of animals in their labs. Detailed studies by PCRM have documented blatant and repeated violations in the care and treatment of animals in the labs of eight Ivy League universities. These include Princeton University, University of Pennsylvania, Yale University, Harvard University, Cornell University, Brown University, Dartmouth College, and Columbia University. To these should be added non-ivy-league repeat violators, University of Kansas, University of Wisconsin, and Temple University, as well as others (National Anti-Vivisection Society [NAVS] 2012, 13; PCRM 2011,6–8).

Experiments involving mistreatment of animals at my own university, Columbia University, were revealed in 2001 by a whistleblower, a postdoctoral veterinary fellow at Columbia, who was appalled by what she found in the lab. Being a university associated veterinarian, she was one of the few not on the research team who had access to the lab. The animals, baboons, she discovered had been subjected to experiments in the treatment of stroke. The experimenter, an assistant professor of neurosurgery, had artificially induced strokes in the animals by removing their left eyeballs and, using the empty eye sockets to reach a critical blood vessel to the brain, clamped it off. The intended purpose was to attempt to then treat the resulting stroke with an experimental drug. What the veterinarian found were creatures left over the weekend in their cages, hunched over, unable to drink or lift their heads and without veterinary care. They were also left with inadequate anesthesia, in spite of the fact that eye removal is so painful that human eye surgeons routinely give morphine to their patients for up to three days after the surgery. Neurologists have commented that such artificially induced strokes are useless for understanding strokes in humans, which have altogether different causes, such as predisposing conditions like arteriosclerosis, high blood pressure and diabetes. Dr. Carl Van Petten, neurologist at the University of Southern California, said of the Columbia stroke experiments, "There is very little probability that this study or others like it, will produce results that will help in the prevention or treatment of stroke in humans." Another neurologist, a Stanford professor, said that the experience for the animals was extremely painful and "obviously terrifying, and useless" (Akhtar).

When once looked into, it appeared that Columbia's animal experiments had been going on for many years. Monkeys had had metal pipes surgically implanted in their heads to study the effects of stress on women's menstrual cycles. In experiments extending over two decades experimenters at Columbia had been pumping nicotine and morphine into pregnant baboons strapped inside their metal cages to see the effect on the fetal infant. A letter to the President of Columbia, inquiring about what had come to light, received the not surprising answer from a university public relations staff member with the assurance that Columbia was conducting an internal investigation to correct any mistreatment of animals, and that it would continue using animals for medical research because "research on life threatening catastrophic diseases such as stroke is necessary for improving health and finding new cures for these crippling diseases" (private correspondence).

This appeal to possible health benefits as a justification for unlimited animal experimentation does not seem to go away. It gets hauled out again and again. And the universities never apologize. The noted bioethicist, Daniel Callahan, has shown that the same appeal repeatedly serves as an imperative justifying all kinds of dubious experiments on humans. What he says about defending proposed research on humans because it just might have health benefits, applies equally as well to animal experimentation:

> The proposed research is called morally obligatory, and it is either said or implied that the chosen research is the only or the incontestably superior way to go; its proponents dismiss the critics of the research as ignorant, fearful, or biased and make only superficial changes to mollify them; and when the research fails to pan out or is slow in coming, they take that to show that more research money is needed or that ethical hand-wringing and groundless anxieties have stood in its way. (Callahan, 177)

Medical schools have for decades used animals, especially dogs, goats, and pigs, for surgical training of their students. Often these animals have been obtained from shelters. A note of good news is that out of scores of medical schools that once used animals for training in surgery and trauma response, only about 25 medical schools now use animals for these purposes. The others have found—mainly through the efforts of such animal welfare organizations as the Physicians Committee for Responsible Medicine—that live animals can be replaced by much more effective, artificial human simulators. Still among the medical schools that continue to use animals for surgery training are the prestigious University of Tennessee Health Science Center, University of Mississippi Medical Center, Johns Hopkins University, and Rush Medical College.

3. PSYCHOLOGICAL EXPERIMENTATION AND MILITARY INTELLIGENCE

Among the strictly medical researchers, psychologists have also been very much involved in animal research. In appealing for funds and for public support, they, too, use the same type of argument as their medical colleagues; namely, that psychological experiments on animals promise benefits for the understanding and treatment of humans, in this case, the human psyche. This is the same "human benefit" argument with which we are familiar. It is difficult to know whether at a deeper level pure "scientific curiosity" is not just as powerful a motivating force in many scientific animal experimenters: "How will the animals respond if we do this to them; how, if we do that?" This kind of question seems to be very strong among the psychologists. Whatever their justification for animal research, the psychologists have moved in force into the field.

As early as 1950, Harry Harlow, professor of psychology at the University of Wisconsin, was developing what came to be called "maternal deprivation" studies, and, later, "depression" studies, both using infant rhesus and macaque monkeys. One of his earliest studies, as Jean Kazez describes it, was to separate infant monkeys from the mothers and keep them in wire cages with a choice between two mother surrogates, one a wire frame with a bottle to feed from, the other a wire frame simply covered with a soft terry cloth. Harlow and his colleagues found that the baby monkeys went for the bottle for only about an hour and spent the rest of the day clinging to the cloth mother. This was thought to show "the importance of tactile comfort to rhesus monkeys, and therefore (by analogy) to human infants" (Kazez, 142). Then Harlow and his colleagues wanted to know what would happen if the surrogate mothers were made even more unpleasant, and they set about to create a variety of "monster mothers." Peter Singer quotes from an article Harlow and his colleague wrote in which they describe how they had the "fascinating idea" of inducing depression by "allowing the baby monkeys to attach to the cloth surrogate mothers who could become monsters." The following passage is quoted by Singer from their article.

> The first of these monsters was a cloth monkey mother who, upon schedule or demand, would eject high-pressure compressed air. It would blow the animal's skin practically off its body. What did the baby monkey do? It simply clung tighter to the mother, because a frightened infant clings to its mother at all costs. We did not achieve any psychopathology. However, we did not give up. We built another surrogate mother that would rock so violently that the baby's head and teeth would rattle. All the baby did was cling tighter and tighter to the surrogate. The third monster we built had an embedded wire frame within its body that would spring forward and eject the infant from its ventral surface. The infant would subsequently pick itself off the floor, wait for the frame to return into the cloth body, and then cling again to the surrogate. Finally, we built our porcupine mother. On command, this mother would eject sharp brass spikes all over the ventral surface of its body. Although the infants were distressed by these pointed rebuffs, they simply waited until the spikes receded and then returned and clung to the mother. (Singer 2009, 33)

They didn't stop there. As Singer describes further, they decided to create a real monkey mother who was a monster. They reared female monkeys in isolation, but because these monkeys did not have normal sexual relations with males, they had to be made pregnant by a technique they referred to as a "rape rack."

When the babies were born the mother either ignored them and their cries to feed at the breast, or they killed them in ways that were brutal.

Then after these experiments on abuse and deprivation, Harlow and his colleague began to develop experiments on depression. They designed a literal "well of despair" to reproduce the state of depression that they described as a state of "helplessness sunken in a well of despair." They built a vertical stainless steel chamber with a rounded bottom in which they placed a young monkey for periods of up to 45 days. They described the confinement as producing "severe and persistent psychopathological behavior of a depressive sort" (ibid., 34). In another article they wrote of how they had gone further to create a "tunnel of terror" in order to produce terrified baby monkeys.

Why this attention to Harlow's work? There should be good reasons for dismissing it today. It was carried out in the 1950s and early 60s before the passage of the Animal Welfare Act. His work has actually been very influential, cited in countless college psychology textbooks, but it has also been criticized, not only by animal welfare advocates, but also by fellow psychologists. The criticisms have been made on various grounds. First of all, and most striking, is that human studies of orphaned babies predated the animal studies and had already shown the importance of infant and maternal touch. The monkey studies added nothing. The monkey studies have also been criticized for faulty scientific procedures and interpretations.

Why, then, give attention to them here? Again, for several important reasons. First of all, Harlow's studies were an inspiration to other psychologists. Singer points out that Harlow inspired over 250 such experiments like his in the U.S. in the following years. These included rhesus monkeys, chimpanzees, dogs, cats, and, of course, thousands of hapless rodents, all of which were subjected to every variation of maternal deprivation, separation, and isolation experiments. "These experiments," writes Singer, "subjected over seven thousand animals to procedures that induced distress, despair, general psychological devastation, and death" (ibid., 36).

And, yet, the pressure to perpetuate them continues. In the summer of 2014, at the University of Wisconsin, a proposal was accepted by the university animal care committee (the IACUC) to deprive newborn monkeys of their mothers in a renewal of the maternal deprivation experiments. The protocol was accepted over the objection of two committee members, including the University of Wisconsin bioethicist, who was also chair of the IACUC. The experiment will involve 20 infant monkeys removed from their mothers at birth and a control group of 20 other, mother-raised monkeys. For a year the motherless monkeys will be given tests to provoke and measure anxious behavior. "Provoke" here means inducing anxiety by frightening the young and isolated monkeys with live snakes, and other shocks. Then they will all be killed and their brain tissue analyzed for molecular analysis. "Our hope," says psychology professor Kalin, the research director, "is that we're going to come up with both new medication strategies as well as new psychotherapy strategies" (Wisconsin Center). The study has been granted NIH funding for over 500,000 dollars.

Although the University of Wisconsin seems to receive special funding attention, many other research institutions also conduct maternal deprivation type experiments with baby monkeys. For thirty years the Laboratory of Comparative Ethology, part of the National Institutes of Health (NIH), has conducted maternal deprivation experiments on hundreds of monkeys under the head researcher, Stephen Suomi, Harlow's student and original collaborator. Many of the monkeys in his lab are intentionally bred for increased likelihood of psychopathology, with some being separated from their mothers 24 hours after birth and made to undergo trauma-producing experiences. Jane Goodall has said of these experiments:

> These experiments are unjustifiable from every perspective. They cause baby monkeys crippling emotional trauma, they have never lead to or improved treatments of human mental illness, and they are superseded by modern non-animal research methods that are actually relevant to humans. It's shocking that NIH has allowed these studies to continue for 30 years, but they can't go on any longer. (King)

American psychologists also developed a line of research intended to create in animals what they call "learned helplessness." In the 1950s Harvard psychologists placed forty dogs in a device called a "shuttlebox," a divided cage separated by a barrier. High intensity electric shocks were delivered to the dogs' feet, which, not surprisingly, caused the dogs to jump over the barrier to escape. Then to prevent the dogs escaping the shocks a glass barrier was placed between the two sides of the box and the dogs were again tested. The dogs repeatedly smashed their heads against the glass barrier, while showing symptoms of great distress, such as "defecation, urination, yelping, trembling, and so on. Finally the dogs gave up and did nothing to escape the shocks." The psychologists called this, "learned helplessness." Professor Martin Seligman of the University of Pennsylvania continued similar experiments, with further "refinements," developing from them a theory that identified "learned helplessness" as a cause of human depression. Other psychologists, following Seligman, continued over the years to develop the "helplessness effect," submitted a variety of animals to electric shocks, from fish to cats and, even at the University of Kansas, ponies. The theory linking "learned helplessness" to human depression has been pretty thoroughly discredited by critics, and, in fact, Seligman himself eventually abandoned the theory (Singer 2009, 45–50; Kazez, 114; Hartman).

The idea of "learned helplessness" did not go away, however, nor did the psychologists associated with it, including Seligman himself. They did reappear, however, in a probably unexpected place. In the summer of 2014, James Risen, a New York Times investigative reporter, published a book in which he reveals the widespread involvement of psychologists, and of the American Psychology Association (APA) itself, in the CIA's "enhanced interrogation" program after 9/11. Seligman is a former president of the APA. Risen documents the existence of "a tight network of behavioral scientists [mainly psychologists] so eager for CIA and Pentagon contracts that they showed few qualms about getting involved with institutions that were using pseudo behavioral science to brutalize prisoners." The information that has emerged, says Risen, helps "reveal the close relationship between behavioral scientists and the government that made it easier for the CIA and Pentagon to develop such a large detention and interrogation infrastructure so quickly" (Risen 2014, 192–197).

The 2014 report by the Senate Intelligence Committee on CIA and Pentagon "enhanced interrogation" further documents the participation of the AMA psychologists in it. The Senate Report quotes one high-ranking military psychologist in urging the application of "the full range of harsh interrogation measures" as saying that this would "produce the desired level of helplessness." The CIA, with the psychologists' help, also equipped one detention center, and perhaps more than one, with what was called "the salt pit," an isolation chamber in which at least one prisoner subsequently died. It is striking how the language used by the interrogators echoes almost verbatim that of the psychologists in their university experiments, and with the "salt pit" even harks back to the isolation "pit of despair" in which Harlow put baby monkeys (*New York Times,* "Senate Report," Dec. 10, 2014).

The APA went so far as to alter its ethics rules in order to give professional cover to psychologists who had been helping monitor and oversee interrogations. The most important change in the APA guidelines was to say that if a psychologist was caught in a conflict between the APA code of ethics and the law of the government, he (and it was usually a he) could follow the law rather than the ethics. In other words, the APA went against the Nuremberg principle, which said that personal and professional ethical convictions should in some cases take precedence over "following orders." Today, a chastened APA is now attempting an independent review of its collusion with or in support of the use of torture in the interrogation of prisoners during the Bush administration, Shortly after 9/11 Seligman had held a meeting in his home with a group of academics and national security officials. In following years, however, he has said, according to Risen, that "he was later horrified to discover that his work on learned helplessness had been used as the doctrinal basis for the interrogation program" (Risen 2014, 2015b, 2015c; *New York Times,* Nov. 14, 2014, A6).

This little excursion into the collaboration between U.S. military and intelligence agencies and psychologists with a history of animal torture might seem to have only tangential relevance to our larger consideration of animal welfare and animal experimentation. But it is directly relevant—and revelatory—for at least one main reason. It demonstrates how lack of compassion and common decency in relationship to animals translates effortlessly into similar attitudes toward human beings. It is further validation, if any were needed, of the warnings of early anti-vivisectionists, going back a couple of hundred years, that inflicting such experimentation on animals would quickly pave the way for like experimentation on humans, especially on the vulnerable and those deemed inferior. As C. S. Lewis prophesied years ago in an article on vivisection, "no argument for experiments on animals can be found that is not also an argument for experiments on inferior men. If we cut up beasts simply because they cannot prevent us and because we are backing up our own side in the struggle for existence, it is only logical to cut up imbeciles, criminals, enemies, or capitalists for the same reason" (quoted, Linzey 1994, 95).

If humans have no unique responsibility for the weak and helpless animals, if we can experiment on them in any way we want and are able, then this "might makes right" ethic can be turned upon all defenseless, vulnerable beings, including human beings. And we have seen, just as the early anti-vivisectionists said we would, that there have repeatedly been experiments on both human and animal subjects, and always upon the weak, the defenseless, and those defined as inferior. For more than a century, which has seen, in Andrew Linzey's words, "the most sustained and ruthless use of animals in scientific research," there has also been repeated instances of experiments on Jews, people of color, prisoners of war, the mentally ill, embryos, and children, especially poor and orphaned children (recall the poor children on whom the polio vaccine was first tried out). The popular ethic that asks—accusatorily—of animal defenders, "How can you be concerned about animal suffering when so many human beings in the world are suffering?" turns out to be not only thoughtlessly conventional, but also shortsighted, with the most dire of consequences. The lack of compassion in the one realm is part and parcel of the same lack in the other (Linzey 2013, 21; Lederer 1995; Goliszek).

4. MILITARY–ANIMAL RELATIONSHIP

When we turn directly to the military–animal relationship as such, we find a highly undiluted expression of the view that animals exist solely for the satisfaction of human desires. We need not dwell at any length on the military use of animals beyond a few, telling examples. After having learned from a newspaper ad in 1973 that the US. Military was planning to purchase, as subjects for a nerve gas test, hundreds of beagle puppies, with their vocal cords tied to prevent barking, Representative Les Aspin of Wisconsin campaigned successfully to force the Department of Defense to replace the beagles with other experimental animals. Another personal note: Before the time of Les Aspin's campaign I had the dismal experience of being present in the late 1950s on a military base in Maryland just as a poison gas test had ended with some two score or more of beagle puppies laid out on the ground in various stages of seizure and dying. Aspin's efforts, however, did not end the military's other experiments on either beagle dogs or monkeys, and other experimental animals (Singer 2009).

The history of military experiments and other use of animals is long and many-sided. It has been estimated that the military kills more than 10,000 live animals in combat and trauma training every year. Animals have been subjected to radiation, rifle and explosive wounds, temperature extremes, and poisons, among other things. Pigs and goats have been favorites for training in various battlefield surgical techniques, and have had inflicted on them, accordingly, limb fractures, amputations, burning, hemorrhaging, and wounds of various kinds. The University of Wisconsin (again!) has been funded for twenty years by the U.S. Navy for the study of decompression sickness. Many other examples exist of the government (military and police) colluding with academics and industry to conduct painful, death-dealing experiments of dubious value on animals. One recent instance (2004) involved a professor at the University of Wisconsin (!), who, with the support of a $500,000 grant from the Department of Justice, attached electrodes to the skin of pigs and opened their sternums to insert taser darts or catheters near their hearts to measure the effects of Taser shocks. A variation of this experiment was a little later performed by a professor at the University of Missouri in Columbia. This experiment also had the support of the manufacturer of Tasers. Live pigs were electrocuted to death with very high charges of electricity to show that Tasers, with lower charges, are safe when used on humans (Bekoff 2007, 141; "stopanimaltests").

Animal protection groups, such as the Physicians Committee for Responsible Medicine, have been leading campaigns to end the use of live animals in combat and trauma training by the use of more effective, cruelty-free medical, simulation methods, such as, for example, the "cut suit" designed for trauma training, which accurately replaces the experience of emergency procedures on a living victim. Also, to its credit, the Department of Defense has issued guidelines for *Use of Animals in DoD Programs*, although it is not clear to what extent these are followed (Finkelmeyer; *PETA's Animal Times* 2012; PCRM 2014). The Navy continues to conduct sonar tests in whale breeding and birthing ocean areas, in spite of the fact that it disorients the animals and may be responsible for large whale beachings and death. The military has enlisted at least 1800 dogs for protection, pursuit, tracking and search and rescue, and bomb-sniffing detection. A number of these have been killed in action. Some good things can at least be said about the use of these dogs: It is a use of the animals that has some clear meaning and purpose; and the dogs and their soldier handlers seem sometimes to establish close, mutually protective relationships—although a number of these dogs have also been abandoned when their handlers were sent home (*New York Times*, May 12, 2011).

5. MICE AND RATS AGAIN

The suffering of larger animals, such as dogs and apes, quickly and easily arouses our sympathy. But the little animals, mice and rats especially, that make up 99 percent of laboratory animals deserve at least equal attention. From the standpoint of the experimenter they make the ideal lab animal: they are intelligent and readily learn puzzle-solving tasks that can be useful in research; they are not covered, along with birds, fish, and farm animals, under the Animal Welfare Act, which makes it easier not to attend to their suffering; they are relatively inexpensive to acquire and to house; they can be designed to order—engineered, for example, to be obese or to have specific disease proclivities; they are defenseless and easily controlled and manipulated; and they are in full supply, easily acquired, easily used, and easily disposed of—some 80 to 100 million of them each year. Moreover, they do not motivate the larger public, apart from a relatively few, vexatious animal advocates, to inquire what is going on in the labs, since the public regards them anyway mainly as vermin, preferably to be exterminated. Ethologist Marc Bekoff sums up their fate: "The vast majority of these animals live most of their lives in extremely small cages, bored and lonely, and they will die in the lab when researchers are done with them; almost all are killed by researchers either deliberately, because dissecting them is part of the research and sacrificing them outright clears the way for naïve new subjects, or as an unintended consequence, because the animals just couldn't cope with what was being done to them" (Bekoff 2007, 139).

Joel Marks, Professor of Philosophy Emeritus at New Haven University and a Bioethics Center scholar at Yale University has made a small, detailed analysis of animal experiments cited in a major book on neuroscience research. Among the experiments are those that involve damaging areas of an animal's brain through surgery or the administration of drugs in rodents, apes, and frogs to see the effects on the animals' behavior. Sleep deprivation experiments were also performed. At one point, for instance, Marks quotes the book's author as describing "a grisly set of experiments with rats," which "showed that total sleep deprivation will cause death in three to four weeks." After his survey of a whole range of such experiments, Marks concludes, "The laboratory for medical or basic research is a horror house for rodents and nonhuman primates." And he goes on further to observe that never is there any expression on the part of the experimenters or of the scientist reporting on them of feeling for the animals, and certainly no sense of gratitude for them or recognition of the moral debt owed to the animals for the harm done to them (Marks, 6–8).

The ethologist Jonathan Balcome relates an experiment that has a double, albeit ironic, significance. Scientists sought to determine if mice show evidence of empathy in witnessing the pain in other mice. They injected painful irritants into the stomach and paws of mice and then put them into a clear, plastic tube where their writhing response could be observed. Other mice could also watch their writhing and showed clear signs of recognizing and responding to the others' pain. The scientists also observed that the mice exhibited the sympathetic reaction only if they knew the writhing mouse. This difference in response, the scientists concluded, showed that the mice weren't simply expressing an automatic reaction to pain as such, but seemed to have a close empathic relationship to family and friends. At the end of the experiment, all the mice, as usual, were killed, some hundreds of them (Balcombe, 131–132). The irony is clear: a total lack of empathy among the humans trying to demonstrate empathy in mice by causing excruciating pain to other mice. One cannot help wondering how they were able to recognize it when they saw it.

6. Animal Confinement

In discussing the natural enjoyment the animal takes in its bodily nature and experience, Rudolf Steiner remarks that the animal seldom injures itself because the wisdom in its body and soul leads it usually to the right food, to the right shelter, and so forth. "The animal," he says, "injures itself very much less than it is injured by man." And he adds, "Animals are injured most of all when man keeps them in captivity" (Steiner 1910a). The harm done to animals by keeping them in captivity today is especially acute in three main areas of our treatment of them: in the research and experiment lab; in zoos, circuses, and other displays of animals for our entertainment; and in the high-density containment of animals in factory farming. We will look at the effects of captivity on animals in the second and third of these areas. We need first to conclude our review of animal experimentation to briefly take account of the confinement of animals in the laboratory, an issue often neglected even by persons otherwise deeply sensitive to the animals' suffering in the experiments themselves.

Perhaps among the most qualified persons to speak to this issue is Bernard E. Rollin, professor of animal science, professor of bioethical sciences, and university bioethicist at Colorado State University. His book, *The Unheeded Cry: Animal Consciousness, Animal Pain, and Science* is considered by many a classic. Rollin eloquently describes the confinement situation of experimental laboratory animals:

> Even if, as the research community claims, the vast majority of experiments performed on animals do not cause significant pain, 100 percent of research animals suffer because the environments in which they are kept fail to respect their biological and psychological needs or natures. Social animals are kept in isolation; nocturnal animals are kept in twenty-four-hours-a-day light; housing and husbandry conditions are designed in accordance with human convenience, not animals' needs. Cage design is primarily determined by ease of cleaning, not animal comfort. Appallingly, even the death of the animals in the service of research is not the most painless and comfortable death possible. The vast majority of animals do not get a "good death"; asphyxiation or suffocation by inhaled carbon dioxide is by no stretch of the imagination humane, despite its being approved by the American Veterinary Medical Association. (Rollin 2012)

He goes on to show that suffering is much more than just physical pain—it includes separation from family and other animals of the same species, denial of opportunities to move and to play, unnatural diets, stress, boredom, and so on (Rollin 2012).

7. BIOMEDICAL ANIMAL EXPERIMENTATION: CONCLUDING REFLECTIONS: RUDOLF STEINER AND OTHERS

Can a compelling case be made for biomedical-animal experimentation? And so we come back to the "big ethical question": "Do we have the right to use animals in research and experimentation at all?" In many respects the entire biomedical-animal experimentation enterprise has been so compromised as to make a simple and unequivocal "yes" answer extremely difficult. Most of these compromising aspects we have looked at. One is the use of the concept and practice of "experimentation" itself as a legal protection should the use of a new product or medicine go awry. Legal protection means in this instance that experimentation has primarily a "value function," that is, a monetary purpose. To this is added the massive weight of many other, intertwining monetary interests that seek to profit from animal experimentation: industry, especially the pharmaceutical, universities, the public, politicians, science, and the media. Further compromising the whole enterprise has been the unreliability of animal models for predicting human drug and disease response, as well as the many experiments that turn out patently useless, trivial, or obvious. A further compromising factor has been the lack of affect on the part of many scientists—an absence of feeling and compassion for their lab animals. And, not least as a compromising factor is the well-documented and widespread abuse and neglect of animals in many laboratories, and their treatment as mere things and disposable commodities. In addition to all this stands the fact that, while America engages in the most excessive destruction of animals "for the benefit of humanity," it has the lowest lifespan of all Western nations.

We can, however, approach our big ethical question from the other direction and ask if a compelling case cannot still be made for some animal experimentation for human benefit. Granted, the whole undertaking is human, and, accordingly, has its full complement of human foibles and self-seeking motives. Are there not, then, outweighing the negative, also some positive and beneficial aspects in the effort to serve humanity with the help (coerced, to be sure—they don't get to give their consent) of the animals? Do not humans have a first moral responsibility to their own kind, lest human morality, as the primatologist Frans de Waal has feared, "unravel very rapidly indeed if it failed to place human life at its core?" (de Waal 1996, 215). And, finally, are there not medical researchers who take every step necessary to ensure 1) that the potential benefit of a proposed experimental protocol has been established beyond doubt; 2) that alternatives to animals are not available; and 3) that every effort is made to provide proper anesthetics and analgesics, palliative treatment for pain, and "painless euthanasia" (Redmond; Miller; Ringach). Assuming that all possible care and consideration for the animal subjects are taken, can some animal experimentation for poten- tial, human medical benefit be ethically justified in the end? Let us see how various people, including Rudolf Steiner, might deal with this question.

We need to bear in mind, as fundamental to all that fol- lows, Rudolf Steiner's description of the animals' experience of pain. Recall his description of the difference between the animal and the human in this regard. Because the soul of the animal is intimately connected with the animal's physical body, the animal feels physical pain much more deeply and more com- pletely, throughout its whole being, than the human being usu- ally does. This, Steiner remarks, is especially the case with the higher animals, which for him seem to include in this context, the vertebrates and increasing in intensity, on up the phyloge- netic scale through the mammals. The human in comparison is freed enough from the physical body to be able consciously to understand better the reasons for the pain and also to an extent to bring to bear inner forces of consciousness in alleviating the pain. For the human, of course, this is all relative, depending on the nature and intensity of the pain; but, even having the possibility of understanding, and of inner transformation, is not something the animal has available.

Recall Steiner's words quoted earlier: "Those who main- tain that human pain can be more intense than the pain felt by animals are talking without foundation. Pain in the animal is far, far more deep-seated than purely bodily pain in man can be" (Steiner 1910a). The anthroposophic medical doctor, Werner Hartinger, has summed up this understanding of animal pain:

> Animals experience joy with the whole body and show it in the way they express it, and they experience pain not only at the point where it is inflicted. The whole animal is seized by the pain, and because it lacks the intellectual capacity to understand what is going on this pain is magnified into an unbearable fear of death, which no one realizing this would have been prepared to inflict. (Hartinger, 73)

The whole animal, in the lab and on the factory farm, is subjected to an entire lifetime of unrelenting, all-consuming pain. The ethical question becomes ever-more pressing: Do the benefits justify the torturing to death of millions of animals? For factory-farmed animals the answer is simple: the pain and death of these animals cannot be justified. For animals used in biomedical research, however, the answer is not so clear.

How do some of the animal advocates we have looked at regard animal biomedical research? A few are thoroughgoing absolutists, finding no justification for it at all. Their answer to the big ethical question is that the suffering of animals in the labs is out of all proportion to whatever medical benefits are obtained. This is the position taken by animal advocates such as Tom Regan, Gary Francione, and Joel Marks. Peter Singer's portrayal of the suffering inflicted on animals in the laboratory was a major influence in awakening significant numbers of people to the travails undergone by millions of lab animals. Singer himself, however, is not an absolutist rejecting all medical research on animals. Singer's utilitarianism—calculating costs and benefits, balancing suffering and pleasure—does provide some openings for at least limited biomedical animal research. As a good utilitarian he says, that "if one, or even a dozen animals had to suffer experimentation in order to save thousands, I would think it right and in accordance with equal consideration of interest that they should do so" (Singer 1980, 58). But this opening does become a rather large gap, for, as we have noted, his emphasis on "self-awareness" as a deciding principle for what beings count in the utilitarian calculus leads him to justify the killing of babies (infanticide) within one month of age before self-awareness can develop. And it opens the gates to experimenting on, and even killing other, weaker human beings lacking in self-awareness. Thus Singer seems to add confirmation to the contention of C.S. Lewis that animal experimentation leads inevitably to experiments on vulnerable humans, though Singer himself would seem to resist this radical extension of permitted experimental subjects (Singer 2000, 323).

Another approach to animal, biomedical experimentation is that of the Anglican theologian, Andrew Linzey, whom we have already met. Linzey is not an absolutist against all biomedical experimentation, but he is firm in insisting that the ethical question and an ethical concern be kept at the center at all times. Many possibilities exist in nearly all aspects of the human–animal relationship to sidestep or divert discussion of the ethical issues. Central to the ethical question, for Linzey, is, of course, the reality of animal pain. On this, Linzey is close to Rudolf Steiner and Dr. Hartinger in their assessment of animal pain:

> There is ample evidence in peer-reviewed scientific journals that all mammals at least experience not just physical pain but also mental suffering, including terror, stress, fear, anxiety, trauma, anticipation, and foreboding, and that only to a lesser or greater degree than we do ourselves. (Linzey 2007, 5; Rollin 1989)

Linzey is very clear about the centrality of the ethical issue. "What is not legitimate in my view," he writes, "is the infliction of suffering on some animals to benefit others (either humans or other animals), and in so doing to simply use them as means to an end, even a laudable one" (Linzey 2013, 156).

As a Christian theologian, Linzey derives his ethics from his understanding of the divine-human–animal relationship. Animal rights and human rights are all an expression in his understanding of "God's rights" (*Theos-Rights*, in the term he has coined).

As the creator of the Earth and all its creatures, God's right is preeminent—his right to have all his creatures' rights respected and protected. Animals are, like us, God's creatures, and so, "we have no absolute right over them, only the duty to look after them as God would look after them" (Linzey 2000, 12). God's care is expressed, for Linzey, in Christ, the being of love who privileges the poor, the oppressed, the weak and vulnerable. The animals are among the most innocent and most vulnerable. The animals are those least able to give their consent to being experimented upon, unlike human beings for whom the giving of consent to any experimental procedure is a legal requirement, or for whom special legal provision is made for those humans unable to give consent. The animals are totally helpless before the experimenters.

Linzey, however, does not accept the view that humans and animals are equals morally or intelligently. This, however, actually heightens in his view our responsibility for looking after them. Our special value as a species in Linzey's view consists in our being of special value for others, including the animals. While he is not an absolutist in rejecting all animal experimentation, his theological and ethical commitments demand the most stringent and responsible limitations on what is permissible. He rejects utterly the common and comfortable attitude that easily justifies all animal experimentation because it just might benefit humans. The idea that scientific curiosity ought also to rule supreme, allowing nothing to stand in its way, is deeply ingrained in modern consciousness, so much so that it functions as an untouchable doctrine in the scientific belief system. This Linzey also rejects. The lure of possible medical benefits joined with satisfying the itch of scientific curiosity together make possible the rationalization of any and all animal experimentation. "If we are to have ethical science," Linzey writes, "then it must be a science that recognizes certain moral constraints. Not everything that could be done, should be done" (Linzey 2000, 95). The anthoposophical doctor, Werner Hartinger, expresses the same conviction: "An immoral action does not become morally acceptable through being justified as serving one's own requirements or classified as 'scientifically necessary'" (Hartinger, 62).

What then can we conclude about Rudolf Steiner's position on animal biomedical research? For Steiner the human being is responsible for all the suffering he or she causes other beings, humans and animals. Steiner emphasizes this especially in relationship to the esoteric understanding that the human being after death must undergo a period of soul purification in which cravings and desires that would obstruct the individual's spiritual progress must be eliminated. This also involves living through and experiencing the suffering we have caused others as our own suffering. Steiner borrows the Indian term, *Kamaloca,* "the region of desire," as shorthand for this period of soul purification. The Kamaloca experience brings out unmistakably our responsibility for the animals as well as for other human beings, and for the suffering we cause both. Steiner writes:

> Consciously or *unconsciously,* intentionally or *unintentionally,* he [the human being] causes pleasure and pain, joy and sorrow, to animals and men. All such occasions he will encounter again as he lives through the Kamaloka period; he returns to the place and moment when he was the cause of pain to another being. At that time he made someone else feel pain; now he has to suffer the same pain in his own soul. All the torment I ever caused to other beings I now have to live through in my own soul. I enter into the person or the *animal* [my italics] and come to know what the other being was made to suffer through me; now I have to suffer all these pains and torments myself. There is no way of avoiding it.... A vivisectionist has a particularly terrible life in Kamaloka. (Steiner 1970, 30–1)

Steiner puts the practice of vivisection in its historical context. Until the rise of the modern mechanistic worldview many traditional cultures maintained a deep respect and reverence for nature and its creatures, with injunctions and divine commandments to care for the animals and to avoid inflicting gratuitous cruelty upon them. The rise of the mechanical worldview, however, eliminated all vestiges of the sacred and any connection with the feeling heart of the cosmos. The consequent view of the animal as an unfeeling machine resulted in the relatively sudden practice and spread of vivisection among many scientific circles.

"In this way," observes Steiner, "we come to understand it, but we should never excuse or justify it."

> The consequences of a life that has been the cause of pain to others are bound to follow, and after death the vivisectionist has to endure the same pain he inflicted on animals. His soul is drawn into every pain he caused. It is no use saying that to inflict pain was not his intention, or that he did it for the sake of science or that his purpose was good. The law of spiritual life is inflexible. (Steiner 1970, 31)

We have already seen how, since Steiner wrote, animal experimenters have been exceedingly inventive in devising ever-new forms of vivisection and in expanding its scope through genetic engineering to encompass the whole of an animal's life. Of course, the prospects of a period of purification after death are of little concern to the experimenter, whose mechanistic and materialistic assumptions rule out such a thing from the start. For his own part, however, Steiner's description of an inexorable experience of Kamaloca, whether we believe in it or not, underscores his insistence on our responsibility for the animals and how we treat them.

In this light, it would seem that Steiner would be opposed to animal experimentation of any kind, including biomedical research for potential, human benefit. However, at one point there does seem to be an opening in his thought for some careful consideration of animal biomedical experimentation. This appears at the beginning of his discussion of vegetarianism and meat eating. Steiner is adamant that vegetarianism is not a requirement for being an anthroposophist or for membership in the Anthroposophical Society. This is fully in keeping with his emphasis on individual freedom and his insistence that the Anthroposophical Society be a completely open society. He says, in fact, that for some people—a relatively small number—some meat eating may be necessary for their health. This is not Steiner's last word on meat eating, which we will look at in much more detail later. But, at this point—allowing that meat eating may be necessary for the health of a small number of individuals—Steiner clearly puts genuine human need above the claims of the animal. Steiner does not hold, however, that medical advance in itself justifies the torture and death of millions of animals. If some experiment must be carried out then the reasons for it must be clear and compelling, and the most stringent and humane conditions and procedures must be followed. The burden of proof, for establishing a compelling case for the experiment and the humane means of conducting it, rests upon the experimenter. Given the uncritical, popular pressure for any possibility of medical advance, given the extremes to which vivisection has been developed and practiced, and given all the ways, as we have seen, in which the medical experimentation enterprise has been compromised, by itself and by various vested interests—the odds against the experimenters being able to successfully meet that burden of proof are high indeed.

2.

Wild Animals

Every year wildlife and other animal welfare organizations send out full-color calendars with striking, beautiful pictures of animals of all kinds—some featuring wild animals, others concentrating on pet and domestic animals. These organizations do this to inspire commitment to the work. I have three of these calendars pinned on the wall beside my desk, and a pile of nearly a dozen others with such awe-inspiring photos that I am loathe to get rid of them. Sometimes, however, I wonder if, in a way, these calendars with the beautiful pictures of handsome and imposing, or cute and lovable, creatures, do not do something of a disservice to the cause. The beautiful photos can convey an impression of wellbeing far removed from the actual situations and conditions of the animal world today. Of course, these organizations have made the right decision in their choice of photos, for to present at first too stark a picture of reality would be more than anyone would want to look at and to hang on the wall, and would probably dampen rather than encourage enthusiastic response to the organizations' requests for support. And these organizations, in their many fine publications, do go on to present their readers and donors with much of the full reality confronting animals in today's world. And it is important, of course, to attempt to hold both perspectives together at the same time, to try to grasp at once both the beauty and awesomeness of the animal world as well as the worsening situation of the animals, and ourselves along with them.

1. The Sixth Great Extinction Event

The overriding reality facing all wild life today is the imminent threat of extinction. This includes the threat to plants along with animals. As far as is known, the Earth has seen, what has been called, five great "extinction events" during the past 400 to 500 million years. Each of these appears to have destroyed 50 to 95 percent of the Earth's life each time. It has been estimated that after each event it took at least 10 million years for biological diversity to begin to recover. The last such event saw the disappearance of the dinosaurs. The present event under way is sometimes labeled the Holocene extinction event because the Holocene is the most recent epoch of calculated geologic time and reaches into the present (Kolbert; Whitty; Robbins; Center for Biological Diversity).

The new extinction period is under way and proceeding apace; it is not a far distant occurrence. It has been estimated that the world has lost half its wildlife since the 1970s. The World Conservation Union (usually known by its initials, IUCN), which every two years updates a "Red List" of endangered species derived from its worldwide tracking efforts, estimates that 40 percent (40,160 total number assessed) of the examined species of the planet are in peril of extinction in the not too distant future. Harvard biologist, E.O. Wilson, predicts that "our present course will lead to the extinction of half of all plant and animal species by 2100" (Whitty). Other scientists estimate that as many as 30 to 50 percent of all species are possibly heading toward extinction by half-century (Center for Biological Diversity).

Increasingly, many scientists and environmentalists are beginning to refer to the present rate of extinction not so much as the Holocene but rather as the Anthropocene extinction event, and that for a very simple reason: nearly every cause of the growing extinction rate has been brought about by human attributes and activities. The list of human causes of extinction is long and growing. Even a partial list would include: habitat loss; over exploitation (as in, over-fishing); urbanization; industrialization; mono-agriculture; pollution of nearly every conceivable kind;

deforestation, especially by mining, farming, and timber interests; poaching; hunting; wildlife trade; climate change; human-borne invasive species; and so forth. In this light it would appear that humans are the most dangerous of all invasive species—and are now approaching a world population of some nine to ten billion. Many of these causes of extinction overlap with one another, thus increasing their impact exponentially.

In their publicity and fund-raising the major wildlife organizations often feature the great dramatic animals—lions, tigers, elephants, rhinos, leopards, cheetahs, gorillas, whales, great white sharks, bald eagles, and the like. They feature these animals for good reason. They call forth immediate attention, compassion, and concern. Some biologists have even begun to refer to them as the "charismatic fauna." They command admiration and sympathy, and help the wildlife organization then introduce more effectively the plight of the myriads of less "charismatic" species, which are equally threatened and equally essential to the biological diversity and health of the planet. These other species range from birds, reptiles, and amphibians down to the tiny marine creatures that, for example, build coral reefs and provide subsistence for the larger oceanic species. Furthermore, the so-called charismatic creatures are not emphasized simply as a clever publicity technique, they are themselves in great trouble. Human activities are again the chief cause—human population pressure, destruction of forests and habitats, and, today especially, hunting, poaching, and trade in exotic species as well as in such wildlife products as ivory, rhinoceros horn, and tiger penis. The demand, for example, for rhinoceros horn, for supposed health benefits, has meant a quadrupling of rhino deaths in the last four years to 1,215 killed in 2014 alone (Editorial).

The list of land animals threatened with imminent extinction is huge. Here we can only point to a few notable examples.

Primates. The IUCN estimates that almost 50 percent of the world's primate species are at risk of extinction. Ninety percent of primates—monkeys, lemurs, orangutans, gorillas, chimpanzees, and other apes, live in tropical rain forests that are fast disappearing. Wild chimpanzees are facing catastrophe. Under assault from all sides, they are hunted for their meat ("bush meat"), for raiding farmers' fields that are encroaching upon their living space, and for the exotic pet trade. The most pressing threat to the wild chimpanzee is, again, the loss of habitat, which squeezes chimps into ever-smaller territories, making them prone to inbreeding or being wiped out by a single epidemic. Part of the sorrowful irony is that many poverty-stricken Africans turn to hunting "bush meat" to feed their families, which in turn further decimates the ape population ("Visiting an Ailing Relative"). It has been estimated that only 170,000 chimps are left in the wild. Mountain gorillas may be in even greater difficulty. Poaching is a major threat, their coats selling for thousands on the international black market, with fewer than 900 gorillas remaining in central Africa after decades of hunting and habitat destruction. Orangutans in Indonesia, to take but one more example, are in desperate straits with the loss of their forest homes to logging and timber interests and to palm oil production.

African Elephants. The ivory trade has opened the floodgates for the poaching of elephants. From an estimated 10 million African elephants in 1900, their population has plummeted to 420,000 in 2014. The ivory tusks of each dead elephant bring at least $30,000 each at final sale. Militias in the Congo and Sudan fund much of their operations by poaching elephants. Political elites in East Africa, Mozambique, Gabor, Tanzania, the Congo, and other African countries clandestinely support and profit from the ivory trade. At the end of a worldwide ivory trafficking network, the largest market for ivory is China, with its newly recent, wealthy middle and upper classes, hungry for the status symbols of ivory jewelry and sculpture. The most rigorous analysis of elephant poaching places the number of animals now being killed as between 35,000 to 50,000 a year, at the rate of around 100 a day.

Most heartrending is the impact of the slaughter on the social and emotional lives of these highly communal creatures. The orphaned young suffer especially, suddenly bereft of the companionship and guidance of their elders, and particularly of their nurturing, matriarchal mothers. The impact on numbers of orphaned elephants, expressed in great displays of sorrow and often violent anger, has been described as nothing less than extreme post-traumatic stress by those who work closely with these magnificent, intelligent, and feeling creatures (Bradshaw 2009; Showmatoff; Bornfree). To his credit, President Obama in July 201 issued an executive order stepping up efforts to combat wildlife trafficking, and, as a result the United States Fish and Wildlife Service has begun to implement a ban on commercial elephant ivory trade in this country (Chris Gibson letter). This is commendable on the part of the Fish and Wildlife Service, but as we shall see, this government agency has an extremely mixed record on wildlife protection. The Multination Species Conservation Fund is the funding line under which the African Elephant Conservation Act, the Asian Elephant Conservation Act, the Rhinoceros and Tiger Conservation Act, the Great Ape Conservation Act, and the Marine Turtle Conservation Act are all funded in the annual Interior Appropriation bill. The general lack of serious commitment that characterizes much government action on behalf of wild life can be seen in that the total funding for all these efforts is $9 million dollars, meager in the extreme. This underfunding has resulted in a drastic decline of the number of wildlife investigations in just the last year. "This means," concludes a *New York Times* editorial, there is scant letup in the smuggling frenzy that has resulted in the slaughter of more than 100,000 elephants for ivory since 2010" (editorial 2015b).

Tigers. During the past 100 years tigers have been extirpated from vast areas of the Earth, from about 93 percent of their original, historic ranges. Estimated to number 100,000 at the beginning of the twentieth century their numbers have sunk to about 3,000 to 3,900 today. Again the main causes have been human encroachment, habitat loss, and poaching. Ironically, tigers are among the most popular of the world's charismatic megafauna. Along with the endangered tigers should be added the polar bear and the grizzly bear, the polar bear in peril from climate change and the grizzly from creeping human civilization.

Marine Mammals. It has been estimated that nearly 1200 ocean mammals are endangered, especially whales, dolphins, and porpoises. Japan has been using a loophole in international law to slaughter 850 minke whales, 50 endangered humpback whales, and 50 endangered fin whales, officially for "scientific research," although most of the whale ends up on the domestic fish market for food. The slaughter of whales, it should be noted, is especially gruesome in that it involves driving an explosive grenade on the end of a harpoon to explode deep within the animal, which then takes about 45 minutes to finally die. Thousands of whales are also killed each year through collisions with naval and tanker ships.

Over-fishing is destroying entire populations of fish stocks. Fishing nets, bottom trawling, and giant factory ships, which literally vacuum entire schools of fish, all decimate entire species, until, when the number of one species has become too low to be profitable, the fisheries turn to another species. Each year more than 650,000 whales, dolphins, porpoises, and other marine animals are caught and killed as collateral damage by being trapped in fishing gear. Japanese sushi eaters, along with their gourmand imitators now worldwide, have almost wiped out the Blue Fin Tuna, one of the great wild fish. In a class by themselves, sharks are on the brink of extinction because sharkfin soup is considered a delicacy by the elite around the world. Sharks are taken in large numbers, pulled aboard ship and their fins cut off. They are then thrown back into the ocean to sink to the bottom where they die a slow death. Shark fin trade was recently outlawed in California, but the Obama administration asked the Court through the Department of Justice to overturn the California law, arguing that only the federal government, not the states, can regulate shark-based products in state markets. Pollution, trash, chemicals, and global warming put all marine animals, and the sustainability of their ocean homes, at great peril (McCarthy; Whitty; Zimmer 2015).

Amphibians and Reptiles. Amphibians—frogs, toads, salamanders, and others—are at great risk because of water and air pollution, climate change, the introduction of exotic species, disease, and exposure to ultraviolet light owing to the thinning of the ozone layer. Biologists urge that amphibians should be given special attention because they—like the canary in the mineshaft—probably give advance warning of changes taking place unsuspected in the larger ecosystem that can affect other animals and humans. Reptiles are at similar risk. The IUCN reckons that 21 percent of the total species they have evaluated must be considered endangered. Again human activities have so destroyed and/or fragmented, or polluted, their habitats that the reptiles are increasingly unable to flourish.

Birds. The Center for Biological Diversity reports that bird populations are declining worldwide, again because of human activities. Habitat loss, pesticides and other pollutants, as well as invasive species, and the wild bird trade, are among the major causes. In the U.S. alone, reports the Center, 251 (31 percent) of the 800 species in this country are at risk.

Reflections. Why the emphasis here on this looming threat of mass extinction? From an anthroposophic point of view the answer, if not simple, would seem to be straightforward. We have seen repeatedly how Rudolf Steiner stresses and describes the oneness of the human being with the entire Earth and its creatures from primal origins on. We have also seen our commonality in soul with the animals. And, as bearers of an independent and potentially free self, we have begun, perhaps, to recognize our special responsibility or the Earth and its creatures. This responsibility becomes all the more pressing today in light of the extent to which we have neglected it, and because of that neglect now as humans threaten the whole future of Earth evolution.

There was a time in which it was fairly easy to distinguish between wild nature and the human sphere. That has long become an untenable distinction. Human attitudes and activities have long encroached upon every corner of the natural world. Some students of the environment even say that nature as such no longer exists. The Christian theologian and environmentalist Christopher Southgate has given eloquent expression to the need of coming to an understanding of the interaction between human activities and nature. "Human activity," he writes, "is affecting the whole course of planetary evolution, and almost every environment on Earth. Our activities continually alter and jeopardize the health of all sorts of ecosystemic contexts. This generates a strong imperative to understand these contexts as fully and accurately as we can, and to take action to maintain the flourishing of creatures. It is even more unlikely that the action of simply 'letting be' will prove sufficient" (Southgate, 250). This is a view that anthroposophists can readily embrace, given Rudolf Steiner's many calls to be awake and to seek greater understanding, in short, to reject simply "letting be."

With this call to awaken, we can look briefly at two, further related topics These are 1. Zoos and circuses and 2. Alteration of human–animal-environmental relationships.

Zoos and Circuses. Here we are reminded again of Rudolf Steiner's statement that "the animal is injured most of all when man keeps them in captivity." Zoos offer an important case in point. Traditionally, zoos have served mainly for human entertainment and amusement, keeping animals penned up, usually for life, in small, barren enclosures with little, if any, possibility for large muscle movements or emotional stimulation. Today, however, many leading zoos are seeking to convert from mainly providing public entertainment to taking a leading part in wildlife conservation. A recent article in the *New York Times* has documented both of these aspects—entertainment and conservation—in many of the 250 accredited zoos and aquariums in this country. On the one hand, in visiting many zoos the author found again and again animals confined and alone, suffering from a variety of afflictions: depression, anxiety, fear and unease, phobias, obsessive compulsive behavior, and what behaviorists call "stereotypy"—ritualized behavior brought on by frustration or confinement—for example, the constant lifelong pacing around and around in a small enclosure, a scene many of us may vividly remember from childhood visits to zoos. At the same time, the author witnessed in many zoos a serious effort to transition to a more animal-nourishing environment. Zoo exhibit designers are often attempting to replicate the natural habitats of animals and to give them more enriched and stimulating surroundings.

Many zoos are in transition in which old conditions persist even as the new are being introduced. Zoos in this country, the author reports, have changed immensely in the last 30 years

(Haberstadt 2014). In addition, a number of zoos are beginning to see themselves as having a key role to play in preserving some species, and not only the "charismatic megafauna" but also all kinds of mammals, amphibians, birds, and even insects, whose numbers are crashing. This also has forced wrenching decisions on zoo officials. They must decide which among different species are most crucial to save and which they are equipped to care for as a chosen few, and those that out of necessity they must reluctantly abandon. "Some days," one official has said, "the burden feels less like Noah building an ark and more like Schindler's list" (Kaufman 2012). As important as their conservation efforts are, zoos as such can only make a relatively small contribution in the larger fight against extinction.

As for circuses, suffice it to point out that a number of animal welfare organizations have been leaders in exposing the mistreatment and extreme confinement that exists in most circuses.

Altering the Human–Animal–Environment Relationship. Some environmentalists are exploring possible plans to alter beneficially the relationships among humans, animals, and the environment itself. A major cause of the threat to animals is the proliferation of human settlement and all that attends it—urbanization, agriculture, logging and gas and oil development, shopping malls, ski resorts, and the growing maze of roads and thruways that crisscross and intersect throughout the countryside, and so on. All these fragment and deprive animals of their natural homeland, and, with roads and thruways, throw up insurmountable obstacles blocking the animals' natural migration paths and foraging areas. The result is isolation, which deprives wide-ranging animals especially of necessary hunting space, and for many eventually leads to inbreeding and the ultimate weakening and demise of entire species.

An especially endangered wildlife path of movement is the borderland between the U.S. and Mexico. Some of North America's most threatened wildlife—jaguars, mountain lions, Mexican wolves, and others need to cross here in order to survive. The tragic conflict between humans and animals once again surfaces because this is where Mexican workers, migrant families, and children also cross. The 700-mile border fence being built to keep the humans out also threatens a major catastrophe for the wildlife. In all the deliberations and controversies in Congress over the creation of the fence, the threat to the animals has never been mentioned. A similar border fence between India and Pakistan has forced starving bears and leopards, which can no longer cover their feeding territories, to attack villages, which further exacerbates the human–animal conflict.

One proposal for providing land for the animals has been called "rewilding." This may be one of the boldest attempts to recover and protect animal territory. Rewilding consists of finding, connecting, and safeguarding large land areas that are still relatively open for animals. A conservation group, The Wildlands Project, is leading this move for rewilding in North America. It envisages four broad mega-linkages in North America reconnecting what can be considered remaining wilderness areas, such as parks, refuges, national forests, local land trust areas, and so forth. The idea is to reconnect these with protected corridors and overpasses providing safe passage for wildlife. This project is clearly both short- and long-term, perhaps requiring decades for the completion of certain aspects. It has the backing of a number of wildlife organizations, and has the potential for making a critical difference in the survival of major North American species, but time is pressing (Whitty).

A third, still more radical proposal for preserving endangered species is what is called "assisted migration." This involves moving entire species from one part of the globe, where their survival has become impossible, to another, more hospitable region. The polar bear is an obvious, prime candidate. Transfer of the polar bear from the melting arctic to the Antarctic could well be the polar bears only hope, but, alas, that would hinge on a slower melting of the Antarctic ice. Transfers of other animals might not be quite so daunting. Assisted migration in any case would be incredibly complicated, and would require large-scale international cooperation and support. Given the course of climate change, assisted migration could out of necessity attract serious attention and thought, but this itself would depend on a heightened human sensitivity to the plight of the animals than exists at present (Southgate).

2. Hunting and Wildlife Management

Rudolf Steiner does not address the issue of the hunting of animals, or, if he does, I have not discovered the relevant passages. Of course, if some exist, I would welcome being alerted to them. Nevertheless, it seems to me important to reflect on hunting in the modern world in light of Steiner's underlying emphasis on "reverence for everything living" and "compassion for all creatures." The few paragraphs that follow are, therefore, my own attempt to reflect on what "compassion for all creatures" might mean for the pursuit of hunting in our modern world. I say modern world because hunting in our scientific, technologized, and economically globalized world has acquired its own peculiar characteristics that distinguish it decisively from hunting in earlier ages of human history.

For thousands of years, humans are thought to have lived as hunter–gatherers, foraging from the land and hunting animals for subsistence. From what we know of the hunter gatherers, they considered the animals to be part of the larger communion of being in which humans and animals were mutual participants. The hunting, killing, and consumption of animals appear, therefore, to have been conducted with great respect, even awe, toward the animals, and enwrapped in rituals of gratitude, propitiation, and remorse. Gradually as civilization began to replace the hunter–gatherer society, the rituals reflecting a sense of communion between humans and animals seem to have melded with more formalized, religious sacrifice of animals oriented more around guilt and atonement (Rogerson). The literature on hunter–gatherers has given some support to the modern idea of some biologists that the human being is by nature a hunter (stretched by some into the notion of the human as "the killer ape"). This idea, however, has been called into question by some new findings and speculation. One leading authority on early hunting has even argued that, "The hunting hypothesis originated as a myth concocted out of antique preconceptions and wishful thinking" (Cartmill, 224).

What does seem to be noncontroversial is that hunting gradually, perhaps very early, came to be associated with the "warrior virtues" of bravery, boldness, strength, and so on. This image of the hunter as the brave warrior-type appears, for example, in Greek mythology in the figure of Orion, who was said to have been a young man of huge stature and great beauty, and a mighty hunter who out of love for the daughter of the King of Chios cleared the island of wild beasts. Or one finds the early portrayal of the hunter as a great and bold leader in the brief mention in Genesis of Nimrod, "a mighty hunter before the Lord," "the first on Earth to be a mighty man" (Genesis 10:8–12). Nimrod's prowess as a hunter and as a ruler of kingdoms is clearly presented as of a piece. This association of the hunter with the mighty warrior may have had some basis in the fear among ancient peoples of the threat of dangerous wild animals that were encountered in the vast places thought of as the wilderness.

In our time four main forms of hunting warrant looking at: 1) subsistence hunting; 2) trophy hunting; 3) sport/recreational hunting; and 4) so-called game management hunting.

Subsistence hunting, which involves the killing of animals for meat in order to survive hardly exists in the industrialized, developed world. Sports hunters do sometimes eat their kill— venison, for example—but few of them do so out of necessity. Genuine subsistence hunting exists today only in a relatively few unsettled areas of the world, say, for example, among people in the Amazon rain forest, or among the impoverished of some developing countries, who must hunt to feed their families (with "bush meat" for instance). Subsistence hunting as essential for survival is extremely rare in the modern world. Some so-called sport hunters do claim that they try always to eat the results of their kills, but such do not seem to be a big majority, and in their case the hunting is not prompted by survival needs but by pleasure in the hunt and in the killing and by the taste of wild flesh.

Trophy hunters hunt for the pleasure of killing and of exhibiting the heads, horns, tusks, and skins they take from the carcasses of the animals they have slain. Trophy hunting is big business and a global enterprise. Large organizations, including gun manufacturers, are devoted to promoting and sustaining trophy hunting, organizing and outfitting safaris, conventions, and award ceremonies—all with the support of the governments and game agencies. One of the largest organizations of trophy hunters is Safari Club International (SCI) with thousands of members in this country (Scully). Much trophy hunting, if not most, is what is known as "canned hunting," in which animals are confined within a closed area, sometimes only a few square yards in size, others, thousand of acres. There the animals are "hunted," often by hunters perching in tree blinds or hiding behind vehicles, luring the animals to feeding stations, or taking advantage of their familiarity from having been around humans in captivity. Many ways exist to make the shooting and kill a sure thing.

Trophy hunting is a worldwide business. Zimbabwe has dozens of hunting lodges that cater to wealthy trophy hunters from Germany, Saudi Arabia, and, notably, from Texas. South Africa, one report describes as "making a name for itself as the canned hunting capital of the world" ("Canned Hunts"). The United States, however, is no slacker in the field of canned or captive hunts, with more than a thousand captive hunts in at least 28 states in the U.S. Texas is the leading state with among 12 other states granting permission for hunting endangered species, which takes place on "game ranches," with exotic species trapped and flown to the ranches from as far away as Nepal and India. Trophy hunters can, thus, kill their own exotic species right here at home. It costs a lot, but many game ranches have a "no kill, no pay" policy, which helps ensure that the owner will do all it takes to make sure the kill takes place, using guides who know where the animals feed and sleep, permitting the use of dogs, and supplying feeding stations that lure the animals while the hidden hunters lie in wait.

Much of the canned hunting in the U.S. takes place on private property (for-profit hunting reserves or game ranches), which is not regulated by Federal law. There are an estimated 1,000 such game "preserves" in the U.S. On Ted Turner's 2 million acres, hunters can pay thousands of dollars to kill bison, deer, African antelope, and turkey ("Canned Hunting"). Especially popular for those who can afford it are guided safaris to various African countries. There hunters can acquire trophies from what are known in the trade as the "Big 5," elephants, rhinos, buffaloes, lions, and leopards. Trophy hunters seem to have an especially strong attraction for elephants, even though elephant herds are being decimated. The mentality of trophy hunters was displayed vividly by one exuberant elephant killer, who, after sneaking up to within 30 or 40 yards of an elephant in the trees, dropped it with a shot to the head and exulted:

> We did it! Oh man! Big-game hunting is one of the most exciting things there is in the world. You got your grizzlies, you got your lions, you got your leopards, you got your buffalo. But I'm here to tell you, baby, ain't nothing like the elephant. (Showmatoff, 133)

This hunter has a special attraction to killing elephants but the general trophy-hunter mentality would seem to be the same in varying degrees for all trophy hunters. Matthew Scully comments, with the elephant specifically in mind, but he makes clear throughout his wonderful book, *Dominion*, that his words are not unrelated to the general trophy hunter mentality:

> How could anyone find pleasure in shooting an 8,000-pound mammal who has been walking the Earth for fifty-odd years, who lives in a complex family structure, needs fourteen or fifteen years to rear the young, charges only in defense of the calves or of the herd, has been observed bringing food to sick members of the herd and even aiding the young of other species. (Scully, 75)

It is hard not to think that trophy hunting reveals a depth of decadence nearly inconceivable to most non-hunting people.

Our third category, sport or recreational hunting, is probably the most popular and accessible of all forms of hunting. It has a resemblance to trophy hunting in that both claim to involve sportsman-like competition with the animals. And both are deficient on this score. So-called sports hunters, however, have marshaled a number of arguments that claim moral justification for their activity. One of these is that hunting for recreation and pleasure is really an exercise and training in sportsmanship, and the latter especially for young hunters. This argument claims that the hunter must pit his or her skills in a mutual competition with the animal: That hunting requires skills of tracking an elusive opponent; that both animal and human have to master the natural surroundings, which can pose unexpected challenges for both, and that hunting can entail hardship and physical challenges that the hunter must learn to encounter and surmount.

For the hunter–gatherer much of this may well have been true. How much, however, does it hold for the modern hunter? In the first place the animal is grossly disadvantaged in comparison with the hunter. The hunter is equipped with all kinds of sophisticated weaponry—shot guns, precision-tooled, high-powered rifles, binoculars, telescopic sights, walkie-talkies, GPS positioner devices, and compound bows, to name a few. President Kennedy once commented sardonically on the one-sidedness of the hunt. Having reluctantly yielded to L.B.J.'s insistence that he go deer hunting on the latter's Texas ranch, Kennedy is said afterward to have ruefully remarked to the effect that, "Hunting will be a sport when the deer have rifles." Hunters also resort to trickery of all sorts, much of which is unsporting by any definition. They use snowmobiles to run down elk, airplanes to exhaust and drive wolves to the ground, and dogs to tree cougars. They shoot unsuspecting animals from hidden blinds and tree stands, and attract them with bait—corn for deer, honey and meat, and frequently doughnuts, for bears. They will use special call devices mimicking a young animal in distress to bring out protective mothers, which can then easily be shot, and they will use special sex lures for the male and female of many big species. And they will shoot animals when they are eating or sleeping—not very sporting (Williams, 58–9).

Hunters, however, have special arguments to justify and commend their sport to the public. One such argument is that hunters bring us closer to an awareness and appreciation of the natural world. Hunters, in this view, come to know in detail the lives of the hunted animal—its nature and way of life, its habits and skills, its social life and surrounding environment. Implied in this is that the hunter's intimate and detailed knowledge of the animal helps bring to awareness and cements the bond between humans and animals. Unfortunately, however, it is not likely that hunters have a compelling command of the animals' fully complex life and nature—certainly not the many weekend hunters that pour into the woods when hunting season opens. A few hunters may well be accomplished trackers, but they would be rare. And in the end, whatever knowledge of the animal world the hunter may have garnered, the sole purpose of it is to facilitate the kill. And the kill does take place, even if the hunter's aim is sloppy, as it often is, and the wounded animal has to drag itself into the woods or grass to linger and die.

When I asked a hunter friend whatever became of the camera as providing a fitting end to the hunt that would preserve both the animal and perhaps some new knowledge about its life, the response was a disdainful, "You don't understand, that would be so anticlimactic and such a letdown." The kill itself seems to be the irrepressible yearned-for climax to the rhythm of the hunt. Many photos may be taken afterward to document the hunter and his or her kill, and to provide pleasure for the folks at home.

The myth of the mighty, manly-man, hunter warrior continues from time to time to be hauled into service. A most pathetic example was the photo-op picture in 2004 of Presidential candidate John Kerry, outfitted in the obligatory camouflage fatigues, a new gun slung over his shoulder, dragging by its neck a poor goose he had shot—all to show that he has what it takes to be able to kill innocent and powerless beings, a *sine qua non* requirement, it seems, for modern statesmen.

Another argument for hunters, not widespread probably among most run-of-the-mill hunters, but popular and well developed among certain individuals and groups, such as the Safari Club International, is that, at heart, hunting is a spiritual endeavor, that it is a path to the deepest of spiritual experience. Matthew Scully is perhaps the most adept at exposing the sanctimony and hypocritical cant in this effort to cloak hunting in spiritual significance. "The touchiness about the sport," writes Scully, "has lately led many hunters to search for higher ground, to ultimate meanings and spiritual self-justification. The result is a mix of feel-good moral relativism, informercial-type self-empowerment, and half-baked mysticism." For example, Scully quotes from a book by James A. Swan, *In Defense of Hunting*, that is a favorite of the Safari Club members, including General Norman Schwarzkopf, a champion of manly spirituality in hunting. Swan states,

> "And what about the poor animals?" the critics of hunting scream. Anyone can declare an animal to be special, even sacred. But a thing can become truly sacred only if a person knows in his or her heart that the object or creature can somehow serve as a conduit to a realm of existence that transcends the temporal. If hunting can be a path to spirit, unhindered by guilt, then nature has a way of making sure that hunters feel compassion.

To this, Matthew Scully retorts:

> Like, wow, is that deep or what? Things are "sacred" only when the hunter has made them so in his heart.... The creature becomes a "conduit" to the transcendent. Guilt now becomes a *hindrance* to compassion, which is achieved in the very act of killing, and so on further up into holy realms unattainable, one assumes, to the non-hunter. (Scully, 54–5)

Besides claiming as some hunters do to being, as hunters, on a spiritual path, almost all hunters are inclined to present themselves as protectors, par excellence, of the Earth and the environment. Their claim is that they are the true conservationists and environmentalists. This is especially evident, they maintain, in their cooperation with government wildlife agencies in wildlife management, population control, and wildlife conservation. This claim deserves a close look.

The very numbers killed by hunters in themselves belie their conservationist, environmentalist posturing. Hunters kill more than two hundred million animals each year—among the annual death toll: 42 million mourning doves, 30 million squirrels, 28 million quail, 25 million rabbits, 20 million pheasants, 14 million ducks, 6 million deer, and thousands of geese, bears, moose, elk, antelope, swans, cougars, turkeys, wolves, foxes, coyotes, bobcats, boars, and other creatures. These figures don't include the millions of animals wounded and left to die (In Defense of Animals). We have already noted the powerlessness of the animals at the hands of the heavily armed, technologically equipped, and tricky hunters with their lures, ambushes, and vehicular chases.

"Game Management" is especially slippery and elusive, both in concept and practice. Conflicts of interest are rampant, especially in that government wildlife agencies and hunters often act in collusion. Government wildlife agencies receive much of their funding from hunters—hunting licenses, fees, and from politicians responsive to hunter lobbyists. The wildlife agencies frequently work to manipulate animal environments and populations so as to favor hunters. They also work assiduously to retain the support of agriculture and ranching interests by eliminating possible pests (prairie dogs, for example) or predators (coyotes especially), although the actual predator threat to cattle and sheep is quite small, still it is good to have powerful people like western ranchers and politicians on your side. The irony is seen in that after getting rid of predators the increasing numbers of "prey animals," such as elk and deer, then also have to be "culled."

Collusion between hunters and government agencies is apparent at many points. One example is the twisted relationship between national wildlife refuges and the public, on one hand, and hunters and government agencies, on the other. Instead of being sanctuaries for the animals, as the name suggests and as most of us of the public normally assume, more than 440 wildlife "refuges" are open to hunters who enter them and kill millions of animals annually. In other words, hunters can hunt on public lands—national parks and state forests—paid for by the non-hunting public (Williams, 69). Another example: No government program kills more wildlife than the United States Wildlife Services (cynically named, says the Center for Biological Diversity). The millions of animals killed by this agency annually include coyotes, bears, beavers wolves, otters, foxes, prairie dogs, mountain lions, birds, and others. Most of these animals are killed on behalf of hunters, ranching, and commercial interests. The methods used for the killing include gassing, traps, and exploding cyanide caps. And most of this is conducted out of view and with little accountability to the American public ("Targeting Wildlife Services").

Nevertheless, overpopulation by some animals—notably deer and bear in a few areas of the U.S. and elephants in Africa and parts of India—can be a genuine and perplexing problem. Deer get killed crossing roads and highways and occasionally cause the death of the human drivers. Deer also can be nuisances and, for example, eat the azalias and rhododendra around the house, though one could wonder whether a death sentence is proportionate to the crime. Too many bears in an area are mainly a nuisance. Herds of orphaned elephants, often quite angry and desolate without the care of their poached mothers, can be dangerous to persons and destructive of property. Sometimes, moreover, overpopulation is a threat to the survival of the animals themselves.

The standard game management protocol calls for the "culling" of the surplus animals. One thing, however, bears repeating and should be kept in mind in considering the issue and practices of game management: The overpopulation of some animals is almost always a direct result of humans. Often hunters have eliminated the natural predators that would keep populations controlled naturally. In addition, the expansion of human settlements has deprived many animals—deer, bears, elephants, lions, and others—of suitable habitats and have thus forced the animals to move ever closer to humans. The knee-jerk reaction to animal overpopulation is to call for the hunting and killing ("culling," "thinning") of them.

Most wealthy communities—the ones that complain the most and loudest about too many animals—understandably don't want to reintroduce predators. They are also, however, not disposed to pay for fences or to resist developers who support local politicians. Instead the usual reflex action is to call in the hunters, or, as is becoming something of a fad, to sponsor "the suburban deer bow hunts" (never mind that the bow—usually technologically powerful has been shown to be one of the cruelest and least effective of the hunter's killing apparatus). For those communities, however, that are concerned to develop humane methods of dealing with animal overpopulation, there is a feasible and highly promising alternative: namely, to replace bullets with birth control.

Birth control can take two main forms: sterilization and contraception. Both have been used with success in several important American communities, and both are being further developed and their use extended with the help of local community authorities and animal welfare organizations, such as the Humane Society. Sterilization methods are being offered to communities on Long Island; and Maryland, Virginia, California, and New York have granted licenses for surgical sterilization (after tranquilization). A major test of an immunocontraceptive, *Porcine zona pellucida* (PZP), is underway in Hasting on Hudson, the first place, the Humane Society reports, where "it is being used to reduce a free roaming population of deer in an open community versus at a fenced site or on an island." On Fripp Island, South Carolina, PZP has drastically reduced deer numbers (Lange 2015a). Also wildlife managers in South Africa have begun to administer PZP to elephants in what appears to be a promising effort to balance the needs of rising numbers of elephants with the needs of other species in limited preserved areas (Lange 2015b).

It should also be borne in mind that the success of managed hunts themselves has not been well established. A major complicating factor is what has been called "compensatory reproduction," observed also in human populations during wartime. Many animals will compensate naturally to make up for unusual losses in their numbers. In the case of deer, for instance, the females will tend to "compensate" for a dent in their population by breeding at an earlier age and having bigger litters. The momentary reduction in numbers owing to culling may make more space and food available for the remaining deer with the result that the deer population compensates to become larger than originally. One leading authority on deer has written, "Most natural populations respond to reduction in numbers by increased productivity." He explains:

> If population levels are lowered artificially, the density-dependent brake on population growth is released: the reproduction increases, mortality declines. Lack of selectivity in the cull...may also exacerbate the pest problem by disrupting the social structure and organization of the pest. This may have two consequences: a further increase in population density, and an increase in damage caused because the animals display abnormal behavior in response to a distorted social structure. (Putnam, 171–2; also, Linzey 2009, 91; Scully, 103)

So-called game control is, without doubt a real and difficult problem. The need for it is usually the result of human attitudes and activities. Much remains to be understood about it, and no one seems to have easy, conclusive answers. The case for killing as the automatic, reflex solution to control is much weaker than frequently presented and assumed. A good deal more is needed in the way of knowledge, ethical scrutiny, and humanely inspired creativity.

When all else is taken into account, the case for hunting in general seems to rest at bottom on the pleasure and joy in killing. Then it has to be assessed in the context of "reverence for all creatures."

3.

FACTORY FARMING:
THE ANIMAL–ACADEMIC–INDUSTRIAL COMPLEX

Just as the "wild" animals are declining in numbers and are on the brink of extinction, the "mild" animals (in Jean Kazez' nice distinction)—the ones we raise to kill and eat—are greater in numbers than ever, and they are killed for consumption in equally great numbers. The number of land animals slaughtered each year, and each day, for meat, is stunning. The introduction of mechanized agriculture—factory farming, known more sedately as Concentrated Animal Feeding Operations (CAFOS)—has made it possible during the past half century to produce an enormous amount of flesh for humans to eat. Nearly 10 billion land animals were raised and slaughtered for food in 2010 in the U.S. alone, more than 25 percent of the world's total, with the U.S. having only 5 percent of the world's population. Though there may have been a slight decrease between 2010 and 2014, the numbers, nevertheless, remain huge, and they are growing worldwide.

Globally, the number of land animals killed for food each year has exceeded 65 billion. This number is likely to rise exponentially as the newly developing countries, such as China, India, and Brazil, become more affluent and their people more and more demand the status attached all over the world to meat eating. While China, for instance, has not yet instituted full-fledged factory farming, it is moving rapidly in that direction. Chinese meat consumption has quadrupled over the past thirty years and is now the second largest segment of China's retail food market. China has recently also welcomed investments by major multinational meat and dairy producers associated particularly with the U.S., including Tyson Foods, Smithfield, and Nova International. In addition, China has entered into an agreement with the U.S. government to receive slaughtered chickens from the U.S. to be further processed in China, and then the products to be shipped back to the U.S. for sale to the U.S. consumer (in the form presumably of "chicken nuggets," etc.) ("China's Encounter"). It should perhaps be noted in passing that in countries like China, India, and Japan, which are increasingly adopting Western-style, meat-heavy diets, the rate of Western-type diseases is also soaring—heart failure, diabetes, obesity, cancer, and so forth.

With world population predicted to be some 9 billion humans by 2050, the only possible way to sustain the growing demand for meat consumption will be through industrializing its production, that is, through factory farming. But this will be possible only if the nations of the world fail to take into account the true costs of factory farming. In 2006, the United Nations Food and Agricultural Organization issued a study of the impact of meat consumption on the health of the planet. The study was entitled, "Livestock's Long Shadow." The UN study concluded that, "The livestock sector emerges as one of the two or three most significant contributors to the most serious environmental problems, at every scale from local to global" (United Nations Report). In 2008, in a follow-up of the UN Report, the Pew Commission on Industrial Farm Animal Production issued a two-year study of factory farming, which concluded that the food industry today is unsustainable because of its effects on 1) the animals raised for food; on 2) humans; and on 3) the environment (Pew Commission). We will consider each of these in due course.

The development of factory farming represents the latest triumph of the mechanical worldview. The animals themselves are defined by the industry as machines, literally as, "units of production," for the production of meat, milk, and eggs. These animals are managed by a system wholly organized and conducted by the dictates of industrial–technological–scientific efficiency and profit.

The dominant form of farming until recently was that of the age-old practice of "husbandry." *Husbandry,* as Wendell Berry describes it, meant "connection"—connection of the farmer with the soil, with the animals, and with the local community. Animal husbandry involved the farmer maintaining a relatively few animals having access to natural environments to live and move around in. It also involved care and concern on the part of the individual farmer for the individual animals, as well as for the herds and flocks. Husbandry also entailed a mutually beneficial relationship between the farmer and the wider community (Imhoff, 44–51).

All of this changed with the large-scale introduction of factory farming after World War II. Animal agriculture began to be industrialized and to be dominated by concentrated animal feed operations" (CAFOs). As its name suggests, the CAFO consists of huge numbers of animals crammed and caged in essentially factory-like buildings. The CAFO is basically a feeding operation and has its chief objective the most efficient increase in animal weight possible. The CAFO system takes its intellectual lead from land-grant universities teaching science and applying the mechanistic conception of nature directly to the development of factory farming. Veterinarian and philosopher of science, Bernard Rollin, quotes a university colleague as saying, "The worst thing that ever happened to my department is betokened by the name change from Animal Husbandry to Animal Science" (Imhoff 2010, 11). The result of the shift away from animal husbandry has been the rise of an "industrial–agricultural–academic complex" comprising an alliance of commodity groups, academic scientists, and government officials. The government, furthermore, provides subsidies for the whole operation.

1. The Suffering of the Animals

The consequences for the animals have been horrific. For one thing, farm animals, like the lab rodents and other little animals, are not covered by the Animal Welfare Act, and are hardly regarded, much less treated, as animals. They are unfeeling, units of production, to which anything can be done to increase efficiency and profits. As of 2013, nearly 65 million animals—cattle, pigs, and chickens—were crammed in CAFOs. Sows that normally may cover the equivalent of a square mile a day in foraging are confined their entire lives in cages, "gestation crates," barely larger than the pigs themselves, so small that they can hardly turn around. They spend their lives in these crates on a concrete floor with slots so that their excretions can drop through to a catchment pit below. They are repeatedly artificially inseminated and then separated from their piglets as soon as the little ones are born. The insemination is then repeated until after a year or two the sows are worn out and slaughtered, often for pet food. They live their entire lives in unrelieved pain, sickness, and boredom, and go crazy as a result, chewing and banging on the metal bars of their cages. As the piglets are fattened to full-grown hogs, they live by the hundreds and thousands in large warehouse-like barns in rows of wall-to-wall pens. There is no sunlight, straw, fresh air, or earth. As many as forty fully grown 250 pound male pigs will be crammed together in a pen the size of a small apartment (Imhoff, 104–124). One Smithfield food operation in Utah contains 500,000 pigs. In such crowded conditions, even minor wounds give rise to cannibalism.

Cattle are also destined for the CAFOs. Calves are first turned out on pasture for a few months, and then separated from the mothers, to the great distress of both, and transferred to a "cattle feed lot." There they stand together in their own manure with other cattle, as many as 100,000 in some lots. In the feedlot, the cattle are placed on a grain-based diet, mainly corn, supplemented with synthetic growth hormones, antibiotics, feather meal, pig and fish protein, and even chicken manure. This grain-based diet, et al., which is unnatural for cattle, fattens them up faster than a natural grass-based diet, but causes constant digestive problems, which then have to be treated with antibiotics and more supplements (Imhoff, 92–108). At a little over a year in age, having gained enormously in weight, the cattle are sent to the slaughterhouse to be killed and processed.

Dairy cows fare little better. The push with them has been to obtain as much milk as possible out of each cow. Selective scientific breeding has been impressively successful in this regard.

Because of this, from 1960 to 2008 (years for which figures are available), the amount of milk produced increased from 120 billion to 190 billion pounds, while the number of cows decreased from 18 million to 8.5 million (Imhoff, 134). At the same time the size of dairies also increased enormously. Compared to small dairy farms before World War II, which commonly had 20 or so cows, today a dairy farm in California or Colorado may milk 15,000 or 18,000. A sardonic critic of these operations has suggested that it would be most accurate to describe a modern dairy farm as "an agricultural engineering center" and the cows within it, not as cows, but as "bovine assembly-line components with the drawback of being alive."

The emphasis on ever more milk from individual cows results in herds stricken with mastitis, an inflammation of the teats and udders. To combat mastitis dairy owners have to test cows regularly and administer heavy does of antibiotics. The heavily concentrated protein diet, as opposed to a natural hay and grain diet, also causes digestive disturbances and liver abscesses, which often lead to a painful foot inflammation called laminitis. Laminitis is probably the cause of "downer cows," which in the slaughterhouse collapse on their way to the killing area. The Humane Society filmed, undercover, downer cows at a California slaughterhouse being goaded to their feet with electric prods or fork-lifted onto carts and taken to slaughter—and this was undoubtedly not a unique occurrence. Although the normal lifespan of a cow is about twenty years, most factory-farmed dairy cows, trapped in an unrelenting cycle of impregnation, calving, and milking, are "burned out" by the age of two and sent to the slaughterhouse (Mendelson).

Of all the animals in the CAFO, chickens (along with turkeys) are probably the least likely to elicit sympathy (compared to pigs and cattle), or to inspire concern about their use and abuse, or about their fate in general. To many people, who would not say the same for cows and pigs, chickens come closest to fitting the image of the machine—without pain, essentially stupid, and without emotions or a life worth living in itself. Even erstwhile, wannabe vegetarians will often be heard to say, "I'm a vegetarian.

Of course, I do eat fish and chicken." Chickens have in fact become increasingly the "meat of choice," displacing somewhat the demand for cattle and hogs. Chickens make up about 90 to 95 percent of all land animal meat eaten in the U.S., and eggs from layer hens are a major source of protein for millions of Americans.

In the CAFO two main, designated types of chickens are kept. One type is the egg-laying hen and the other is the so-called "broiler chicken," raised and sold for meat. Life for both is, in the philosopher's expression, "solitary, poor, nasty, brutish, and short." About 300 million egg-laying hens are raised in the U.S. every year, along with some eight to nine billion broiler chickens. What is CAFO life for these birds like, starting with the hens?

The laying hens spend their lives in "battery cages" lined up in rows and stacked in tiers in huge warehouse barns, with usually six to eight birds in a cage. Each bird has a living space no larger than the length and width of a letter-size sheet of paper. They cannot stretch or flap their wings; indeed, they can barely move. They cannot build nests or find a small private place to lay eggs, though forcing hens to lay eggs in crowded cages—"in public" as it were—is much as it would be for a human to have to excrete in public. The noted ethologist Konrad Lorenz has said, "The worst torture in which a battery hen is exposed is the inability to retire somewhere for the laying act. For the person who knows something about animals, it is truly heartrending to watch how a hen tries again and again to crawl beneath her fellow cage mates to search in vain for cover" (Davis, xii). The floors of the cages are made of wire on an angle so the eggs can roll down onto a conveyor belt, and to make the removal of manure easier. The slanted wire floors of cages cause broken bones, foot and leg injuries, and severe arthritic-type pain. The hens are painfully debeaked shortly after hatching because their frustration in the crammed battery cages would otherwise lead them to peck and injure each other. The building containing the hens reeks at all times of manure, ammonia, and the smell of decaying birds, to such an extent that it is difficult for the workers to breathe in them, although the birds must live their entire lives in the fetid atmosphere, developing from it various lung diseases.

By manipulating the light—sometimes dark, sometimes light—the farmers are able to bypass the normal egg-laying cycle and to increase the number of eggs produced by each hen from as few as 30 eggs a year for the normal hen to as many as 275 a year for the battery hen. In natural settings hens can live ten years or longer, but after a year and a half in the battery cage the hens are "spent," and are removed and sent to slaughter where their bruised and broken bodies can be shredded to make low-grade meat products like chicken soup or pot pies, or pet food. Every year, also, millions of male chicks, useless for laying, are sorted and macerated (put through a shredder, usually alive), or suffocated or gassed; and, turned into a saleable product such as chicken feed, fertilizer, or cat and dog food.

The broiler chickens are no better off. They spend their entire lives in filthy sheds containing tens of thousands of birds where the intense crowding leads easily to the spread of disease. These "broiler birds" are bred and drugged to grow so quickly that their breasts become so out-sized that the rest of the bird—legs and organs—can't keep up, making heart-attacks, organ failure, and crippling leg deformities not uncommon. Turkeys are especially unfortunate, bred to produce enormous breasts, so large that it is impossible for them to mate naturally and reproduction has to take place by means of artificial insemination. On Thanksgiving Day, that great annual, American family fetish, more than 46 million turkeys are eaten with no awareness or care on the part of the diners of what these artificially bred and oversized birds have been put through in order that every American can enjoy his or her white meat and crispy drumstick delectations. What all of these birds have been fed to stimulate growth on the cheap might itself well give us pause. The F.D.A. allows as protein for poultry, as well as for pigs and other non-cattle: cattle blood, brain, and spinal cords of cattle not older than thirty months, restaurant plate waste, and poultry litter. "From a human standpoint alone," writes philosopher Evelyn B. Pluhar, "the mere knowledge of what the animals we eat themselves eat is enough to make us sick" (Pluhar).

Chickens and all other poultry are not only excluded from the Animal Welfare Act but also are not protected under the

Humane Methods of Slaughter and Transportation Acts. At slaughter time, after having been packed and transported, often violently with many injuries and broken bones resulting from their human handlers, the birds are shackled by their legs and feet and placed onto a conveyor belt, moving at the rate of as many as 5,000 birds an hour. On the conveyor belt they pass through a "stunning tank" of electrified water, which is supposed to render them unconscious, and come to a mechanical blade that cuts their throats. Not infrequently, the birds are not sufficiently stunned or even killed by the mechanical blade before being plunged into boiling water. "The U.S. Department of Agriculture records show that millions of chickens are boiled alive every year" (Baur, 158; Kristof 2015).*

The everyday slaughterhouse experience of cows and pigs is just as awful. Here is a description of the culminating experience for these animals on the killing floor by two advocates of the meat industry. While they are spokespersons for the meat industry, they do try to be as realistic as possible:

> No matter how much new technology is developed, and no matter how nicely meat is packaged, the central facts of the meat business cannot be changed. This is an industry built around noisy, foul-smelling animals whose fate is to have an eight-inch-long pin fired into their foreheads at point-blank range. Their blood and guts will spill forth on the killing floor, and their carcasses will be stripped and carved and chopped during a process that, although it is governed by "humane slaughter" laws, can be nothing other than gross and brutal. (Gruzalski, 126)

While they do make an effort to be realistic about the system for which they advocate, they, nevertheless, do hold back from the full horrors of the slaughterhouse that take place regularly, in violation of the Humane Slaughter and Transportation laws. Gruzalski, in quoting these spokespersons for the meat business, summarizes a documented account by Gail Eisnitz, a major

---

* For my description of procedures and conditions in factory farming I have drawn freely on a number of sources, but especially on Baur, Foer, Scully, Davis, and Imhoff, with others cited specifically.

authority on slaughterhouses, of the full treatment undergone by the animals on the killing line. "Workers who are supposed to stun pigs and cattle before they begin to kill and butcher them, often fail to do so. As a result, fully conscious animals are regularly stabbed, skinned (cows), or scalded (pigs) to death. In addition, to keep the assembly line moving quickly enough (so as not to be fired), workers hit cows with whips, chains, shovels, and boards, as well as beat hogs with lead pipes, sometimes beating them to death" (Gruzalski, 127).

Workers in factory farms of all kinds, and in their associated slaughterhouses, are also victimized. Often illegal immigrants, factory farm laborers are subject to low pay and work conditions that undermine their health. The most dangerous job in America today is that of the slaughterhouse worker. They are in constant danger of injury and death, owing in large part to numbing repetition and unrelenting speed and volume involved in the killing and dismembering operations. Cattle, for example, are slaughtered at the rate of about 1.5 million a day. Sadly, as documented by Temple Grandin, who has designed many slaughterhouses so as to ease the animals' final moments, full-time slaughterhouse workers are so brutalized by their jobs that in their anger they often become sadistic toward the animals, brutalizing them in turn (Pollan, 233).

And it should not be forgotten that farm animals are not protected by law from any kind of experimentation aimed at finding ways to increase meat production. The *New York Times* has recently exposed in great detail the extreme suffering inflicted on animals—sheep, cows, pigs—at the Nebraska-based, Meat Animal Research Center of the U.S. Department of Agriculture. Grotesque experimentation, gross neglect of animals in pain, even sadistic enjoyment by researchers of the animal's distress are described by the *Times* editorial board, which commented on the shocking revelations of their own article a few days after its publication:

In engineering animals to maximize industry's bottom line, the Center, at a sprawling, secluded site in Nebraska, has created pigs that bear freakishly large litters of frail piglets,

which are often crushed by their mothers. Cows give birth
to triplets, many of them deformed. Lambs are born in open
fields, where they starve, are eaten by predators and are
overcome by the elements. These so-called easy-care sheep
are bred to eliminate the need for shelter and human help at
birthing time.... How does the consumer benefit from the
center's research? Lower prices, as well as bigger lamb chops,
leaner pork loins and more tender steaks. The cost to tax-
payers of the research at the center seems negligible...but
the cost borne by the animals in pain and suffering is clearly
horrific. (Moss 2015a; editorial 2015)

This is scientific, agricultural research at work, and all under
the auspices of the U.S. Department of Agriculture in cooperation with the meat industry. Following the *Time's* exposé, a bill
has been introduced in Congress to extend the Animal Welfare
Act (AWA) to shield cows, pigs, sheep, and other animals used
for agricultural research at federal facilities. From the beginning
these animals have never been included under the AWA. The
new bill is still pending in Congress. Secretary of Agriculture,
Tom Vilsack, meanwhile, has declared a moratorium on further
research at the Center until it strengthens its internal oversight,
which many critics have noted is fraught with conflicts of interest
(Moss 2015a, 2015b, 2015c).

A bit more encouraging, is that some headway has been made
in providing a minimum of protection for animals caught up in
factory farming. Countries in the European Union and Canada
have banned pig and veal crates and battery cages for poultry.
In this country only a few states have moved in this direction.
The way has been lead by California's 2008 Proposition 2, which
bans crates and requires that by 2015 "farm animals be able to
stand up, lie down, turn around, and fully extend their wings." A
few other states have followed California's lead in banning veal
creates, gestation crates, and battery cages. These laws, which
may take 10 years to be fully in place, are being vigorously fought
by the meat industry with the help of politicians. In California,
many factory farm managers are resisting by relying on litigation
to slow or abolish the Proposition 2 requirements. New Jersey

passed a Proposition 2 type of ban on crates only to have it vetoed by Governor Chris Christie. (Speculation has it that Christie, eyeing a run for the presidency in 2016, does not want to offend the voters of Iowa, a main venue for Republican primaries and a major factory-farming state.)

Nor should one be misled by the labels that are given the Department of Agriculture stamp of approval, but that mean less than they suggest. "Free range" may mean access to outdoors but this may be only a slab of concrete. "Cage free" hens may live in hen houses, but seldom, if ever, actually go outside. This labeling deception is yet another example of the collusion of the government with giant food companies.

2. FACTORY FARMING, LABORATORY EXPERIMENTATION, AND THE WAR ON TERRORISM

Some present efforts to protect agribusiness could almost justify expanding our earlier subject heading of "The Animal Industrial Complex" to "The Animal Industrial, Military Complex." Elements in the national and state governments have attempted to brand animal activists as "terrorists" and view them as enemies in "the war on terrorism." The "Animal Enterprise Terrorism Act of 2006" makes it a federal crime to "damage or interfere with the operation of an animal enterprise." The phrase "Animal enterprise" is a broad, covering term for any U.S. business that processes, sells, or uses animals. In 2006, four California activists were indicted for chalking the sidewalks, leafleting, and joining a demonstration against the University of California in protest of its vivisection experiments on animals. Charges were later dropped, but activists still had their passports confiscated and had to bear legal expenses. One was held under house arrest.

Some of the worst abuses of animals on factory farms would remain unknown to the public were it not for undercover investigations by such organizations as the Humane Society HSUS) and People for the Ethical Treatment of Animals (PETA). Their investigators have often worked undercover as regular farm and slaughterhouse laborers to covertly video what they saw and experienced as happening to the animals within. Their videos have brought to light scores of otherwise hidden instances of extreme and gratuitous cruelty to animals in these farm and food operations. Such undercover investigations have led directly to some of the largest meat recalls in the country and the closing of several slaughterhouses (Oppel).

Resistance to these efforts has come from several state leg-islatures, in cooperation with agribusiness corporations. Several states have enacted laws that would make it a crime to secretly videotape livestock farms or apply for a job at one without dis-closing ties to animal rights groups. Some version of these bills also would have violators placed on a "terrorist registry." Mark Bittman in the *New York Times* has dubbed these as "Ag-Gag" laws (Bittman 2011). Six states have passed Ag-Gag laws, while others have rejected them. These Ag-Gag laws would effectively shut down efforts to find out what is actually happening to ani-mals on factory farms or in slaughterhouses (Oppel; Hightower). Just as ominous, documents uncovered through the Freedom of Information Act have revealed that the F.B.I. Joint Terrorism Task Force has kept files on activists who expose animal abuse on factory farms and has recommended prosecuting them as ter-rorists (Potter).

3. Environmental and Health Hazards of Factory Farming

Along with the suffering of the animals, factory farming poses a direct danger to human beings. One is the pollution of ground water, streams, lakes, and even the ocean, by massive manure and urine disposal from factory farms. Not only is the manure disposal a carrier of disease, but the stench arising from it affects the health and wellbeing of whole communities for miles around. Another direct threat comes from the antibiotics administered to millions of animals to promote growth and to reduce sickness, which always threatens to spread rapidly under the conditions of close confinement and the high-growth diets the animals are fed.

About 80 percent of the antibiotics sold in this country are for factory-farmed animals, more than for people. The rapid spread of antibiotic resistant bacteria among humans is, consequently, becoming a major issue for modern medicine, which relies on antibiotics to treat many life-threatening infections. Furthermore, the antibiotics don't always kill the disease-bearing bacteria in the animals themselves, so the consumer must ingest with their meat (pig, cow, and chicken—and, don't forget, battery produced eggs) untold quantities of both antibiotics and with them the swarms of e-coli, staph, salmonella, campylobacter, and listeria that teem within the animals. Mark Bittman reports a food safety lawyer telling him, that "almost all chickens and turkeys produced in the U.S. is tainted with a bacteria that can kill you" (Bittman 2012).

In addition to the human costs—individual and social—of industrial agriculture, the danger it poses to the wider environment and natural ecosystem is no less serious. The 2006 United Nations study, "Livestock's Long Shadow," and others that have followed it, show that high confinement meat production is a major source of greenhouse gasses and a chief cause of global deforestation and general degradation of water quality. The release of methane directly from the billions of confined animals—such as huge numbers of feed lot cattle emitting tons of methane gas—and from the disposal of their enormous quantities of manure constitute a major source of greenhouse gasses. Methane is estimated to be 70 times more damaging to the Earth's atmosphere than CO_2 (Cummins). Added to methane is the release of nitrous oxide from vast amounts of pesticides and synthetic fertilizers used to grow genetically engineered soy and corn, the major foods for CAFO animals. The 2006 U.N. Report estimated that 18 percent, or nearly one-fifth of greenhouse gases come from "the livestock sector." In fact, as Mark Bittman has pointed out, animal agriculture is a larger source of the pollutants causing climate change than the greenhouse gases from all forms of transportation combined, 18 percent as compared to 14 percent (Bittman 2008). At the same time enormous areas of the Earth's tropical forests are being cut down to clear land for large-scale cattle ranching and the planting of corn and soy. According to the U.N. Report, an estimated 30 percent of the Earth's ice-free land is directly involved in livestock production.

This ongoing destruction of wild animal habitats, owing to the expansion of the livestock sector, reveals the direct link between the domestic CAFOs and the denizens of the wild. The suffering of our CAFO animals and the looming extinction of our wild animals are inextricably woven together. And the use of the possessive "our" in both cases is fitting because we are responsible for both.

With meat consumption rising worldwide—and with meat consumption in America still twice the global average—more and more knowledgeable experts are calling on people to at least cut back on the amount they eat. If people were to cut back by only 20 percent, a beginning brake might be put on the incessant demand for more land for the livestock sector (Cummins). The philosopher Jean Kazez has deftly captured the connection between, as she puts it, our wild animals and our mild animals (the ones we eat): "You can decline the hamburger to save the cow, but just as reasonably, to save the tiger" (Kazez 167).

The Pew Commission on Industrial Farm Animal Production, which we looked at earlier, called in its 2008 Report for a major reform to take place over a period of ten years leading to more humane treatment of CAFO animals. Five years later (2013) a further review of the Pew Report by the Johns Hopkins Center for a Livable Future scolded the powerful meat companies and their allied legislators for resisting at every turn the Pew Commission demands for stricter regulations. The situation, therefore, still stands with the earlier conclusion of the United Nations and Pew Commission studies that the food industry as it exists today is basically unsustainable. Its effects on the animals, on humans, and on the environment are too destructive (Bittman 2008).

One argument often made for factory farming in today's world is that it is efficient and so is able to keep costs down and make relatively low-priced food available to almost everyone, an increasingly important consideration in a world of expanding human population. This argument, however, is invalid on at least two counts. In the first place, if all the external costs borne by the wider society were taken into account—pollution, waste, disease and antibiotic-resistant bacteria, greenhouse gases, to name but a few, factory farming would be seen to be far from efficient and inexpensive. The huge costs that society takes on for the agricultural sector are not reflected in the supermarket prices. Added to this, secondly, is the important fact that the reason factory-farmed meat can also be marketed at deceptively low grocery-sticker prices is because the growing of corn and soy, the main food sources for factory-farmed animals, is heavily subsidized by the federal government. Take away the generous government subsidies, and factor in the external costs to the whole society, the illusion of inexpensive, factory-farmed food would evaporate.

Continuing with the present system of agriculture unchanged is a sure prescription for ever-deepening catastrophe, for humans, for animals, and for the Earth. What are the options? Two are the most discussed: humane food animal farming and vegetarianism. We will explore each with an eye both to practicality and to ethical validity.

Before looking at these two possibilities, let us set aside a third that is sometimes presented as an option to eating meat; namely, satisfying the desire for meat by eating fish instead. This disqualifies itself from the start simply because fish is meat. Furthermore, the world's fish stocks are already seriously endangered by over-fishing and pollution (Zimmer 2015). Switching mainly to seafood would further accelerate the present scouring clean of the oceans of all fish. And, finally, the death throes of the fish as they flop and gasp for oxygen after being landed signal that their deaths must be agonizing. Not a scintilla of evidence suggests that the fish do not feel pain, or that their deaths by asphyxiation out of the water are pain free. It may be, as some have claimed, that certain invertebrates, such as scallops and mollusks, probably lack the nerve-system complexity to feel pain. Octopuses, however, are mollusks, and octopuses have been shown to possess a surprisingly complex consciousness and behavior (Zimmer 2008; Mather 2008). "Eat more fish," may be good advice for health reasons (if one sets aside the mercury problem), but ecologically it cannot be an acceptable global policy (Zimmer 2015). And it skirts all the ethical questions entirely, just as it ignores completely the deaths of millions of marine mammals that become entangled and trapped in giant fishing nets or swept up by giant factory fishing ships.

So we have the two main alternatives to factory farming: humane animal farming and vegetarianism.

4.

Humane Animal Farming

Before we look at the potential of humane animal farming as an alternative to factory farming, let us consider briefly the emotional and spiritual lives of the animals involved. They are the same animals for each method of farming—cattle, pigs, poultry, and others. That these animals might have an inner life that matters to them is seldom considered, even by most proponents of smaller, humane animal farms. Even when talk turns to such things as "grass fed," "antibiotic-free," "organic," "cage free," "free range," and similar labels, it is usually hoped that these will be guarantees both of humane treatment of the animals and healthy food products for human consumption. Beyond this "assurance-labeling" for the benefit of the humans, however, these animals are still mainly looked upon, for the most part, as convenient parcels of tasty, healthy protein for human enjoyment and benefit. Because these animals lack the pazzaz and romance of the wild, "charismatic megafauna," it is easy to ignore or pass them by in so far as their own intrinsic needs and value are concerned. Silent, gentle, and mild as they are, these cattle, sheep, pigs, chickens, turkeys, and the like, will never remind us vociferously and dramatically of their very being as can the lion, tiger, wolf, and others. Once they have lived out their short but "humanely raised" lives, the gentle animals are easy to ignore and tend to fade into the background—much like the wallflowers at the high school prom. The less we hear and know about them, the more we can concentrate on the kitchen and the dinner table, and maybe on the latest gourmet recipe from the *New York Times* food section.

But should they receive from us more than just a fleeting awareness? Since we have come to rely on them so much, perhaps it might behoove us, perhaps out of an elementary sense of gratitude and common courtesy, to learn something about who they are in themselves. Do their lives as such matter, not only to us, but also to them? And, if to them, maybe they should also to us, and in their own right. Let us make a slight excursion to look at what we can glean from ordinary observation of the inner lives of the main farm animals so close to us. Although there are others, for the sake of space, I will focus here on poultry, pigs, and cattle.

1. The Lives of Farm Animals

We have learned from Rudolf Steiner that all the animals are immersed in the spiritual realities of the cosmos. They are guided by their own group "I"-beings and group souls, and are blessed with a powerful, group-species wisdom. Their delight in digestion, their mating and nesting, and their care of the young are all deep spiritual experiences, a participation in cosmic rhythms, cosmic feelings and thoughts, and cosmic being. Much can also be learned from their lives as *individuals*.

Chickens. This following description applies to chickens in their natural state. Chickens are the possessors of a complex group-species intelligence to which they give expression with many individual variations. They live in small groups of familiar chickens with very complex hierarchies, the famous "pecking order." They recognize over 100 other chick faces, even after months of being separate. They recognize human faces too, and remember their experiences with different people. Even after three days they recognize other chicks with whom they have been hatched and whose company they prefer. When a hen is about to lay an egg she recruits her rooster mate and together the two search for a suitable place to build their nest. Chickens have more than thirty different call types, each with a distinctive meaning: distress and warning calls, nesting and laying calls, warning and "all-clear" calls, and others. A hen also "talks" to her eggs and the embryos answer with peeps from within. Chickens love dust bathing, basking in the open air, scratching, stretching their wings, preening, and enjoying the company of others.

In a wonderful article on the situation and treatment of chickens in factory farms, Deb Olin Unferth reports on findings of animal studies that show that chickens all have different dispositions. Some are social and fearless, others more shy and watchful. Some enjoy human company, others are more stand-offish. Some have best friends, some rivals. Ethologists have shown that chickens have complex cognitive capacities. They are able to recognize a whole object even when it is partially hidden, a capacity previously thought only humans possess. Some experiments have shown that chickens have the ability to count to a certain extent and to use geometric type information to find food, and to relocate it if necessary. They are also capable of using their calls honestly, and, when it serves them, deceptively. Dr. Chris Evans, administrator of the animal behavior lab at Australia's Macquarie University, says, "As a trick at conferences, I sometimes list [chickens'] attributes, without mentioning chickens, and people think I'm talking about monkeys." Think on these little birds the next time chicken is your default order from the diner menu.

If we had the space we would find that geese, ducks, and turkeys are equally as interesting in their abilities and capacities as chickens, but with their own species differences. Domestic turkeys, to take but one example, in addition to the many capacities they share with chickens, are known by those who work with them in their natural state to be exceedingly affectionate and friendly toward humans, love to be caressed, and have even been known to "hug" humans and make a purring sound when they are content (Hatkoff; Unferth; Balcombe, 3).

Cattle. A tendency seems to exist to unconsciously regard cows as something of a huge digestive system, a kind of "digestive reactor" turning out hamburgers and milk for human enjoyment, and also turning out copious quantities of manure. At first glance, Rudolf Steiner might seem to lend some support to this attitude. If we observe the cow's whole form, he says, "we see it is in fact what I may call an extended digestion system...The cow is all digestion." But this system is integral to the deepest of spiritual reality and experience. The digestive system provides the cow with the deepest experience of the spirit, an astral soul joy that partakes of the astral soul of the cosmos itself. "For it belongs to this digestive process in the cow," Steiner explains, "to develop a wonderful astrality. The cow becomes beautiful in the process of digestion. Seen astrally, something immensely beautiful lies in this digestion. And when it is said by ordinary philistine concepts, indeed by philistine idealism, that the process of digestion is the most lowly, this must be indicated as an untruth, when from a higher vantage point, one gazes with spiritual sight at this diges-tive process in the cow. For this is beautiful, this is grand, this is something of an immense spirituality" (Steiner 1970, 25).

The joy of the cow in digestion makes real in the world the soul reality of the cosmos, for "she [the cow] is the animal that continually spiritualizes the Earth, which continually gives to the Earth the spiritual substance that she herself takes from the cos-mos." Elsewhere, Steiner also describes how other animal forms give expression to different aspects of the relation between the Earth and the spirit, but it is the cow that reveals par excellence the spiritual reality of the entire animal kingdom. "You see," says Steiner, "the cow has seen to it that, in her weight [the result of her remarkable digestive system], she is the expression of animal nature as such, she is as thoroughly as possible the expression of what is cosmic" (Steiner 1970, 24-5, 61-2). "The animal that chews the cud!" In this the cow is emblematic of all the animals. At the level of what is often regarded as the most material of all material processes, the digestive and metabolic systems, the cow reveals that all the animals in their being and experience are themselves a manifestation of the spirit, and themselves partake of the spirit.

As far as the individual cows are concerned, they participate in their cow soul—in the group-species soul—in many rich and differentiated ways. Cows are perceptive, sensitive, and highly attuned to one another, and to those humans, with whom they must deal. They form close, lifelong relationships with one another, and they have their distinct preferences for those they associate closely with. When they are separated from those close to them they will bellow and walk back and forth for some time. The mother–calf relationship is especially strong. In industrial agriculture those calves destined to become beef steers are weaned suddenly and prematurely, taken from their mothers where they have been together on pastures, and transported to a feed lot with thousands of others to be fattened for slaughter. This premature weaning and sudden separation are causes of great distress, to both calf and cow. Michael Pollan, who bought a young calf to follow it through the factory farming steps from calf to beef writes that "weaning is perhaps the most traumatic time on a ranch for animals and ranchers alike; cows separated from their calves will mope and bellow for days, and the calves, stressed by the change in circumstances and diet, are prone to getting sick" Pollan 2006, 71).

Cows' sensitivity to others is also seen in their excellent recall abilities. Cows can recognize at least fifty different other cows and ten different humans for several years, and can tell people apart based on posture, clothing, faces and height. For long periods of time, they maintain a sense of the location of things, such as paths, water, shelter, fences, etc. They will hold a grudge indefinitely if mistreated, and are known to sulk and act vain. Cows also learn from one another. They will avoid an electric fence, for example, just by first seeing another cow get an electric jolt from the fence. And, like chickens, cows will try new foods, or avoid harmful ones, by observing what others eat. They even show excitement when they succeed in solving problems, such as, when they unlatch a gate to obtain food. The emotional sensibility of cows is also reflected in that milk production increases when they are being spoken to and handled gently, and it declines when they are stressed by rough handling, prodding, and hollering. Cows are far from the stolid, obtuse creatures they are often portrayed as (Bekoff 2007, 55; Pollan 2006, 71; Hatkoff).

Pigs. Winston Churchill is reported to have said: "I like pigs. Dogs look up to us. Cats look down upon us. Pigs treat us as equals." Apocryphal or not, these words ring true to anyone who has grown up in close contact with pigs. Those of us who have grown up on a family farm with pigs know, too, that pigs are smart. The veterinarian and philosopher of science, Bernard Rollin, maintains that "Pigs are arguably smarter then dogs," and Gene Baur, founder and director of Farm Sanctuary, says, "In my experience, they're more like human beings than any other farm animal."

Pigs combine a strong individualistic streak with an equally strong social disposition. Baur observes that they can be very loyal as well as ornery. Sows build nests for themselves and their litters, taking fresh straw or dried leaves in the mouth and move it into a pile to sleep and give birth in. They also, however, raise their young cooperatively and take turns with other sows watching over the piglets. They develop one-on-one relationships and also form cliques, both of which may last for years. Pigs are known to be emotionally devastated when a close companion dies, and sometimes die themselves not long after from "unknown" causes. Contrary to popular prejudices, pigs are clean; they are not dirty, their houses are not sties. Baur reports that pigs on his Farm Sanctuary use the center of the barn for their common latrine, thereby keeping their own nests clean. Pigs love to root in the soil, and because they don't have sweat glands they need mud and water to cool off. While they form friends and groups, they also develop rivalries (Baur; Hatkoff).

People who take on pigs as pets know that they are not only clean and smart, but also can be extremely affectionate. With other pig companions, they enjoy touch and physical contact, and like to sleep together, often snout to snout. With humans they also express affection and loyalty, and love to be scratched behind the ears and have their bellies rubbed. Like many animals, young pigs love to play, fighting, nipping, and chasing. To signal their desire to play they use bouncy running and head twisting. Also, like many other animals we have looked at, pigs have a sense of fair play, with larger piglets handicapping themselves by sitting, kneeling, or lying down when playing with piglets smaller than themselves (Hatkoff; Baur; Balcombe, 130).

The intelligence of pigs is apparent even to a somewhat more than casual observer, but in test situations with animal researchers, it is striking. They are highly motivated and persistent, and capable of what is called "one trial learning," such that, if, for example, they pull a lever once and it gives them food they have no need to repeat the action. They can identify and fetch objects on request, and can respond to commands that involve objects, as in "push the dumbbell onto the mat" (Hatkoff, 94). They can make comparisons and maintain relationships among objects based on color, order, or location, and can identify the same object three years later. Some ethologists have taught pigs to play video games, using their snouts to move a joystick directing a cursor to hit targets on the screen. In video game tests the pigs can outperform chimpanzees. After a year, though a little rusty at first, pigs were able to take up the video game again and repeat what they had learned (Baur, 126–9; Bekoff 2007, 97; Balcombe, 130; Hatkoff, 92–121).

These are the animals that in factory farming are confined to pens and crates so small they cannot turn around in them, and for their entire lives are denied contact with other pigs, and have their litters taken from them as soon as possible. All animals in factory farming have every aspect of their natural lives violated in the cruelest ways.

I am aware that because of space limitations I have given short shrift to other farm animals, such as sheep and goats. The descriptions, however, of their emotional and social lives would be similar.

2. The Problem of Land: There's Not Enough of It

Neither a proliferation of small family farms nor vast, grassland ranching, singly or together, can solve the food problems of a growing world population, if meat is seen as essential to the diet. A major problem is simply that not enough land exists on the Earth to supply a meat-eating world with pastured, grass-fed meat. One food-production authority has calculated what would be needed:

> It requires 2 to 20 acres to raise a cow on grass. If we raised all the cows in the United States on grass (all 100 million of them), cattle would require (using the figure of 10 acres per

cow) about half the country's land (and this figure excludes space for pastured chickens and pigs). A tract of land just larger than France has been carved out of the Brazilian rain forest and turned over to grazing cattle. Nothing about this is sustainable. (McWilliams)

Mark Bittman has similarly observed that the 1.3 billion cattle now raised and slaughtered for food in CAFOs would be far too many for the available pasture on Earth (Bittman 2009). To complicate the picture further, unless their numbers are radically reduced, the pasturing of cows and chickens will produce as much methane as the grain-fed CAFO animals. The environmental argument for natural farming collapses, unless the number of animals involved is cut back drastically. On the sustainability issue, one conclusion seems unavoidable: Meat-eating, worldwide, cannot continue on its present and accelerating rate.

3. LIFE AND DEATH ON THE FAMILY FARM

How do small family farms stack up with respect to the lives of the animals on them. Without a doubt, the animals are spared most of the horrors of factory farming. For the duration of their lives on the small farm they are able to enjoy, more or less, the natural life for which their entire being is formed and intended. Even this, however, is limited. Their natural life is cut short long before its normal life span is completed. The animals on these farms live a little longer than those in the factory, and thankfully, without the torture. Still the family farm animals are killed in the prime of their lives. The normal life span of a pig is between ten and fifteen years, yet pigs raised on the small farm for food are killed, often after six months, and certainly by two years of age. Although a chicken can live for almost seven years, broiler chickens are killed at about seven weeks. Dairy cows will live for some years on the small farm, but beef steers will be slaughtered after some months. Although their lives are short, compared to their natural lifespan, the lives of the family farm animals are a far cry from those of the steers in the feed lots, the hens in the battery cages, the sows in the gestation crates. On this score alone, small humane farming is to be welcomed and encouraged as far as the quality of the animals' lives before their destined end is concerned.

All of this, however, is cut off prematurely. Herein lies a major, hidden question, hidden because seldom raised, seldom addressed: Can the killing be justified ethically by people deeply concerned with the welfare and lives of the animals? The animal has been living and enjoying life, under the care of trusted humans, when suddenly, from one day to the next, the animal is removed from this life, confined, and killed by its erstwhile caretakers. Something seems amiss here.

In the story I told in my introduction of my father's relationship with a favorite pig, I think he momentarily touched upon this key question, albeit unknowingly and with no sense of its wider implications. For months he and the pig had developed and enjoyed a close and affectionate relationship. When each day he called her by name to feed her, scratch her behind the ears, and rub her belly, she would come immediately and excitedly, stand up on the fence and reach through to touch him with her snout or hoof. Then one day after all these months, he killed and butchered her. When my mother served her up for supper the next day, as I related, my father looked at his plate, placed his hands on the table, and pushed his chair back, saying, "I can't eat this." I think (now I do, not then), that for a brief moment he had the feeling, even if he did not articulate it to himself, "I have betrayed a good and trusting friend." My father's flash of remorse points to a similar problem in the whole of small, "humane" meat production, where, in the end, betrayal of the trusting and vulnerable is a defining quality.

A central argument for justifying the killing of animals raised humanely is that killing is distinct from causing suffering. This argument holds that, as long as we have done everything to avoid pain and suffering for the animal during its lifetime, killing it, as painlessly as possible of course, is morally justified. Once the animal is dead we need no longer be concerned about its pain and suffering, for the possibility of these is over. The deeper assumption here is that the animal's life as such is of no value; what is of value is helping it to avoid pain and suffering as a sentient being while still alive. All told, its main and overriding value in our eyes all along has been its value for us as future food.

One of the earliest challenges to this argument came from the philosopher Ros Godlovitch in her coedited book of 1971, *Animals, Men, and Morals.* Peter Singer says Godlovitch was a first inspiration for his book, *Animal Liberation.* Andrew Linzey credits Godlovitch with a justifiable claim to being "the intellectual founder of the modern animal movement' (Linzey 2013, 158). One of her basic ideas is that it doesn't make sense to value alleviating the suffering of animals without valuing positively its life. Linzey quotes her at length as she addresses our question head-on:

> Although it seems coherent, absurdities follow from holding that animal suffering is to be avoided, but denying that animal life has value. For if a man were to consider his duty to prevent animal suffering without holding that animal life has value, then it would follow that he ought to exterminate all animal life. It seems an inevitable fact that all sentient creatures suffer to a greater or lesser extent at some points in their lives. Suffering is accepted as a concomitant of living and, as such (except for extremely severe and prolonged suffering) is considered worth tolerating. But it is considered worth tolerating because a value is placed on *living.* (quoted, Linzey 2013, 159)

As Godlovitch indicates, this does not mean that all killing is wrong. Defense, as when being mauled by a lion (not too common) and euthanasia when an animal's suffering is prolonged, intense, and unrelievable, may be justified. Even these exceptions can be seen to be in the interest of life.

The philosopher and veterinarian, Bernard Rollin, develops the argument further, and always from the standpoint of the animal. "Animal life," he writes, "is of value in and of itself, and killing animals even without pain is morally questionable." Rollin argues that animals have a number of interests more important to them than avoiding pain. "It is well known," he gives as examples, "that animals will chew off limbs to escape from traps, suggesting that concern with freedom—or life—trumps concern with pain. Animals will also choose sexual contact at the cost of pain. Biologically, as well as morally, it makes sense to suggest that life is more important to an animal than anything else.... By taking life, we take away the possibility of actualizing those interests that would be experienced as good by an animal" (Rollin 1989, 173). This would apply to all animals, including our farm animals, not least the chickens. Holding that the animal's life as such is of value is not merely an animal rights question. Of course, it implies that the animal has a right to live its life. Beyond a rights question, however, it is more a question of human responsibility—responsibility not to destroy but to protect something that as moral beings we have recognized as having intrinsic value of its own, whether useful to us or not.

What, then, are small farmers to do with their animals?

4. Biodynamic Agriculture and the Animals

This is an especially pressing question for biodynamic farmers because the animals on the farm are essential and integral to this method of agriculture. Biodynamic agriculture was initiated by Rudolf Steiner in Germany in the 1920s in response to groups of farmers asking his help in dealing with what they were experiencing as increasing depletion in soil and food quality. Since that time, biodynamic agriculture has spread around the globe and has been especially instrumental in pioneering the introduction and growth of community supported agriculture (CSA), an innovative way of developing a full-fledged, close relationship between producers and consumers.

While biodynamic agriculture is one part of the large and growing, general organic movement, it also contributes its own unique and important insights and practices to the larger movement. It shares most of the central aims of the general organic movement: the production of foods superior in nutrition and taste; foods free of pesticides, antibiotics, and disease-carrying bacteria; conservation of soil and water; no pollution; an intimate reciprocity between the farmer and the community; and humane treatment of the animals. To these aims, biodynamic agriculture adds at least three further contributions of special importance for noting here because they involve the farm animals directly. These include: a detailed understanding of the life forces of the Earth and practical methods for nurturing and renewing those forces; a deep understanding of the wholeness in the interaction of the cosmos, earth, plants, animals, and humans; and the presence of animals as essential to healthy and vital agriculture.

The animals are integral to biodynamic agriculture. The farmer, the soil and crops, and the animals form a unity with each contributing to the whole. By their presence, the animals make palpable the experience of the whole farm as a living entity. The manure from the animals ensures the renewal of the soil from year to year without synthetic fertilizers. The animals are also the source of special preparations recommended by Steiner for treating the soil to preserve and enhance its life forces. And the animals provide a direct connection to natural and cosmic rhythms so essential to an agriculture in harmony with the fullness of nature.

It is not surprising that biodynamic farmers honor their animals and feel a personal connection with them. The farmers provide them with shelter and healthy food—hay, green fodder, legumes, and so forth—free, of course, of antibiotics and pesticide residue. The farmer respects the bodily integrity of the animals and practices none of the mutilating practices so common to industrial agriculture. There is no painful dehorning of cattle, debeaking of chickens, or docking of pig and dairy cattle tails. And care is taken to ensure that the animals have ample space—in meadows, fields, and surrounding farmland—in which to move, play, and forage.

The consumers of the farm products are also viewed not merely as costumers, but also as part of the wholeness of the farm life. All are shareholders, who, buying a "share" at the beginning of the season, enjoy the bounty of the crops and also assume part of the yearly risk that all farming entails. Share holders may be local or part of a city group, and may number in the hundreds for a single farm. Shareholders and other recipients of the farm products are encouraged to visit the farm, take part in farm festivals, and for a few hours each season volunteer to help out in certain of the farm tasks. They are also encouraged to visit the animals.

Still, at the end, the animals are, as a rule, killed, butchered, and their meat sold to shareholders and others. At this point, a certain disjunction, or disconnect, appears in the experience of those who receive the animal products. Parents and children may visit the farm together for their food pick-up. While there, the parents may admire and enjoy views of the cows and pigs in the fields or at feeding time; the children may pet the sheep and squeal with the piglets. They then pick up their vegetables, which are usually beautiful and abundant, and, if they have purchased a meat share, pick up their nicely wrapped packages of chicken, beef, pork, or lamb. And it is here that the disconnect appears. A gap, a yawning space, separates the picture of the whole, vital animals flourishing on the farm and the neatly wrapped packets of separate animal parts at the pick-up. Seldom do the farm customers show evidence of any thought or curiosity about what has transpired in the in-between. The packaged flesh in their hands has no connection to the bucolic memory of the farm animals in their heads.

If biodynamic farmers—and all small farmers—were to become convinced that the killing of the animals cannot be morally justified—especially the pre-mature killing that is now common to all farming—what are they to do with the animals? It is feasible that the animals can be retained for their necessary manure and permitted to live out the entirety of their lives on the farm. Small vegetable farmers the world over have done this, or something like it, for centuries. This possibility has its own challenges, however, for the animals must still be cared for, and this can be a constant, labor-intensive responsibility, and inconvenient, especially in the provision and care for ailing or aged animals. It would also be necessary to adjust to the fall-off in shareholders who still demand their meat.

Nevertheless, a few biodynamic farmers have chosen not to kill their animals. They demonstrate that it is a feasible and workable, to embrace and enjoy the animals as fellow members of the whole family, farm community. Nevertheless, for those like myself, who hope that all farmers would be able to choose this option, it is incumbent upon us to recognize that it is not necessarily an easy solution, and that it deserves all the support we can give to the farmer, including political.

5.

VEGETARIANISM

The term *vegetarianism* first made its appearance as such in the 1840s. It was derived from the Latin *vegetus* to mean "one who lives a healthy life." In 1847, the Vegetarian Society was founded in England. It first prohibited alcohol and tobacco as well as meat, but the first two prohibitions were dropped about thirty years later. Long before the founding of the Vegetarian Society, however, the rejection of meat eating had already a millennia-long and venerable history. Important among the ancients was the Greek philosopher Pythagoras (570–495 BCE). He required that his disciples refrain from meat eating both because he saw the animals as having souls that would reincarnate, perhaps as humans, and because he considered meat-eating an indulgence of the senses at the expense of higher states of consciousness and spiritual development. Plato followed Pythagoras in his portrayal of the ideal society in *The Republic*, in which Plato maintained that the sensual indulgence of meat-eating is a hindrance to the development of intellect and spirit. The Neo-Platonists, such as Plotinus, Plutarch, and Porphyry (234–305 CE) continued the tradition. Like the other Neo-Platonists, Porphyry, in his essay, *On Abstinence from Animal Food*, presented the ancient tradition as "a way of living and thinking that recognizes the value of all creatures, human and otherwise, with whom we share the world" (Porphyry, 148). In his view, as with the others, meat-eating is a harmful, sensual gratification that impedes clarity of consciousness and spiritual development, and that, moreover, encourages the killing of animals, who have their own rightful claims on life and justice, and that we kill them for no better reason than that we like the taste of their flesh.

The Neo-Platonist tradition surfaced again in the Renaissance in such thinkers and artists as Marsilio Ficino, Giordano Bruno, and Leonardo da Vinci. By the early seventeenth century some of the most important Enlightenment thinkers and scientists were advocating a meat-free diet. Their numbers included, amazingly, leaders of the emerging mechanical philosophy, such as Descartes, Pierre Gassendi, and Francis Bacon. Much of their rejection of meat-eating was because they concluded for scientific reasons, based ironically on new discoveries revealed by human and animal dissection, that the human body was designed to be herbivorous. By this time also, however, travelers to India had discovered the ancient Indian teaching of *Ahimsa,* "nonviolence to all living beings." In his magisterial history of vegetarianism from 1600 to modern times, *The Bloodless Revolution,* Tristram Stuart points out that Indian vegetarianism had a powerful impact not only on the intellectual elite of Enlightenment Europe but also on a wide popular audience. Sir Isaac Newton himself was among the numbers of philosophers and scientists who, responding to the Indian philosophy, adopted a plant-based diet out of regard for the animals. "Sir Isaac Newton's reading about Indian sages," reports Stuart, "helped to convince him that 'Mercy to Beasts' was one of God's first and most fundamental laws from which Europeans had long since apostatized" (Stuart, xx.). By the early nineteenth century, Stuart concludes, "most of the philosophical, medical, and economic arguments for vegetarianism were in place and exerting continual pressure on mainstream European culture" (Stuart, xx, ccvi).

Stuart, interestingly, also points out that the actual coining of the word *vegetarian* and the founding of the Vegetarian Society in 1847 had a serious, dampening effect on the spread of vegetarianism. After that, he writes, "'vegetarianism' was applied to a distinct movement that could easily be pigeonholed, and ignored. Before that, meat-eating was an open question that concerned everyone and it affected not just people's choice of diet but their fundamental ideas about man's status on Earth" (Stuart, xvii). It is probably safe to say that only in the last half-century or less has vegetarianism begun to attract renewed attention in mainstream

Western culture, and then mainly during the past few decades. This growing attention is probably owing in some large part to a mounting preoccupation of the many with matters of health and longevity. But it also reflects to an extent a widening awareness of, and discomfort with, the extremes of cruelty and suffering meted out to billions of helpless animals every moment. It is only during the past couple of decades that there has begun to appear in significant numbers, hitherto a rarity, vegetarian and vegan restaurants in large cities, and in university towns even in Midwest America. Many ordinary restaurants have also begun to include a meatless salad or entrée on an otherwise still meat-packed menu. The agricultural, factory farm industry, with its myriad of fast-food outlets is, nevertheless, still powerful and pervasive, but it is no longer totally unchallenged. The number of vegetarians in this country and in Europe is still relatively small, but continues to show significant gains. A 2008 survey by the *Vegetarian Times Magazine* found that 7.3 million Americans, about 3.2 percent of the population, count themselves to be vegetarian, and one million or .5 percent vegan. It is not clear how many of those claiming to be vegetarian refuse only red meat, but continue to eat fish and chicken. While relatively small in numbers, vegetarianism is becoming a more and more significant presence in the food-animal-cultural complex.

Throughout our exploration, our guiding question has been, "How does Rudolf Steiner help us understand our relationship and responsibility to the animals?" We have looked at many specific areas related to this question. We are now at a juncture to ask another very specific, critical question, "What help does Rudolf Steiner give us, if any, on the vegetarian option?"

Before taking up this question directly, however, there is one area having to do with eating animals in which we do not need Rudolf Steiner's help, assuming that we are basically decent people with a modicum of conscious awareness. This is the realm of factory farming. All that we know about the awfulness of factory farming demands a fundamental refusal to eat any animal products—meat, dairy, and eggs—that have their origin, or may have, if we only knew, on factory farms. The only decent response to factory farming on all counts is veganism. This is simple, it is absolute, and it is categorical.

RUDOLF STEINER AND VEGETARIANISM

Now we can explore Rudolf Steiner's position on vegetarianism in general. I will focus on my understanding of what I take to be three main areas of Steiner's view about vegetarianism. The first area concerns Steiner's insistence on the freedom of the individual in the choice, for or against. The second has to do with his insights on the place of vegetarianism in a disciplined path of meditation and spiritual–moral development. And the third area, the more pressing and difficult, is that of our actual obligations to the animals with respect to our killing and eating them, or not.

Vegetarianism, Ideology, and Individual Freedom

Rudolf Steiner was adamant that vegetarianism is not a requirement for being an anthroposophist nor for membership more specifically in the Anthroposophical Society. This is fully in keeping with his fundamental philosophy of freedom and of ethical individualism. He wanted Anthroposophy as a movement and the Society itself to be truly free and open. The Statutes that he drew up for the Anthroposophical Society stipulated that "the General Anthroposophical Society is in no sense a secret society, but an entirely public organization, "without distinction of nationality, social standing, religion, scientific, or artistic conviction.... A dogma in any sphere whatsoever shall be excluded from the General Anthroposophical Society" (Steiner 1963, 5). More specifically, Steiner emphasized, "No dogmatic rulings shall be given in regard to vegetarianism, meat-eating and so on, for these things must be relegated to the sphere of individual judgment and it is really only in the sphere of individual experience that they have value. I mention this in order to avoid giving rise to the opinion that Anthroposophy entails standing for this or that kind of diet, whereas what it actually does is to make every diet comprehensible" (Steiner 1970, 201).

Steiner did not stop there. Some people, he said, actually need some meat for reasons of health because from heredity their bodies are unable to assimilate all they need from plant sources alone. Some people have a strong craving for meat because the *body* needs it, much like animals, perhaps, which in their natural surroundings go to the foods that are good for them. But Steiner did not say that just because a person likes meat, he or she needs it. In fact, most people think that they need far more protein than is necessary, and tend to eat meat to supply that protein. Too much protein is "poisonous to the body," and contributes for example to arteriosclerosis (Steiner 1987b, 101–2).

Steiner leaves no doubt that if a person can do without meat the advantages for emotional and physical energy are clear, but this is a matter, which individuals must decide for themselves. Steiner, nevertheless, stressed: "If he [a person] does decide he can do without it and changes over from a meat to a vegetarian diet, he will feel stronger than he was before.... If one does become a vegetarian, he feels stronger." Steiner even told of his own personal experience to a group of workers he was speaking to: "I know from my own experience. I could not otherwise have endured the strenuous exertion of the last twenty-four years! I could never have traveled entire nights for instance, and then given a lecture the next day" (Steiner 1987b, 100–1). When one considers the more than 6,000 lectures that Steiner gave during these twenty-four years and the many new fields he opened up in education, medicine, agriculture, the arts, and religious renewal, there would seem to be strong support in that alone for a meatless diet.* Still, Steiner repeats, "But now don't get the idea that I would ever agitate for vegetarianism! It must always be first established whether a person is able to become a vegetarian or not; it is an individual matter" (Steiner 1987b, 101).

Steiner's position on making an exemption for those genuinely needing meat for medical reasons would seem to be in accord with

---

* A modern historian of German culture, surveying Steiner's prodigious activities throughout his life, remarks of Steiner that he was "possibly one of the most indefatigable people who ever lived." Peter Watson, *The German Genius: Europe's Third Renaissance, the Second Scientific Revolution, and the Twentieth Century*, Harper, 2010, 676.

a basic mandate of most spiritual traditions, namely, to do what is necessary "to guard your health and life" (Kalechofsky, 173–4; Steiner 1947, 116–7). But an individual's decision to eat meat would not be at the expense of the other dimensions of Steiner's account of our kinship with the animals, and our responsibility to care for them. Nowhere does Steiner give any leeway to eat meat for frivolous and self-centered gastrocentric desires.

The health issues as such, for and against meat-eating, are difficult to referee. Perhaps the two most outspoken groups representing directly opposing outlooks on this issue are the Physicians' Committee for Responsible Medicine (PCRM), on one side, and the Weston-Price Foundation, on the other. The PCRM has mustered copious data pointing to the disease consequence of meat eating, especially red and processed meat, such as cold cuts, bacon, sausages, and so forth. The PCRM has also taken a leading and very successful role in working for alternatives in animal experimentation and medical school surgical and other training. They have also been leaders in urging for health reasons the adoption of a wholly plant-based, vegan diet. In direct opposition to the PCRM position on meat-eating is the Weston-Price Foundation, which argues that meat produced organically is essential to a complete and healthy diet. Perhaps, depending on how one slices and dices the evidence, a respectable case can be made for either of the two positions. In my understanding of Rudolf Steiner on the health issue, a genuine medical need, which would affect a small minority of persons, would have to be established to qualify as a bona fide medical reason for meat-eating.

The Place of Vegetarianism in Spiritual–Moral Development

Rudolf Steiner is very clear that meat-eating can be a serious hindrance to spiritual–moral development. By tending to increase the influence of the body over consciousness, meat-eating can contribute to a dulling of the clear consciousness so central to the attainment of spiritual clarity and insight. Here Steiner seems to represent a modern version of the Neo-Platonic vegetarian tradition, with important qualifications. He describes the place of vegetarianism in a genuine spiritual path of discipline:

Vegetarianism will never lead anyone to higher worlds; it can be no more than a support for someone who thinks to himself: I wish to open for myself certain ways of understanding the spiritual worlds; I am hindered by the heaviness of my body, which prevents the exercises from having an immediate effect. Hence I will make things easier for myself by lightening my body. Vegetarianism is one way of producing this result, but it should never be presented as a dogma; it is only a means that can help some people to gain understanding of the spiritual worlds. (Steiner 1983, 9–3)

It is something of a puzzle to me that some anthroposophists of my acquaintance take with utter seriousness Steiner's warnings of the harmful effects of alcohol on body and spirit but ignore, as if they were never spoken, his words on how a meat-free diet might lend strength to their meditative life.

Steiner goes immediately, however, to an important caution. Vegetarianism by itself cannot produce spiritual progress. It can only help if a certain spiritual progress and a beginning loss of pleasure in meat have been achieved. "Anyone," writes Steiner, "who develops spiritually with the aid of vegetarianism will be stronger, more efficient in daily life; he will be not merely a match for any meat eater but will be superior in working capacity." But, he warns, as long as a desire for meat is unattended to, vegetarianism is useless. It does not produce spiritual results by itself; it works only when grounded in genuine effort to overcome the desire for meat. Otherwise the soul has not changed, and remains stuck at where it was at the beginning of the path. "When pleasure in eating meat has gone, then to abstain from meat may be of some use in relation to the spiritual world. Until then, breaking the meat-eating habit can be helpful only for getting rid of the desire for meat. If the desire persists, it may be better to start eating meat again, for to go on torturing oneself about it is certainly not the right way to reach an understanding of Spiritual Science" (Steiner 1983, 92–3). To want to overcome a desire for meat, and to work toward that, could well be mandated as also a part of our spiritual commitment to help the animals in light of all the harm that we have done to them.

Vegetarianism and Our Obligations to the Animals

Rudolf Steiner goes further with respect to vegetarianism. He approaches this issue with reflections on the origin of humans and animals. The animals made possible the development of the human being as capable of possessing a true, free, and individual self. The animals made this possible in two ways that we have looked at. They took on for themselves physical forms that would have been useless and a hindrance as a vehicle for a free and independent self. And they took on extreme emotions and passions that would have overwhelmed the human "I." In the process we also left the animals behind as beings that have the capacity to suffer and to feel pain. Having a free and independent "I"-being, the human can work with pain, to bear it with understanding and to transform it. This the animals cannot do. "We have left behind us the animal as something that already has the capacity to feel pain but does not yet possess the power to raise itself above pain, and to triumph by means of it." The animal is trapped in its pain. When we develop a cosmic feeling for how the animal has made possible our possession of a self, and how, as a result, we can deal with our pain in ways the animal cannot, "we then experience a great and all-embracing feeling of sympathy for the animal kingdom." Traditional peoples preserved a memory of the original relation between human and animals, and, with their memory, a deep feeling of connection and sympathy for the animals. Humans gradually lost a sense of this connection and the sympathy for the animals that went with it. This loss of connection with the natural world and the animal kingdom was necessary for a time to enable the emerging human "I"-consciousness to come into its own, independent selfhood, determined neither by the natural nor by the spiritual worlds.

Now, however, the time has come for the human I to complete the process of its development: to transcend the initially necessary sense of isolation and self-centeredness and to fulfill its own true potential in being able to open up and reach out to include others in its embrace—including other humans along with the other creatures of the Earth. Originally we could not give the animals an individuality, which can compensate for the pain the animals have to suffer. But when we realize more and more the freedom and selflessness actually possible to the individual self we can begin to give what we could not before.

Our response to the animals is a two-stage process. In the present stage we can only begin the process by showing kindness and compassion to the animals. We can begin to realize, as Steiner puts it:

> It is to the animals that I owe what I have now become. As the animals have fallen from an undivided existence to a shadow existence, I cannot repay them what they have sacrificed for me, but I must make this good, so far as it is possible, by the treatment I extend to them. (Steiner 2000, 47)

This is our duty to them in the present, in the interim we might say.

Then there will be a second stage reaching into the far, far future. In this future stage we can help the animals attain their own independent individuality, their individual I. We will have a better relation between ourselves and the animal than now exists, "especially in the West." "There will come a treatment of the animals whereby man will again uplift those he has pushed down." This will be the second stage in our relation to the animals. We will look more closely at both these stages in our final section.

Before that, however, I want to briefly take note of a peculiar expression Steiner uses in his discussion of what we owe the animals now. It is an expression that warrants our close attention, because, in my view, it is often badly misunderstood and as a result can be seriously misleading. In discussing the modern world's lack of sympathy for the animals, Steiner uses a rather odd turn of phrase, which seems to throw many people off from his real intention. He describes how in the modern, materialistic world human beings, as a rule, have lost any real, inner feeling connection with the animals, to whom we owe our existence. And, so, he says, "Man has paid in a strange fashion his debt to the animals. He has eaten them" (Steiner 2000, 46). Though it is hard for me to grasp, some anthroposophists of my acquaintance interpret this to mean that Steiner is saying that we *should* repay our debt to the animals by eating them. Could there be a more confused and complete misunderstanding? Surely Steiner is here being ironic, or, more strongly, outright sarcastic. And it is with this ironic, I would say sarcastic, comment that I think Steiner is radically calling attention to our human obliviousness and insensitivity to all that the animals suffer at our hands—and at how unconscious we ordinarily remain about all that is entailed in our casually eating them.

Perhaps in the end, the strongest basis for vegetarianism, all things considered, is very simple: pity and mercy.

In the concluding section, I propose to explore further our relation to the animals in the present and long, but foreseeable future, and then what our hope and responsibility can be for them in the far-, far-distant future.

PART V

THE REDEMPTION OF THE ANIMAL WORLD

OUR RESPONSIBILITIES
NOW AND IN THE FAR FUTURE

Rudolf Steiner affirms the importance of animal rights, but insists further that "there are responsibilities that go beyond the realm of rights and the law." Steiner holds that there are two kinds of responsibility, or, perhaps better, two levels of responsibility. We have our responsibility to work for the welfare and rights of animals now in this present stage of Earth existence. But we also have the responsibility to *redeem* the animals in the far distant future from their lives of bondage and innocent suffering. Redemption of the animals in Steiner's vision means that the present group "I"-beings of animals will attain in the next stage of Earth existence their own independent "I"-beings, their own free and individual selves. The first responsibility we can practice now in the present stage of the Earth. The second responsibility, however, we cannot fulfill now, but we can begin preparing for it.

This is the way Steiner explains the relationship between these two sets of responsibilities. The concept of rights can apply only in the immediate sense world. The concept of animal rights has its origin in the recognition of human rights, and we have seen how Steiner concurs with those who have extended the rights concept to include animals as, also, moral beings. Rights have to do with regulating the outer sense relationships between humans, and by extension, between humans and animals. These rights concepts can only apply, therefore, in the outer sense world. This confronts us, nevertheless, with the present task of working in this world to ensure that the animals' welfare and rights, negative and positive, are honored and protected. But our responsibility for the redemption of the animals cannot be carried out under the conditions of the present sense world.

This is how Steiner describes the situation:

> Our responsibility to redeem the animals emerges out of a totally different world. But in our present existence, we cannot assume this responsibility at all. We can do nothing in this present existence to redeem the animals that suffer because of us. We can redeem them only when we look forward to the end-condition of the Earth—a condition in which natural laws do not hinder us from intervening in the redemption of the animal world and removing the suffering from it. (Steiner 2010, 127)

Here we are directed by Steiner to the far-distant future in which our present sense world will have been transformed and new spiritual–physical conditions hold sway. This is a vision of the final transformation of Earth conditions, which Steiner has in common with a number of other spiritual and philosophical traditions.

This is not a vision, however, that a purely materialistic and mechanistic metaphysics can deal with or tolerate. Steiner recognizes this: "From the perspective of natural science"—which today is dominated by a materialistic metaphysics—"everything we say is impossible." Steiner urges, however, that we can begin to glimpse the possibility of such a vision by working on ourselves to realize that an awareness of "this suffering without guilt of the animal world is already a first step in perceiving the spiritual dimension of our present world." Materialistic, mechanistic science cannot grasp even the reality of suffering or its meaning, and the reality of guilt is far beyond its ken. "Thus," says Steiner, "we must now move forward to grasp an end-condition of the Earth, into which physics has no right to speak. Thus we expand what lives in us to a grasp of our cosmic connection" (Steiner 2010, 127). So we need not wait passively for our final redemption of the animals, but we can begin now to prepare ourselves for it by striving to make ever-more real our connection to the deeper spiritual dimensions of the world in which we live.

THE SPIRITUAL–PHYSICAL CONDITIONS
OF OUR PRESENT WORLD

Steiner describes how we have received from earlier stages of Earth evolution a planet pervaded, held together, and governed by an immense wisdom and intelligence. Steiner speaks of the present Earth as a "planet of wisdom." "Wisdom, though hidden, permeates the foundations of earthly existence" (Steiner 1987b, 70). We see this wisdom in all of nature, we see it in the great wisdom of the animals, and we see it closest to us in the intricacies of the human, physical body. If it were not an intelligence-wisdom-filled world, our own intelligence could not connect with it. "When human beings need wisdom in order to understand things—that is, when we extract wisdom from them—this shows that wisdom is inherent in the things themselves" (Steiner 1997, 192–3).

For our present stage of Earth existence, Steiner repeatedly underscores the great wisdom at work in the natural world. This puts him in substantial agreement, it seems to me, with those environmentalists today who stress the natural and intricate balance achieved by the beings of the world with each other and with the Earth. In the natural order of things, this balance involves life and death, joy and pain, cooperation and predation. This balance is the working of the great wisdom woven into world existence. Since it has also been greatly disturbed and upset by the intrusion into it of human beings, Steiner would probably also look favorably on many of the efforts of some environmentalists to restore something of this wisdom-filled, world balance.

Steiner describes the interplay of life and death in maintaining this balance. The biologist, Wolfgang Schad, building on some of Steiner's insights, discusses the central role of death itself in creating and maintaining this balance. Death is clearly important in making room for new life, in what would otherwise be the swamping of the entire Earth by the incredible fecundity of the Earth's living beings. Schad writes: "The life shell, the biosphere of the Earth is limited. The great abundance of her microbes, plants, and animals is only possible through the fact that the majority of the successors serve as nourishment for other organisms." In other words, death not only makes room for the successor, but also makes possible the provision of subsistence that ensures their further life.

Schad describes how this life-role of death works from the mineral world on up to the human. The mineral world experiences a kind of death in that the structure of crystals is broken up to produce water-capable clays and humus on which plants can grow. The plant world, in turn, gives itself partially up so that animals can live from her. Predation among the animals, when also not unduly disturbed by humans, helps maintain the balance. And the human, Schad says, undergoes a kind of "practical" death process in standing up and achieving erect posture, thus leaving the animal bearing behind. Schad also directs attention, as does Steiner, to the fine or delicate dying processes in animal and human physiology that make possible feeling and consciousness. Steiner expresses it this way: "Consciousness only arises when there is conflict between the external elements and the inner life forces, causing a breaking down of tissue. Consciousness can only arise from the destruction of life" (Steiner 1987b, 44–5). Feeling and consciousness would otherwise be overwhelmed by the all-enveloping vitality of unrestrained life forces. This feeling and consciousness that arise from the delicate dying processes are also the source of the pain and suffering that run through all of existence. The life- and death-balance of Earth existence is wrought by the presence and working of wisdom in the world (Schad 2009).

Steiner looks beyond the present stage of Earth existence, however, in envisioning the emergence of a new world order. This would put him at odds with one group of theologians, sometimes known as "eco-theologians." These eco-theologians accept the present world order, with all its pain, suffering, and predation as bearing the final seal of divine approval. Eco-theologian Matthew Fox, for example, says that all aspects of creation are of equal value, and he endorses predation as carrying the final blessing of God, and hence to be reveled and gloried in. A certain truth is contained in this in that under present Earth conditions predation is part of the balance of things. And, as Andrew Linzey, Anglican theologian and leading animal advocate—certainly not himself an eco-theologian of the likes of Fox—acknowledges, it is often held against animal rights people that "they don't face up to the realities of the natural world" (Linzey 2007). This charge is also turned, in a related but somewhat different direction, to justify the eating of meat, as in, "In killing and eating the animals, I'm just following the laws of nature," a sentiment often heard around the dinner table on Thanksgiving Day to put a stop to any further, uncomfortable discussion of the matter.

Steiner is realistic about the death, pain, suffering, waste, and futility of much in nature, but he is also realistic about the life and joy in existence experienced by the beings of nature. And he goes radically beyond the eco-theologians in looking toward a future new world, to a transformation of the "planet of wisdom" to a "planet of love." We will look more closely at how he envisages this transformation. First, however, let us revisit briefly our responsibilities toward the animals in this present world.

An essential, first step in our immediate responsibility to the animals in the present conditions of Earth existence is to deepen our moral–spiritual connection with them. This is primarily a felt-connection. Recent ethological research has helped bring this home by revealing the rich feeling, moral, and cognitive capacities that we have in varying degrees in common with the animals. Many animals have been shown to express a whole range of spiritual–moral capacities, which include altruism, compassion, empathy, nurture, fair play, and desire for community, among others. It is also our responsibility to extend an affective connection to animals less complex than the higher vertebrates. These less complex animals also belong to the larger spiritual community of which we are all members. This means that we recognize the intrinsic worth of all animals, and that they have being and worth in their own right. It is primarily through a feeling grasp of our commonality and kinship with the animals that we can acknowledge and take up the fundamental ethical question of whether we can justify our treating the animals merely as means of satisfying our own desires and perceived needs. Part of our present responsibility to the animals is, then, to intensify and enrich our own sensitivities and spiritual, emotional life in order that we can better recognize and respond, on the one hand, to the animals' worth and integrity, and, on the other hand, to their innocence and vulnerability.

3.

OUR WORK WITH THE ANIMALS
BETWEEN OUR DEATH AND REBIRTH

According to Steiner our community of connection with the animals is not broken at our death. On the contrary, after our death we find ourselves, at first and for a time thereafter, directly in the astral realm as such, which is the realm of the animal group "I"-beings. This realm Steiner describes as a "feeling-filled stimulus world," in and from which the dead become intimately familiar with "the inner aspect" of the animal life in their whole world. After death, humans immerse themselves in the wisdom of the group souls and "I"-beings of the animals, which is basically hidden from us in earthly life, apart from the relatively small amount we can observe and come to infer. And from this vantage, humans, after death, work through the inner life of the animal kingdom to help it perfect itself and to evolve. "The very basis of the work of the dead is the furthering of the animal kingdom.... And a large amount of the work of the dead consists in placing themselves in direct relationship to the world of living animals." And he goes on, "Animals exist in the Earth only because human beings die and send their impulses from the spiritual world into the life of animals" (Steiner 2007, 27). He remarks further that the forces identified by Darwinism as the mechanical operations of natural selection and adaptation to the environment are the external expressions of inner forces working from the realm of the dead (Steiner 2007, 27–8). It is in the relationship with the animal kingdom after death that the human can come to comprehend the inner side of animal life in its fullness (Steiner 2008, 25).

Another aspect of the human experience of the animal world after death, according to Steiner, raises a further important issue. In entering the astral realm in the company of the animals, humans, after their death, have the powerful experience of coming face to face with their own "animal nature." Steiner, at various points, depicts the animal nature as the "feeling-filled living element," the surging world of the astral, the world we have in common with the animals, the world of feeling, joy, passion, and compassion. This "feeling-filled living element," however, has a strong aggressive impetus, which gives it a destructive tendency to kill all else that is living around it. By virtue of participation in the astral the human being has an intimate connection with the powerful, destructive forces it contains. In the human, Steiner points out, "a good deal of desire to destroy, to kill the living remains" (Steiner 2007, 27–8).

In earthly life the human being is spared having to face the full force of this destructive tendency. The animals have taken upon themselves the excessive passions and astrality that would otherwise overpower the human "I"-being. In the animal these passions are woven coherently into the wisdom of the animal body and group soul, and, thereby, serve the particular needs and characteristics of the different animal species. Perhaps it is accurate even to say that what would be excessive and destructive passions in the human are taken up and ennobled in the wisdom of the animal—however fierce and violent they may be. Furthermore, the existence of whatever destructive astrality remains to the human is contained in the human subconsciousness , "locked up" below the level of conscious awareness. After death, however, this unconsciousness is unlocked and the human being is confronted directly with the destructive forces that are part of the human's own nature (Steiner 2007, 28–9).

This confrontation with the destructive forces of the astral living in the human calls forth in the human dead the development, as a counter-force, of a "deep reverence for all living things." This counterforce is at first elicited in a way similar to how the growing human child on Earth begins to take hold of its own body, unconsciously and without actively willing it. "What grows up externally in the child to our joy, grows similarly in the dead in that more and more they hold every living thing to be sacred in such an edifying way.... It is the development of the deepest reverence for all living things" (Steiner 2007, 28–9). This reverence for life is indispensable for the transformation also of our own sense-bound thinking, which lacks creative life and in itself visits death and destruction on Earth. The development on Earth of the deepest reverence for all living things is a reflection of, and a contributor to, the same development of reverence for all life that can continue after death.

To make vivid the destructive forces within us, and hidden from us in our subconscious until after death, Steiner uses the imaginative image of the Centaur, the mythological being with a human head and an animal body. It is the task of the human to transform the Centaur in us, to transform the extreme and death-dealing passions within us, which we do have in common with the animal. The difference, as we have noted, is that in the animal these passions are woven into and directed by the wisdom of the animal body and soul. In the human, they are present, but hidden in the subconscious until after death when we have to confront them openly. It is crucial that we accost and transform this element that we have in common with the animals on one level, and in ourselves make it truly human (Steiner 2007, 55–6).

Here we have a possible problem in Steiner's language. "The animal *in the human being*," [my italics] he writes, "is primarily, even in the best sense a destructive one." And in various places he cautions against sinking into "animality" (Steiner 2007; 1941, 157). This language raises an obvious problem. The words "animality" and "animal nature" conjure up all the associations with the centuries-long tendency of humans to regard the animals not merely as inferior to humans but often as outright evil. Is the use of these words evidence of an unexpurgated trace of speciesism in Steiner himself? After all, we still are inclined to use such expressions as "That person is just an animal," or that person is "a beast, beastly." The British moral philosopher Mary Midgley has pointed out that "at a deep imaginative level people still tend to see animals as symptoms of odious, antihuman qualities, and as a consequence to resist the idea of kinship" (Deane-Drummond and Clough, 202). Is Steiner, himself then, perpetuating a deep engrained attitude of speciesism?

My own answer is, No, Steiner is not a speciesist, but he is limited by the available language in his effort to describe what is a genuine issue. The issue is this: If human beings give themselves over to the destructive drives and emotions that we have in common with the animals, especially those that well up out of our own unconsciousness, without our attempting to stand back from them, to evaluate and guide them, we are also abandoning our connection to our own higher self. Because the human being is still on the way to developing a truly free and independent self, we are all too prone to abandon our true selves in just this way. "Our ego ["I"] is submerged," explains Steiner, "in the ocean of the physical material world [not connected with its true, spiritual and higher self] and is anything but free when it follows the dictates of anger, passions, and also love in the ordinary sense. The "I" is unfree because it is ensnared in the toils of anger, of passion, and of the like" (Steiner 2003, 60). When the human being is ensnared in this way the connection with its own true "I" has been cut off. In the animal, the situation is otherwise. In the animal the passions are contained and directed by the wisdom of the animal's group soul and "I"-being. But when the human abandons the guidance of the true human "I"-being, it falls to a level that is neither fully human nor animal. It has lost connection with its own human "I"-being, and it lacks from the beginning the animal's group "I"-being. *It is at once, both subhuman and sub-animal.* The human soul becomes rudderless, driven by the winds of astrality and passion with no stabilizing helmsman at the wheel.

The use of the word *animality* to describe this anomalous state is, in my view, unfortunate. At the same time, I am unable to come up with an alternative that would accurately portray what Steiner is driving at. It is important for anthroposophists especially to attend to the deeper meaning Steiner is aiming to depict. Otherwise, the use of "animality" will simply reinforce centuries-old habitual and conventional thinking and attitudes.

4.

THE "SALAMANDER ANIMALS" AFTER DEATH

What about the animals, the souls of which at death do not merge entirely back into the group soul and "I"? Steiner does not say a lot in this regard, but perhaps enough that we can draw some reasonable conclusions without wildly speculating. Recall how he describes certain animals that, during life, "tear something lose from the group soul that cannot return to it" after their death. Everything that remains behind in this way becomes a spiritual entity with "I"-like qualities, in fact very human "I" qualities. These "I"-like spiritual entities belong to what traditional wisdom calls elementals of the kind known as a Salamander. In Steiner's list of the animals giving rise to this "I" entity, this Salamander, we remember, are included all the apes, as well as some birds, some amphibians, some kangaroos, and some other warm-blooded animals. Released from the group soul, the Salamanders work in the world of nature for the benefit of the wider animal kingdom. They may also work to alert humans more and more to the special needs and capacities of the animal kingdom, and to awaken compassion in the human for the animals. And, perhaps it may be reasonable to suppose that these "I"-endowed animal souls may have a special role to play with us in our working with the animal world after death. It may perhaps be that it is just these animals that will be leaders in cooperation with humans in the ongoing redemption of the whole animal world.

The appearance of the Salamander "I"-being can occur as a given with certain of the higher animals named by Steiner. But it may also occur in another way. The Salamander being can also appear when "a special relationship between man and animal arises," "where a man has that kind of relationship to animals that involve his own feelings, his own concern of soul" (Steiner 1981, 297). The examples Steiner gives are the close relationship that the shepherd has with his lambs, and the relationship of the horseman and his steed—one thinks readily of the long, intimate relationship between Alexander the Great and his courageous war horse, Bucephalus. In relationships of this sort the Salamander is able to embody itself—presumably in the relationship itself—and serve to mediate and share knowledge between the human and the animals in the relationship. "The knowledge that the shepherd has in regard to his flock is whispered to him by these beings" (Steiner 1981, 298).

It would also seem reasonable to suppose that a similar "I"-like entity can arise between the human and his or her companion animals. These relationships are also often replete, in Steiner's words, with the human's "own feelings, his own concern of soul." And the exchange and sharing of feelings is mutual. When one has lived with a companion animal for years, shared the home, not infrequently the bed, come to know each other's habits, moods, likes and dislikes, and idiosyncrasies, enjoyed play time together, and shared affection and empathy with one another—an intimate and enduring relationship, indeed, takes place. When this relationship is broken—when the animal dies or is killed or lost, or when it must be relieved by us of incurable and excruciating suffering from illness or injury, the event can be wrenching. Speaking for myself, "It breaks your heart." This is an experience of grief known to countless people.

The great twentieth-century philosopher and theologian Nicolas Berdyaev describes in his *Autobiography* his reaction to the illness and death of his beloved cat Muri:

I experienced Muri's suffering before his death as the suffering of all creation. Through him I felt myself united to the whole of creation awaiting deliverance.... I very rarely weep, but when Muri died, I wept bitterly. And the death of such a charming one of God's creatures was for me the experience of death in general. I demand for myself eternal life with Muri.

Ptolemy Tompkins, whose lovely little book, *The Divine Life of Animals*, called my attention again to Berdyaev's account of Muri. Tompkins at one time wrote an article for a popular devotional magazine, called *Guideposts*, on "animals and heaven," an extremely popular topic as anyone will know who has visited a "pet cemetery" and read some of the messages to departed pets on their gravestones. Tompkins comments on Berdyaev's grief: "No one would deny that Berdyaev was possessed of a truly formidable intellect. Yet when it came to his feelings on the death of his cat, he sounds practically indistinguishable from the ranchers, corn farmers, and retired grandmothers who wrote in about my *Guideposts* pets-in-heaven piece" (Tompkins, 218).

Perhaps Rudolf Steiner's account of the "I"-like being that arises in a close and feeling relationship between humans and individual animals, often companion animals, offers some possibility of an unbroken relationship between them continuing in the spiritual world—that the animal's death is not a sudden, once-and-for-all separation. Is it possible that the animal after its death exerts its presence in the human soul, sensitizing us to the lives and needs of the animal world around us? And since, as Steiner, along with St. Paul, emphasizes that love is not transient but enduring, is it not possible, and perhaps demanded, that if a genuine relationship of love exists between the human and the individual animal, an enduring spiritual relationship of love between them has also been established?

5.

The Redemption of the Animals

We turn now to a contemplation of the main aspects of Steiner's vision of the far future when humans will have the responsibility to redeem the animals. Following that, we will return to look as clearly and unflinchingly as possible at our present situation and relationship to the animals.

Steiner describes how in the first stage of Earth evolution, that of Old Saturn, certain high beings achieved their "human stage" and how others in the subsequent stages of Old Sun and Old Moon also attained, respectively their "human stage." "Human" in Steiner's usage in this context does not mean that these beings have the appearance or the mode of being of present-day earthly humans, but that they had received a free, independent, individual "I"-being, or self (Steiner 1997, 143). During our present-day Earth stage the now developing human being is destined also to attain full awareness and guidance of its human "I"-being, though at present, we are "still on the way." At the end of the present stage of Earth existence, the animals' group "I"-beings will be redeemed. With the help of advancing humans at that later time, the animals will also attain to their "I"-being, their independent, individual self—in short, their human stage (Steiner 1996).

Steiner's insistence on using the term *human* to describe the state of having an "I" stresses throughout the unique role and responsibility of present-day humans in Earth evolution. It does not mean that the purpose of Earth evolution is solely for the benefit of present-day earthly humans. It is clear that for Steiner the entire realm of nature is of fundamental worth and value and that the animals, among other beings, have their own intrinsic value and worth. The use of "human" to mark the possession of an "I" does point, however, to the unique and crucial responsibility present-day humans have in shaping the future of Earth evolution.

The present and future task of earthly humans is, in Steiner's vision, to transform the Earth as "a planet of wisdom" into Earth as a "planet of love," encompassing all the beings within it. It is not that love will separate from wisdom, but, rather, that love will be guided by "the wisdom that is the foundation of the world." In Steiner's vision, the redemption of the animals—their acquisition of a true and individual self—is integral to the transformation of the present planet of wisdom to a planet of love.

Two dimensions of love as Steiner portrays it are key to our understanding of what is involved in the redemption of the animals. These are the relation between love and individuality and the relation between love and evil.

1. LOVE AND INDIVIDUALITY

Love is only possible among and between individual, independent selves. Love requires individuals—individuals acting freely out of themselves for and with other selves. When individuality is lacking, love is impossible, for lack of independent, individuality means being determined by outer forces and realities. This outer determination and accompanying inability to love can be the result of being engulfed by either external physical or spiritual forces and realities. To be swallowed up in a sea of undifferentiated spirituality, for example, makes the freedom necessary for love no more possible than to be pervaded by physical and emotional forces over which we have no control. Individuality is prerequisite for the possibility of love.

In their present state, the group souls and "I"-beings of the animals have wisdom, but not love. Love is only possible with individuation among and between separate selves:

> No true love is possible where the egos ["I"-beings] are interconnected within the group soul. Beings must be distinct from each other and offer love as a free gift. Only by such a

separation as has come about in the human kingdom, where ego meets ego as an independent individual, has love as a free offering become possible.... the animal species are united with each other within a group soul and their activities are regulated by the wisdom of the group-soul. Only when this group-nature is surmounted, and an individual ego faces another individual ego, can the sympathy present as love be offered as a free gift from one being to another. (Steiner 1987, 12–30)

This is a radical understanding of love. Genuine love is to give oneself to and for another with no expectation of reward or return in kind. "For what else is love," asks Steiner, "than widening one's consciousness to encompass other beings? It is love when we are willing to deprive ourselves, to sacrifice ourselves to whatever extent for the sake of another.... so will we, through widening our life to encompass the lives of others, become able to attain a higher life. There will then, out of what we have given away to others, be born within us love and compassion for all creatures" (Steiner 1987b, 63). So compassion for other creatures is in itself already a first step in developing love within ourselves.

Although the group souls and "I"-beings of animals have only wisdom, since love can only be developed in Earth existence and the animal group souls and "I"-beings are still in the spiritual world, a foundation on Earth has, nevertheless, been laid down. Single, individual animals on Earth are beginning to know love, if even at a beginning and elementary stage. "Wisdom," Steiner explains, "developed before love; as yet love is far from perfect, but even now it is to be found at all levels of existence, in plant, animal, and human beings, from the lowest sexual love to the highest spiritualized love" (Steiner 1987b, 70). In the animal on Earth, love first manifests itself as sexual love and from there the basis exists for love to develop to its highest. "On the Earth love is to develop from the most elementary stage to the loftiest.... At first love appears as sexual love and evolves to the highest spiritual love, but all love, the highest as well as the lowest, is the breath of Gods" (Steiner 1987b, 71). All depends, however, on the human being to develop the fullness of love such that the Earth may become the planet of love encompassing all beings.

The group souls of animals will be raised in this planet of love to receive their own individual, independent selves, capable of freely offering themselves in love. This will be the full redemption of the animals as a long-awaited act of love by humans for them. "For when man has become strong, he will draw the other beings with him" (Steiner 1987, 110).

2. LOVE AND EVIL

Essential to the task of developing love on Earth is the confrontation with evil and its transformation. Love and freedom go together. Love is only love if it is freely given. Freedom, however, requires the possibility of being able to choose between good and evil. It is only in confronting evil that love can emerge as the ultimate transformation of evil:

> The gods endowed us with enthusiasm for what is higher, but without evil we would have no feeling of self, no free choice of the good, no freedom. In order to choose the good, we must also have evil before us; it must exist within us as self-love. When the force of self-love has developed to become love of all, evil will be overcome. Evil and freedom stem from the same original source.... A good is only good if it has stood the test of evil. For love to reach its highest goal, the love of all, it must pass through the love of self (Steiner 1987b, 73).

So if one is to speak about an essential difference between the human and the animal—a difference in kind—one such difference is that the human being knows evil. The animal is not evil, and does not know evil. Moreover, therefore, the human is also different on this score in that the human alone has the ability and task of confronting and transforming evil, and from that to extend love to all beings.

In presenting this radical vision of love, Steiner is by no means unrealistic about the present lack of love among human beings. Humans are "still on the way" in developing love. To work without reward or compensation is still difficult for modern people to understand, let alone to undertake. "That is why," Steiner says, "deeds of pure love are done so unwillingly, why there is so little true love in the world" (Steiner 1998). Nevertheless, daunting as the challenge is, the urgent task facing the human now, and into the future, is to begin to develop love to its highest and to extend it to all beings.

6.

The Christ-being of Love and Freedom

In fulfilling this responsibility, the human being, Steiner emphasizes, does have help from the spiritual world. We have, if we choose to receive and work with it, the help of the Christ, who has entered the realities of Earth existence and remains connected with the Earth and all its beings. The Christ, for Steiner, is not the limited being of any religion. He is, rather, a cosmic being of love, life, and being present in the entire Earth and in every human individual, regardless of religion, race, nationality, or any of the other distinctions humans have been wont to erect. As the cosmic being of love and freedom, the Christ is the ground of the higher self in every human being, the human "I" freed of all self-love. The more humans imbue themselves with the "Christ principle" of love, the more we will be able to transform our narrow self-love. "The Christ Principle has given the impulse for man to love man; thus through being filled with the Christ-principle, human love will be increasingly spiritual. Love will become more of the nature of soul and then spirit and through this man will draw along with him the lower beings of the Earth, will transform the whole Earth" (Steiner 1987, 110, 113).

Yet, there are two large obstacles facing the human being in the development and exercise of love at this point in human history. One has to do with the fact that humans for long periods of time had to go through their own group-soul experience, as a kind of "preliminary schooling" for attaining full "I"-awareness. Before humans had a solid awareness of the "I" they were united, much like the group souls of the animals, in blood-related groups. At that stage, love was still directed by an element of wisdom inherent in the group soul. While this merging and identifying

315

of one's own self with the group was a necessary step in coming to full "I"-consciousness, finding one's source of identity in the group today—in the nation, the folk, the tribe, the religion—is no longer right for modern consciousness. Yet to do so remains a powerful temptation. As nearly every daily news report reveals, the temptation to submerge one's identity in the group, with its offer of certainty in place of the insecurities of the single self, seems for many irresistible. The result is mounting violence as each group claims to have an exclusive claim on the truth.

The other obstacle to love, which is also a particular feature of our modern world, arises from the temptation not to develop the full potential of the self and to remain at the arrested stage of inwardly focused, self-love at the neglect or expense of the other. The "I"-being, as Steiner often emphasized, can be a two-edged sword, and if it stops from developing to the full and remains at self-love, it can be the most destructive force in the world (Steiner 1977).

Steiner emphasizes that it is the Christ-being who makes it possible for the human to overcome both these obstacles. As the being of love and freedom, the Christ is the ground of the true self, and, thus, the uniter of all humankind. The more humans imbue themselves with the Christ-principle of love, "the more we will bear other earthly beings along with us" (Steiner 1987).

The human being is free to work with the Christ-principle—or not—for the being of Christ is freedom and love, and the human being is left completely free. The Christ makes himself available to humans unreservedly, but forces himself upon no one. Thus far in Earth history humans have scarcely begun to imbue themselves with the love now possible to us. Paradoxically, here in this negative aspect of human behavior we also glimpse another fundamental difference, along with all the commonalities and differences of degree, a difference in kind between the human and the animal.

As we have noted, the human alone has the responsibility, among all Earth creatures of saving the Earth. The animals can't save themselves. Unfortunately, the humans also alone have the unique ability to destroy the Earth. We are, alarmingly, far along in bringing the Earth to the brink of destruction through our thoughtless and greedy exploitation of its riches. Not the great apes, not the dolphins, not the elephants, not any of the other animals, can destroy the Earth, nor would they be moved to do so. Responsibility in love remains the human's foremost and unique capacity—uniquely different even in its neglect and profanation. If human beings see only the threat to themselves, the lack of love involved will rebound upon them. The Christian theologian, John Cobb, has said, "The Christian principle that those who seek to save only their own souls will lose them applies to humanity as a whole. If we aim to save only humanity, humanity will die. We will deal wisely with our problems only if we seek the wellbeing of the other creatures out of a real concern for them (Cobb 2001).

7.

Toward a "Planet of Love"

In his looking toward a future, new world, Steiner stands within other spiritual traditions that also envisage a radical change in the spiritual–physical conditions of the Earth. In this he stands fully within the Jewish and Christian eschatological tradition that includes some of the Jewish prophets, such as Isaiah and Hosea, and, with the Christian New Testament writers, St. Paul and St. John. Isaiah's vision includes both humans and animals in a mutual relationship of peace, and freedom from violence and predation, a vision that includes humans and animals living together as members of "a peaceable kingdom." In Isaiah's vision,

> The wolf shall dwell with the lamb,
> And the leopard shall lie down with the kid
> And the calf and the lion and the fatling together
> And a little child shall lead them. (Isaiah 11:709)

This will be the time known variously in Judaism as "the future hope of Israel" or "the Messianic Age." St. Paul expresses a similar vision: "For the whole creation waits in eager longing for the revealing of the Sons of God.... because the creation itself will be set free from its bondage to decay and obtain the glorious liberty of the children of God" (Romans 8).

Central to Paul's vision is that the human being is crucial to the realization of this vision. It is the transformed human beings imbued with the Christ principle of love that will be "the Sons of God," the "Children of God." It is through these Christ-imbued human beings that "the creation itself will be set free from its bondage to decay," that is, that the creatures will participate as free, independent selves in "the glorious liberty of the children of God" (Rom. 8:13–15)

In Steiner's vision of a transformed world, we can see three, but related, meanings in the concept of redemption: 1. The sense of redemption as repayment—redemption as paying off our debt for all that the animals have made possible for human evolution; 2. The sense of redemption as recompense—making up for all the cruelty and suffering we have visited upon the animals; and 3. The sense of redemption as liberation—the release of the animals from a state of "bondage" to the attainment of the freedom of their own, full and independent selfhood. This vision imposes on humans today a tremendous effort of creative imagination, and an engagement with the possibilities of transformation. And as a start, it means a facing of all within us that stands in the way of love of the other. This vision also requires that our work for it begin now.

This "now work" has many dimensions. As we take up the most obvious of the tasks demanded, other equally important ones may reveal themselves. One immediate task is to accept courageously and sensitively our unavoidable uniqueness in having dominion over our fellow creatures. Courage is required because dominion in the light of the Christ-principle means stewardship, care, and responsibility toward and for the others. This conception of dominion also means that we have to begin to sacrifice many things we hold dear—such as, comfort, convenience, ease, control, egoism in general. In Andrew Linzey's phrase it means that we are no longer to be the despotic species but the "servant species." "The uniqueness of humanity consists in its ability to be the servant species. To exercise its full humanity as co-participants and coworkers with God in the redemption of the world. This view challenges the traditional notions that the world was made simply for human use or pleasure, that its purpose consists in serving the human species, or that the world exists largely in an instrumentalist relationship to human beings" (Linzey 1994, 57). Courage is required, for servant-hood entails relinquishing all claims to special privilege and entitlement. No animal has this possibility. In the words of the theologian John Cobb, "in the best of scenarios, we are doomed to dominion." And as Cobb explains further, even if "our ultimate goal is a world in which we will not have dominion," we must work for the foreseeable future in the most responsible way we can for the sake of the Earth and its creatures (Cobb 2001). The Christ-principle calls us to enter into a new interconnectedness with the animals—to a deeper realization of the cosmic community of which we are all members.

Steiner often discusses from various perspectives the functions of thinking, feeling, and willing in the human being. Living with the Christ-principle in interconnectedness with the animals involves the need for a heightened activation of all three. Willing in love expresses itself in concrete actions for the welfare of the animals, and for protecting them from cruelty and unnecessary harm and suffering. Animal activism ought not be beyond the pale for anthroposophists. Feeling also finds expression in a new way. We are called upon to participate in Christ's own feeling for and with the creatures. Today this becomes especially imperative in light of the awareness we have been given in recent years of the rich feeling life of the animals that invites us to enter ever deeper into our common participation in the feeling life of the cosmos. And our thinking is particularly challenged. Part of the "now work" is to give hard rigorous and creative thinking to building a solid basis for the wellbeing of the Earth and our fellow creatures. This entails, among other things, working to preserve endangered species; developing ethical farming; reforming an economic system that turns all living beings into things and commodities for profit; seeking effective means of conservation and ecological health; and much more. The "now tasks" are clearly also long-range, for, during the foreseeable future, there will be many such "now tasks," and so perseverance will be a commanding virtue in carrying them out.

The future of Earth evolution turns on our undertaking now the tasks that can lead to the transformation of the Earth into a planet of love. To draw once more on the philosopher and theologian Andrew Linzey:

> For it may be that Paul was right that humans in some sense hold the moral key to the whole show of creation. It may be that when humans can liberate themselves to a new life of self-sacrifice, moral generosity, and practical humility that the future of the created world can be assured. It can't escape us at the present time, like it or not, the destructive capacities of humankind threaten not only ourselves but the integrity of creation itself. (Linzey 1994, 75)

It is probably no exaggeration to say that if we do not begin now, we threaten the future of Earth evolution.

There is an old Hasidic story that expresses the close connection between the transformation of the Earth in love, the coming of the Messianic Age, and our treatment of the animals in the present:

> A Hasidic rabbi who had moved to Palestine to be right on the spot in case the Messiah should arrive in his lifetime once heard the sound of a trumpet from the Mount of Olives (the traditional sign for the arrival of the Messiah). What had happened was that a prankster had gone up there and thought he would pull a practical joke. So the rabbi immediately rushed to the window, opened the window to see the redeemed world, and what did he see? A driver beating his donkey. And he said, "I don't have to see anything else. So long as people still beat their donkeys, the world is not redeemed." (Cobb 1975)

And so we face two formidable responsibilities:

1. To look without blinking at how we are still "beating our donkeys," and actually in danger of stymying the whole future of Earth evolution. The Earth can never progress to become "a planet of love," as long as our treatment of animals is void of love and compassion, as long as we are still "beating our donkeys."

2. To begin now to develop and express love as the ultimate force—and hope—of true transformation. This alone is the

basis for the redemption of the animals in that through our love grounded in the Christ principle they attain their own individual selves. As the being of love, the Christ is always available to strengthen and guide us. As the being of freedom, the Christ will not intervene to save us. The future of Earth evolution is up to us.

Works Cited

"Beloved New Warrior on the Modern Battlefield," *New York Times*, May 12, 2011.

"Cambridge Declaration of Consciousness," July 7, 2012.

"Canned Hunting," PETA, www.peta.org/issues/animals-in-entertainment/cruel-sports/hunting/canned-hunting/.

"Canned Hunts," Born Free, www.bornfreeusa.org/a9d_hunts.php.

"Chickens Used for Food," PETA, www.peta.org/issues/animals-used-for-food/factory-farming/chickens/.

"China's Encounter with Factory Farming," www.all-creatures.org/articles/ar-chinasencounter.html.

"Judges Hear Chimps Plea, To Be Free and Retired," *New York Times*, Oct. 9, 2014, A32.

"Stop Animal Tests" www.stopanimaltests.com/f-tser.asp.

"Targeting Wildlife Services," *Center for Biological Diversity*," 2014, www.biologicaldiversity.org/campaigns/wildlife_services.

"The Hidden Lives of Chickens," PETA, www.peta.org/issues/animals-used-for-food/factory-farming/chickens/hidden-lives-chickens/.

"Visiting an Ailing Relative," *New York Times*, Sept. 30, 2014.

Akhtar, Aysha, "Why Animal Experimentation Doesn't Work," *Oxford Center for Animal Ethics*, www.huffingtonpost.com/aysha-akhtar/animal-experimenttion_k_3676678.

Almon, Clopper (1998) *A Study Companion to An Outline of Esoteric Science*, Anthroposophic Press.

Amrine, Frederick et al., eds. (1987) *Goethe and the Sciences: A Reappraisal*, Reidel.

Balcombe, Jonathon (2010) *Second Nature: The Inner Lives of Animals*, Macmillan.

Barfield, Owen (1965) *Unancestral Voice*, Wesleyan University.

—— (1982) "The Evolution Complex," *Towards*, vol. 2, no. 2, spring.

Baur, Gene (2008) *Farm Sanctuary: Changing Hearts and Minds about Animals and Food*, Simon and Schuster.

Bekoff, Marc (2007) *The Emotional Lives of Animals: A Leading Scientist Explores Animal Joy, Sorrow, and Empathy—and Why They Matter,* New World Library.

—— (2010) *Animal Manifesto: Six Reasons for Expanding Our Compassion Footprint,* New World Library.

—— (2012) *Psychology Today,* Aug. 10.

Bekoff, Marc and Jessica Pierce (2009) *Wild Justice: The Moral Lives of Animals,* University of Chicago.

Bellah, Robert N. (2011) *Religion in Human Evolution: From the Paleolithic to the Axial Age.* Harvard.

Birch, Charles (1979) "Nature, God, and Humanity in Ecological Perspective," *Christianity and Crisis.* Oct. 29.

—— (1995) *Feelings,* UNSW Press.

—— (2008) "Why Aren't We Zombies? Neo-Darwinism and Process Thought," in Cobb (2008).

Bittman, Mark (2008) "Rethinking the Meat-Guzzlers," *New York Times,* Jan. 27.

—— (2009) *Food Matters: A Guide to Conscious Eating,* Simon and Schuster.

—— (2011) "Who Protects the Animals?" *New York Times,* Apr. 26.

—— (2012) "A Chicken without Guilt," *New York Times,* Mar. 1.

Boardman, Terry (2013/14) "Syriana II," *New View,* winter.

Bornfree, "Ivory's Curse," www.bornfreeusa.org/ivorycurse/a9_ivorys_curse.php.

Bortoft, Henri (1996) *The Wholeness of Nature: Goethe's Way toward a Science of Conscious Participation in Nature,* Lindisfarne Press.

Bowler, Peter J. (1984) *Evolution: The History of an Idea,* University of California.

Bradshaw, G. A. (2009) *Elephants on the Edge: What Animals Teach Us about Humanity,* Yale.

Bradshaw, Gay (2010) "Through a Glass Darkly, and Out the Other Side," *Psychology Today,* Sep. 29.

Burghardt, Gordon M. (2005) *The Genesis of Animal Play: Testing the Limits,* MIT.

Callahan, Daniel (2003) *What Price Better Health? Hazards of the Research Imperative,* University of California.

Carbone, Larry (2004) *What Animals Want: Expertise and Advocacy in Laboratory Animal Welfare Policy,* Oxford.

Cartmill, Matt (1991) *A View to a Death in the Morning: Hunting and Nature through History,* Harvard Univeristy.

Cavalieri, Paola, and Peter Singer (1993) *The Great Ape Project: Equality Beyond Humanity,* St. Martin's.

Center for Biological Diversity (n/d) "The Extinction Crisis," www .biologicaldiversity.org/programs/biodiversity/elements_of_biodiversity /extinction_crisis/.

Clayton, Nicola, et al. (2008) "What–Where–When Memory in Magpies," *Animal Cognition.*

Cobb, John B. Jr. (1975) *Christ in a Pluralistic Age,* Westminster.

—— (1998) "All Things in Christ?" in Linzey and Yamamoto.

—— (2001) "Deep Ecology and Process Thought," *Process Studies,* vol. 30, no. 1, spring/summer.

——, ed. (2008) *Back to Darwin: Richer Account of Evolution,* "Organisms as Agents in Evolution," Eerdmanns.

Cobb, John B., Jr., and David Ray Griffin (1976) *Process Theology: An Introductory Exposition,* Westminster.

Commoner, Barry (2002) "Unraveling the DNA Myth," *Harper's Magazine,* Feb.

Cummins, Ronnie (2013) "Climate Friendly Food Demands Animal-Friendly Farming," *Common Dreams,* Jan. 17.

Darwin, Charles (1872) *The Expression of the Emotions in Man and Animals.* John Murray.

—— (1959) *On the Origin of Species.* Mentor.

Davis, Karin (2005) *The Holocaust and the Henmaid's Tale: A Case for Comparing Atrocities.* Lantern Books.

Davy, John (1985) *Hope, Evolution, and Change: Selected Essays,* Hawthorn.

de Waal, Frans (1996) *Good Natured: The Origins of Right and Wrong in Humans and Other Animals.* Harvard.

—— (2005) *Our Inner Ape: A Leading Primatologist Explains Why We Are Who We Are,* Riverhead.

—— (2006) *Primates and Philosophers: How Morality Evolved,* Princeton University.

——— (2008) "The Thief in the Mirror," *PLOS Biology,* vol. 6, no. 8, Aug.

Deane-Drummond, Celia, and David Clough (2009) *Creaturely Theology: On God, Humans and Other Animals,* SCM.

Demello, Margo, ed. (2010) *Teaching the Animal: Human–Animal Studies across the Disciplines,* Lantern.

Denton, Michael (1985) *Evolution: A Theory in Crisis,* Adler and Adler.

Diamond, Jared (1998) *Guns, Germs, and Steel: The Fates of Human Societies,* Norton.

Dunayer, Joan (2004) *Speciesism,* Ryce.

Editorial (2015) "Farming Science, Without the Conscience," *New York Times,* Jan. 26.

——— (2015b) "Wildlife Slaughter Goes Unabated," *New York Times,* Feb. 15.

Eisenman, Stephen F. (2013) *The Cry of Nature: Art and the Making of Animal Rights,* Reaktion Books.

Eldridge, Niles (1995) *Reinventing Darwin: The Great Debate at the High Table of Evolutionary Theory,* John Wiley and Sons.

Finkelmeyer, Todd (2013) "USDA Inspectors Find Violation at University of Wisconsin-Madison Animal Lab," *The Capital Times,* summer.

Foer, Jonathan Safran (2009) *Eating Animals,* Little, Brown.

Fouts, Roger (1997) *Next of Kin: My Conversations with Chimpanzees,* Harper.

Francione, Gary L. (2000) *Introduction to Animal Rights: Your Child or the Dog?* Temple University.

——— (2006) "The Great Ape Project: Not So Great," www.abolitionistapproach.com/the-great-ape-project-not-so-great.

——— (2007) "Animal Rights: The Absolutist Approach," www.abolitionistapproach.com/vivisection-part-one-the-necessity-of-vivisection/.

Gazzaniga, Michael S. (2008) *Human: The Science behind what Makes Us Unique,* Harper Collins.

Gibson, Chris (2014), letter, Nov. 4.

Glendinning, Lee (2008), "Spanish Parliament Approves 'Human rights' for Apes," *The Guardian,* Jun. 26.

Goliszek, Andrew (2003) *In the Name of Science: A History of Secret Programs, Medical Research, and Human Experimentation,* St. Martin's.

Goodall, Jane (1999) *Reason for Hope: A Spiritual Journey*, Warner.

Gould, Stephen J. (1989) *Wonderful Life: The Burgess Shale and the Nature of History*, Norton.

—— (1996) *Full House: The Spread of Excellence from Plato to Darwin*, Three Rivers.

Greek, Ray and Niall Shanks (2009) *FAQS About the Use of Animals in Science: A Handbook for the Scientifically Perplexed*, UPA.

Greene, John C. (1981) *Science, Ideology, and World View: Essays in the History of Evolutionary Ideas*, University of California.

—— (1991) "Progress, Science, and Value: A Biological Dilemma," *Biology and Philosophy*, 6.

Griffin, David Ray (1988) *The Reenchantment of Science*, SUNY.

—— (2000) *Religion and Scientific Naturalism: Overcoming the Conflicts*, SUNY.

Gruzalski, Bart (2004) "Why It's Wrong to Eat Animals Raised and Slaughtered for Food"; in Steve F. Sapontzis, ed., *Food for Thought: The Debate over Eating Meat*, Prometheus.

Haberstadt, Alex, "Zoo Animals and Their Discontents," *New York Times*, July 6, 2014.

Hartinger, Werner (2005) *The Animals Are Our Brothers and Sisters: Why Animal Experiments are Misleading and Wrong*, London, Temple Lodge.

Hartman, Kathryn (n/d) "Learned Helplessness: A critique of Research and Theory," www.safermedicines.org/reports/Perspectives/vol_1_1989 /Learned%20Helplessness.html.

Hatkoff, Amy (2009) *The Inner World of Farm Animals: Their Amazing Social, Emotional, and Intellectual Capacities*, Abrams.

Heinrich, Bernd (2006) *Mind of the Raven: Investigations and Adventures with Wolf-Birds*, Harper Perrenial.

Heinrich, Bernd and Thomas Bugnyar (2007) "Just How Smart Are Ravens?" *Scientific American*, Apr.

Heisenberg, Werner (1974) "Goethe's View of Knowledge and the World of Science and Technology," in Werner Heisenberg, *Across the Frontiers*, Harper and Row.

Hightower, James (2013) "Gagging on Ag-Gag Laws," www.jimhightower .com/node/8015#.Va_XJrNVhBc.

Holdrege, Craig (1996) *Genetics and the Manipulation of Life: The Forgotten Factor of Context,* Lindisfarne.

—— (2013) *Thinking Like a Plant: A Living Science for Life,* Lindisfarne.

Imhoff, Daniel, ed. (2010) *The CAFO Reader: The Tragedy of Industrial Animal Factories,* Los Angeles: UCLA.

In Defense of Animals, "Anti-Hunting" (www.idausa.org/campaigns/wild -free2/habitats-campaign/anti-hunting).

Jablonka, Eva and Marion J. Lamb (2005) *Evolution in Four Dimensions: Genetic, Epigenetic, Behavioral, and Symbolic Variation in the History of Life,* The MIT.

James. William (1950) *The Principles of Psychology,* vol. 2, Dover.

Kalechofsky, Roberta (2004) "The Jewish Diet and Vegetarianism," in Steve F. Sapontzis, ed., *Food for Thought: The Debate over Eating Meat,* Prometheus.

Kaufman, Leslie (2012) "Zoos' Bitter Choice: To Save Some Species, Letting Others Die," *New York Times,* May 28.

Kazez, Jean (2010) *Animalkind: What We Owe to Animals,* Wiley-Blackwell.

King, Barbara (2014) "Still Now, Should Lab Monkeys Be Deprived of Their Mothers?" NPR, *Cosmos and Culture,* Sept. 11.

Kipp, Friedrich (2005) *Childhood and Human Evolution,* Adonis.

Kolbert, Elizabeth (2014) *The Sixth Extinction: An Unnatural History,* Henry Holt.

König, Karl (2002) *The Animals and Their Destiny,* Camphill.

—— (2013) *Animals: An Imaginative Zoology,* Floris.

Kranich, Ernst-Michael, (1999) *Thinking beyond Darwin: The Idea of the Type as a Key to Vertebrate Evolution,* Lindisfarne.

Kristof, Nicholas (2015) "To Kill A Chicken," *New York Times,* March 15.

Lange, Karen E., (2015a) "Out of Season," *All Animals,* May/June.

—— (2015b) "End of Culling?" *All Animals,* Mar./Apr.

Latham, Stephen R. (2012) "U.S. Law and Animal Experimentation: A Critical Primer," *Hastings Center Report,* vol. 42, no. 6.

Lederer, Susan E. (1995) *Subject to Science: Human Experimentation in America before the Second World War,* Johns Hopkins.

Lewontin, Richard (2000) *The Triple Helix: Gene Organism and Environment,* Harvard.

———— (2011) "It's Even Less in Your Genes," *New York Review of Books,* May 26.

Linzey, Andrew (1994) *Animal Theology,* University of Illinois.

———— (2000) *Animal Gospel,* Westminster John Knox.

———— (2009) *Creatures of the Same God: Explorations in Animal Theology,* Lantern.

———— (2013) *Why Animal Suffering Matters: Philosophy, Theology, and Practical Ethics,* Oxford.

———— (forthcoming) *The Link between Animal Abuse and Human Violence,* Sussex.

Linzey, Andrew and Tom Regan (1988) *Animals and Christianity: A Book of Readings,* Crossroad.

Linzey, Andrew and Dorothy Yamamoto (1998) *Animals on the Agenda: Questions about Animals for Theology and Ethics,* SCM Press.

Lorenz, Konrad (1963) *On Aggression,* Harcourt, Brace.

MacIntyre, Alasdair (1999) *Dependent Rational Animals: Why Human Beings Need the Virtues,* Open Court.

Mak, Nina (2009) "The Role of Ethics in IACUC's Oversight of Animal Research," *AV Magazine,* fall.

Marks, Joel (2011) "On Due Recognition of Animals Used in Research," *Journal of Animal Ethics,* 1.

Marks, Nina (2009) "The Role of Ethics in IACUC's Oversight of Animal Research," *AV Magazine,* fall.

Martin, Ken, et al. (1996) "Ring Bubbles of Dolphins," *Scientific American* Aug. 19.

Marzluff, John and Tony Angell (2012) *Gifts of the Crow: How Perception, Emotion, and Thought Allow Smart Birds to Behave Like Humans,* Free Press.

Mather, Jennifer (2008) "Cephalopod Consciousness: Behavioral Evidence, *Consciousness and Cognition,* vol. 17, no. 1, Mar.

McCarthy, Deidre (n/d) "Earth Matters: End of the Line," www.inmo.ie /MagazineArticle/PrintArticle/8046.

McKinley, Jesse (2014) "Judges Hear Chimps Plea," *New York Times,* Oct. 20.

McWilliams, James E. (2012) "The Myth of Sustainable Meat," *New York Times,* Apr 12.

Mendelson, Anne, "The Milk of Human Unkindness: Industrialization and the Super Cow"; in Imhoff, 131–138.

Miller, R. E. (1986) "The Morality and Humaneness of Animal Research on Stress and Pain," *Annals of the New York Academy of Sciences*, 467.

Morris, Simon Conway (1988) *The Crucible of Creation: The Burgess Shale and the Rise of Animals*, Oxford.

—— (2000) "Evolution: Bringing Molecules into the Field," *Cell*, vol. 100, Jan. 7.

—— (2003) *Life's Solution: Inevitable Humans in a Lonely Universe*, University of Cambridge.

Moss, Michael (2015a) "In Quest for More Meat Profits, U.S. Lab Lets Animals Suffer," *New York Times*, Jan. 20.

—— (2015b) "Lawmakers Aim to Protect Farm Animals," *New York Times*, Feb. 5.

—— (2015c) "Stricter Oversight Ordered for Animal Research at Nebraska Center," *New York Times*, Mar. 9.

Nagel, Thomas (2012) *Mind and Cosmos: Why the Materialist Neo-Darwinian Conception of Nature is Almost Certainly False*, Oxford.

NAVS (2012) *Animal Action Report*, winter/spring.

Nitecki, Matthew H., ed. (1988) *Evolutionary Progress*, University of Chicago.

Nussbaum, Martha C. (2005) "Beyond 'Compassion and Humanity': Justice for Nonhuman Animals," in Cass R. Sunstein and Martha C. Nussbaum, eds., *Animal Rights: Current Debates and New Directions*, Oxford.

Oppel, Richard A. (2013) "Taping of Farm Cruelty Is Becoming the Crime," *New York Times*, Apr. 7.

Pearson, Helen (2006) "Genetics: What is a Gene?" *Nature*, 441, May 25.

Pew Commission on Industrial Farm Animal Production (2008) "Putting Meat on the Table: Industrial Farm Animal Production in America." www.ncifap.org/_images/PCIFAPFin.pdf.

Phelps, Norm (2002) *The Dominion of Love: Animal Rights According to the Bible*. Lantern Books.

—— (2004) *The Great Compassion: Buddhism and Animal Rights*. Lantern Books.

Physicians Committee for Responsible Medicine (2011) *Good Medicine*, autumn.

———— (2013) *Good Medicine*, summer.

———— (2014) "Report from the Field," *Good Medicine*, May.

———— (2014) Physicians Committee for Responsible Medicine, *Good Medicine*, summer.

Pluhar, Evelyn B. (2010) "Meat and Morality: Alternatives to Factory Farming," *Journal of Agricultural Environmental Ethics*.

Pollan, Michael (2006) *The Omnivore's Dilemma: A Natural History of Four Meals*, Penguin.

Porphyry (2000) tr. Gillian Clark. *On Abstinence from Killing Animals*, Cornell University.

Portmann, Adolf (1967) *Animal Forms and Patterns: A Study of the Appearance of Animals*, Schocken.

Potter, Will (2014) "Preface," in Jason Del Gandio and Anthony J. Nocella, *Terrorization of Dissent: Corporate Repression, Legal Corruption, and the Animal Enterprise Terrorism ACT*. Lantern.

Pound, Pound and Ebrahim Shah, et al. (2004) "Where is the Evidence that Animal Research Benefits Humans," *British Medical Journal*, 328.

Putnam, Rory (1988) *The Natural History of Deer*, Cornell University.

Redmond, Eugene D. (2012) "Using Monkeys to Understand and Cure Parkinson's Disease," *Hastings Center Report*, 42, no. 6.

Regan, Tom (1983) *The Case for Animal Rights*, University of California.

Regan, Tom and Peter Singer (1989) *Animal Rights and Human Obligations*, 2nd ed., Prentice Hall.

Ringach, D. L. (2011) "The Use of Nonhuman Animals in Biomedical Research," *American Journal of the Medical Sciences*, 342, no. 4.

Risen, James (2014) *Pay Any Price: Greed, Power, and Endless War*, Houghton Mifflin Harcourt.

———— (2014b) "Psychologists to Review Role in Detainee Interrogations," *New York Times*, Nov. 13.

———— (2015a) "Report Finds Collaboration Over Torture," *New York Times*, May 1.

———— (2015b) "Torture Efforts Were Protected by Psychologists," *New York Times*, July 11.

Robbins, Jim (2014) "Building an Ark for the Anthropocene," *New York Times*, Sep. 28.

Rogerson, J. W. (1998) "What Was the Meaning of Animal Sacrifice?" in Linzey and Yamamoto.

Rollin, Bernard (1989) *The Unheeded Cry: Animal Consciousness, Animal Pain, and Science*, Oxford.

―――― (2012) "The Moral Status of Invasive Animal Research," *Hastings Center Report*, 42, no. 6 (www.thehastingscenter.org/uploadedFiles /Publications/Special_Reports/AnimalResearchEthics.pdf).

Rosslenbroich, Bernd (2006) "The Notion of Progress in Evolutionary Biology: The Unresolved Problem and an Empirical Suggestion," *Biology and Philosophy*, 21.

―――― (2009) "Evolution aus zwei Perspektiven," *die Drei*, 10.

―――― (2009b) "The Theory of Increasing Autonomy in Evolution: A Proposal for Understanding Macroevolutionary Innovations," *Biology and Philosophy*, 24:623–44.

―――― (2012) "Die Biologie der Freiheit; Zur Entstehung von Autonomie in der Evolution," *die Drei*, 10/20/2012.

Rothfuss, Joan, Walker Art Center, www.walkerart.org.

Savage-Rumbaugh, Sue and Roger Lewin (1994) *Kanzi: The Ape at the Brink of the Human Mind*, Wiley.

Schad, Wolfgang (1977) *Man and Mammals: Toward a Biology of Form*, Waldorf Press.

―――― (2009) "Die Evolution der Menschheit," *die Drei*, 10.

―――― (2009b) "Vom Christlichen im Dawinismus" printed MS, Nov. 6.

Scully, Matthew (2002) *Dominion: The Power of Man, the Suffering of Animals, and the Call to Mercy*, St. Martin's.

Seamon, David and Arthur Zajonc (1998) *Goethe's Way of Science: A Phenomenology of Nature*, SUNY.

Showmatoff, Alex (2011) "Agony and Ivory," *Vanity Fair*, Aug.

Siebert, Charles (2014) "The Rights of Man and Beast," *New York Times Magazine*.

Singer, Peter (1980) *Practical Ethics*, Cambridge University.

―――― (2000) *Writings on An Ethical Life*, Harper Collins.

―――― (2009) *Animal Liberation*, Harper, rev. ed.

Southgate, Christopher, "The New Days of Noah? Assisted Migration in an Era of Climate Change," in Deane-Drummond and Clough, 250.

Steinbach, David (2013) "The Money in the Great Ape Debate, *Open Secrets,* Jul. 11, www.opensecrets.org.

St. Fleur, Nicholas (2015) "U.S. Will Call All Chimps 'Endangered,'" *New York Times,* June 12.

Steiner, Gary (2008) *Animals and the Moral Community,* Columbia University.

Steiner, Rudolf (1907) "The Animal Soul," Leipzig, Mar. 16.

—— (1910a) "The Human Spirit and the Animal Spirit," Berlin, Nov. 17.

—— (1910b) "The Human Soul and the Animal Soul," Berlin, Nov. 10.

—— (1912) "The Origin of the Animal World in the Light of Spiritual Science," *Menschengeschichte im Lichte der Geistesforshung,* Jan. 18.

—— (1947) *Knowledge of the Higher Worlds and Its Attainment,* Anthroposophic Press.

—— (1950) *Goethe the Scientist.* New York, Anthroposophic Press.

—— (1951) *The Course of My Life.* New York, Anthroposophic Press.

—— (1963) *The Life, Nature, and Cultivation of Anthroposophy,* Anthroposophical Society in Great Britain.

—— (1968) *A Theory of Knowledge Implicit in Goethe's World Conception,* Anthroposophic Press.

—— (1970) *At the Gates of Spiritual Science,* Rudolf Steiner Press.

—— (1970b) *Man as Symphony of the Creative Word,* Rudolf Steiner Press.

—— (1971) *Theosophy,* Anthroposophic Press.

—— (1976) *From Sympathy to Reality in Modern History,* Rudolf Steiner Press.

—— (1977) *The Apocalypse of St. John,* Rudolf Steiner Press.

—— (1978) *Rosicrucian Esotericism,* Anthroposophic Press.

—— (1981) *The Festivals and Their Meaning,* Rudolf Steiner Press.

—— (1982) *The Influence of Spiritual Beings upon Man,* Anthroposophic Press.

—— (1983) *Metamorphoses of the Soul,* vol. 1, Rudolf Steiner Press.

—— (1987) *Universe, Earth, and Man.* London, Rudolf Steiner Press.

—— (1987b) *The Evolution of the Earth and Man,* Anthroposophic Press.

—— (1987c) *Supersensible Knowledge,* Anthroposophic Press.

—— (1995) *Manifestations of Karma*, Rudolf Steiner Press.

—— (1996) *The Spiritual Hierarchies and the Spiritual World*, Anthroposophic Press.

—— (1997) *An Outline of Esoteric Science*, Anthroposophic Press.

—— (1998) *Love and Its Meaning in the World*, Anthroposophic Press.

—— (1998b) *Bees*, Anthroposophic Press.

—— (2000) *The Temple Legend: Freemasonry and Related Occult Movements: From the Contents of the Esoteric School.* Rudolf Steiner Press.

—— (2003) *Religion: An Introductory Reader*, Rudolf Steiner Press.

—— (2007) *The Influence of the Dead on Destiny*, Steiner Books.

—— (2008) *Death as Metamorphosis of Life*, SteinerBooks.

—— (2010) *First Steps in Christian Religious Renewal: Preparing the Ground for The Christian Community*, SteinerBooks.

Stockmar, Stephan (2009) "Stell dir vor: Ein Tier wird Mensch!" *De Drei*, 10.

Streffer, Walter (2009a) "Das Akustische Spielverhalten der Singvøgel:" *die Drei*, Mar. 2009.

—— (2009b) "'Sie Hätten auch den Vogeltypus Nehmen Können': Die Parallelentwicklung von Vogel- und Säugergehirn zu den intelligenten Leistungen der Singvögel," *die Drei* Oct.

Stuart, Tristram (2006) *The Bloodless Revolution*, Norton.

Summers, Tamler and Alex Rosenberg (2003) "Darwin's Nihilistic Idea: Evolution and the Meaninglessness of Life," *Biology and Philosophy*, 18.

Sunstein, Cass R. and Martha C. Nussbaum (2005) *Animal Rights*, Oxford.

Taylor, Gordan Rattray (1983) *The Great Evolution Mystery*, Harper and Row.

The Week Staff (2013) "Should Apes Have Legal Rights?" *The Week*, Aug. 3.

Tompkins, Ptolemy (2010) *The Divine Life of Animals*, Three Rivers Press.

Unferth, Deb Olin (2014) "Cage Wars: A Visit to the Egg Farm," *Harpers Magazine*, Nov.

United Nations' Report, "Livestock's Long Shadow" (awfw.org/wp-content /uploads/pdf/UNGlobalWarmingReport.pdf).

Verhulst, Jos (2003) *Developmental Dynamic in Humans and Other Primates*, Adonis.

Wesson, Robert (1991) *Beyond Natural Selection*, MIT.

Whitehead, Alfred North (1950) *Science and the Modern World,* Macmillan.

Whitty, Julia (2007) "Animal Extinction: The Greatest Threat to Mankind," www.independent.co.uk/environment/animal-extinction--the-greatest -threat-to-mankind-397939.html.

Williams, Joy (2001) *Ill Nature: Rants and Reflections on Humanity and Other Animals,* Lyons.

Wisconsin Center for Investigative Journalism (2014), Jul. 31.

Zajonc, Arthur (1993) *Catching the Light: The Entwined History of Light and Mind,* Bantam.

Zimmer, Carl (2007) "Time in the Animal Mind," *New York Times* April 3, F1.

—— (2008) "How Smart Is the Octopus?" *Slate,* Jun. 25.

—— (2015) "Ocean Life Faces Mass Extinction, Broad Study Finds, Human Impact Is Rising, *New York Times,* Jan. 16.

Zurlo, Joanne (2012) "No Animals Harmed: Toward a Paradigm Shift in Toxicity Testing," *Hastings Center Report,* 42, no. 6.